for Darren
With warmest regards

Us

Satya Brata Das

Library and Archives Canada Cataloguing in Publication
Das, Satya, 1955-, author
Us / Satya Brata Das.

Includes bibliographical references.
Issued in print and electronic formats.

ISBN 978-1-926755-06-9 (pbk.)
ISBN 978-1-926755-07-6 (pdf)

1. Sustainability.   2. Human ecology.   I. Title.

HC79.E5D68 2014   338.9'27   C2014-905063-1
                                                     C2014-905064-X

 © Copyright Satya Brata Das 2014-19

Published by Sextant, an imprint of Cambridge Strategies Inc.
11607 24th Avenue NW
Edmonton, Alberta
T6J 3R6
www.cambridgestrategies.com

All paper used in this book is certified by the Forest Stewardship Council
1 2 3 4 5 05 04 03 02
Printed and bound in Canada by Priority Printing Ltd., a FSC certified printer

To Mita, my companion on the journey

Also by Satya Brata Das

Dispatches from a Borderless World
(NeWest Press, 1999)

The Best Country: Why Canada Will Lead the Future
(Sextant, 2002)

Green Oil: Clean Energy for the 21st Century?
(Sextant, 2009)

Emancipate yourselves from mental slavery
None but ourselves can free our minds
Bob Marley, *Redemption Song*

Cependant c'est la veille.
Recevons tous les influx de vigueur et de tendresse réelle.
Et à l'aurore, armés d'une ardente patience, nous entrerons aux
splendides villes.

So here is tomorrow's eve.
Let us accept a full measure of vigour and unconditional tenderness.
And as day breaks, armed with ardent patience, we shall enter cities of
splendour.
Arthur Rimbaud, *A Season in Hell*

De pena en pena cruza sus islas el amor
y establece raíces que luego riega el llanto,
y nadie puede, nadie puede evadir los pasos
del corazón que corre callado y carnicero.

From grief to grief love navigates its islands
And sets down roots watered only with tears,
And no one, no one can evade the strides of
the heart as it runs silent and carnivorous.
Pablo Neruda, *One Hundred Sonnets of Love (71)*

Proceeds from the print and electronic sales of "Us" are committed to
endeavours that serve the common good. *These champions of societal*
development are able to raise funds through coded downloads or availing
print books at cost. You may indicate your interest in securing this offer for
your organisation by contacting
satya@cambridgestrategies.com.

Contents

Prologue

Nashville, Tennessee, USA, September 1963

All eyes turn on me as I walk through the door of Chambers BBQ Pit and Steakhouse, walk up to the counter, take a stool. And ask for a menu.

I am a month away from my eighth birthday, by myself, speaking English with an Indian lilt.

We are at the peak of American apartheid. This is a place where only light skinned people dine. Chambers is across the street from the verdant lawns, majestic oaks, and stately buildings of Vanderbilt University. Where none with dark skin has ever been allowed to enrol as a freshman, let alone teach.

The counterman wants to know if my daddy's with me. I pull out the money my father gave me. The diners have pale skin. The cooks, and the servers in their crisp white shirts and black bow ties, have dark skin. And it is the servers who are staring the hardest. I explain my dad asked me to go in by myself. That I am in the third grade at Peabody Demonstration School. My new schoolmates told me about what they eat at home. I wanted to try. This will be my first steak, anywhere. And one of my first tastes of real American food since arriving weeks before from India. The diners turn back to their meals, curiosity satisfied.

The counterman tells me I've come to the right place. The serving is far too large, an old-fashioned cut with a marrow bone in the middle. It is delicious. I tell him so. I get through about a third of it. We talk. I explain that we live across the street, in the Oxford Apartments. That my dad is here as a Kennedy Foundation visiting professor at the neighbouring George Peabody College for Teachers, where my mom is studying for her doctorate.

I do not add, since I did not understand it then, that my father with his open heart and guileless embrace of humanity had given no thought to the disruption my presence might bring when he sent his seven-year-old son to an apartheid era restaurant to dine alone.

Chapter One

Us

White River Junction, Vermont, USA, September 2018

The blackboard menu at Big Fatty's BBQ ("we put some south in your mouth") is so full of options that I ask for a recommendation. Within moments I'm settled at a wooden table with frosted pint of local pale ale; awaiting a trencher of burnt ends and brisket, the meat marinated and slow cooked for hours in this quintessential American cuisine. Fifty-five years on from Nashville, none are looking at the colour of my skin.

I have parked on the slope of an asphalt lot that a more rigorous municipality would have levelled out, once an industrial yard that now holds a locally-owned bar, a nightclub and a barbecue joint: a trifecta of American life that predates the invasion of chain restaurants with their focus-group-tested offerings.

I pull into a main street right out of the 1920s, duly preserved as a national heritage recalling an America from a bygone age: the Coolidge hotel promising rooms with a bath, storefronts with their original trappings, reminders of the time when this railway junction was served by fifty passenger trains a day. It is still a busy working hub for freight along the banks of the Connecticut River, at the confluence of two interstates and two state highways that ended the heyday of passenger rail.

Looking for a late lunch on a bakingly hot day, I twice walk past the door of The Filling Station bar and grill before realising what looks like a home with a residential door is in fact the entrance. It's a comfortable place with a faded linoleum floor, a pool table, a long bar, and two habitués nursing a slow beer through a long afternoon. The apologetic barman says the kitchen is shut until 4 p.m. He sends me down the street to Big Fatty's, where I now face a mountainous heap of lightly charred meat that falls apart with the touch of a fork, glistening with a messily spicy maple habanero sauce.

Although there's far too much of it, this is addictively delicious food, the hoppy crispness of the ale cutting through the richness. And this small moment of perfection, in a railway town still re-inventing itself — a theatre company has a modern hall off Main Street, and there's a school for cartoonists offering a diploma in sequential art — is as good a place as any to start talking about *Us,* and the journey that awaits you and me within these pages.

Us is the story of my life journey, an ordinary life lived in extraordinary times. Well past my sixth decade of life, I am still searching for ways that you and I can share the planet with our fellow humans, without causing hurt or harm to one another and to the natural world.

Us is the story of my explorations, told through vignettes of experiences I have lived or known first-hand. As with M.K. Gandhi's

The Story of My Experiments with Truth, mine is a journey of self-discovery. It is told from the perspective of a privileged life lived in Canada, one of the handful of countries where every stream of the human experience can find mutual accommodation.

You'll get to know me well enough along the way, but let's talk about you. If I'm right about you on even three or four of these things, I hope you'll agree to be my traveling companion.

You try to be a good person.

You care about others.

You want to make a difference, but sometimes you feel like you don't know where to begin.

You know yourself.

You know who you are, and are comfortable enough to know your strengths and weaknesses.

You are true to yourself.

You value honesty.

People you know would consider you a moral and ethical person.

Though you don't always succeed, you try to do the right thing.

You try to be responsible for your own happiness.

You feel at ease with people from cultural backgrounds different from your own.

You try to understand why someone might have hurt you or harmed you: it might have taken a while, but you are learning to forgive.

You value integrity, demand accountability, insist on transparency, respect wisdom wherever it is found.

You might be active on social media.

If you are of a certain age, you might have joined a board or served as an officer for a local club or organisation.

You might have signed at least one petition, written or called a politician about something that matters to you and your community.

You may have been a volunteer.

You have worked with a group; you have spoken in public or shared a public presentation.

Perhaps you have joined a political movement or run for office. You continue to believe politics should be all about public service.

If you are old enough to have lived in the last half of the 20th century, you might have written a letter to the editor of a newspaper or magazine or called a live radio or TV show to express an opinion.

You've actively tried to make a difference in your community or in your politics.

If some of these things sound like you, I hope you will do me the honour of traveling with me on the journey of *Us*.

I will welcome you with all my heart.

And where is the journey taking us?

As we go along, you will choose your own final destination. It will suit who you are, and the change you would like to provoke.

Our general direction is towards a different kind of future. For us, and all who share our planet. Our journey will take us to the mountaintop as we advance towards Dr. Martin Luther King's dream. It will take us towards the transformative energy of empowered truth and love (satyagraha) evoked by Mohandas Karamchand Gandhi. It will take us on the never-ending path of Nelson Mandela's long walk to freedom.

We will consider how each of the three of them faced the existential challenge of their times, of how each responded to circumstances infused with violence. How King and Mandela, faced with violent opposition to their quest for social justice in the 1960s, found different paths: King concluding that moral courage demanded non-violent resistance; and Mandela concluding quite the opposite before embracing non-violence as a necessary political instrument during his long years of imprisonment.

Along the way, we will share experiences that illuminate Gandhi's advice to be the change you want to see in the world. And whatever you may learn is as important as what you unlearn. Indeed, unlearning is the most challenging part of the journey. As Bob Marley told us in his great secular anthem of redemption: emancipate yourselves from mental slavery, none but ourselves can free our minds.

Our destination is within reach: a future where all humans live together, enjoying freedom from fear and freedom from want, in community, with dignity, in harmony with one another and with the natural world. This is what it means to enjoy human rights as a way of life, through the full flowering of our right to be human.

Freedom from fear: this is a place beyond the culture of violence that has infected us throughout our recorded history. Indeed, the absence of fear is the foundation of a community life that brings out the best in us.

Freedom from want: this is more than the basics of food, shelter and clothing. It is the fulfillment of the culture all our spiritual traditions impart to us; a place suffused with the grace and power of mutual love and support.

Living together in community, with dignity: this is a destination that fired my imagination ever since I heard it expressed by the followers of M.K. Gandhi, assassinated seven years before my birth.

Living together in harmony with one another and with the natural world: this aspect of the journey will take us past, through, and beyond what we believe to be the limits of the possible; to discover in the Other the perfect echo of ourselves.

The journey will take us from the dependence of charity to the self-sufficiency of dignity.

Instead of striving to be the best *in* the world, we will explore how to be the best *for* the world.

Thus, we will strive to bring Gandhi's teachings into relevance for our age, for our times, for our challenges.

And we will, along the way, learn together what it might mean to establish and animate the politics of love as the resilient foundation of everyday life.

We will explore what it means to follow the four remedies Gandhi prescribed to begin our own satyagraha, our own experiments with applying empowered truth:

· Understand the suffering of others

· Give wing to the fallen

· Abandon ego and pride

· Serve the divinity within all

In our journey we will explore what Gandhi tried to achieve with these principles. In doing so, we will speak truth to power, armed with the courage of our convictions. Claiming the right to be human.

Like my abundant meal at Big Fatty's, this is rather too much to digest at one go. Let this seed take its time to germinate, nurture the emerging plant to suit your own circumstances and interests.

While you do so, let me lay out a bit more of what lies ahead. The path of *Us* is set out as vignettes. Snapshots of a particular time and place that illustrate truth and love in action: sometimes directly, sometimes tangentially.

You will connect the dots as we go, and in doing so weave your own understanding of what you wish to achieve as an instrument of change. This tapestry of vignettes has one element in common: it is woven from what I have seen, or experienced, or understood. As with all perceptions, there are gaps and flaws; and it is my ardent hope that you will fill the void with recollections of your own.

And we already know something about each other. We know that you have an absolute right to live a life of meaning and purpose: that you were born with your own human dignity which is your inalienable birthright.

You already know this, particularly if you have made the journey within: to truly know yourself, to make peace with and within yourself.

Diners are still ambling into Big Fatty's as three o'clock comes and goes, amiably trading bottles of sauce from the big self-serve rack of them beside my table. This unexpected afternoon is of a piece with my presence in Vermont and New Hampshire: places I never thought to visit and might never have come to. Yet the sojourn here has offered a vivid insight into a life of dignity and community.

I step out into the stunning heat of the parking lot, a blast furnace after the air-conditioned ease of the barbecue joint. I turn back on to Main Street and decide to forsake the faster interstate for the slow route back to Dartmouth Hitchcock Medical Centre in nearby Lebanon, back to the family and friends maintaining a bedside vigil.

This is what I have done every day these weeks past: spent my afternoons exploring a new community in this ample valley, finding a local spot where I can reflect, observe, and gather my thoughts. I am here because calamity befell my beloved nephew Prateek as he vacationed in Vermont with his young family. And in these past weeks, in the community of the hospital and in the communities all around the Upper Valley of the Connecticut River, I have rediscovered an America I thought lost.

Each day, I write dispatches on my nephew's condition to a WhatsApp bulletin board tracked by the many who could not be here in person. This is a community of mutual support, bound by our love and esteem for my nephew. This act of bonding across time zones and continents, and the further spread of our shared experience by members of the support group to their own spheres, have all served to forge a global community that finds and offers solace.

My afternoon interludes give me time to relish this wondrous and profoundly life affirming experience; not least the amazing investment, both personal and professional, of the care teams at Dartmouth Hitchcock Medical Centre in saving our boy from the cusp of death, and impelling him to a condition where he might one day reclaim a life of meaning.

The teams are prodigious, indeed: all summoned to deal with complex and overlapping aspects of my comatose nephew's treatment. I am deeply impressed by the commitment of Dr. Naser Jaleel and his neurosurgery team of doctors Vyacheslav (Slava) Makler, Brandon Root, James Lee, Daniel Dustin, and Daniel Calnan: who went into untried and untested realms of medicine to deal with an unprecedented combination of klebsiella meningitis and ventriculitis with infection rampant throughout Prateek's brain.

Each day, we are offered detailed and precise accounts of his progress by his specialist care doctors James Carroll, Alan Garber, Jeffrey Munson, Laura Paulin, Matthew Roginski, and Robert Westlake. Even as the lead doctors in the care team rotate, the senior residents are always with my nephew — doctors Esther Choi, Emily Harper, Nagma Janish, Peter Liang, Pranav Venkataraman and their colleagues.

Above all, it is both meaningful and moving to observe and experience the steadfast solicitude and unwavering compassion of the two dozen or so specialist nurses offering hands-on care and comfort to my nephew, minute by minute: Paul and Amy, Miriam and Robert, Lindsay and Michelle, dark-haired Amy and Lynn, Rachel and Abigail, Rob and Carly, Becca and Shelley, Lesley and Stacy, Brian and Anna, Brittany and Ann Marie, Jenna and Lauren, Whitney and Keryanne and Anjali.

I am struck by the infinite patience and gentleness of therapists Sarah and Jamme, Jason and Katie, who literally get my boy on to his feet as he finally awakes from weeks asleep, and speech pathologist Erica who helps him find voice. The common thread is the depth of care and commitment: the humanity and dedication so clear and consistent, day in and day out.

Before coming to Vermont and New Hampshire, I myself had developed a sense of cynicism about the United States: dismayed by its embittered politics, the open corruption of its president and his cohort, aghast at the capricious and arbitrary actions of a grand imperium's twilight.

Yet the patterns seen from afar are as far removed as they can be from the quality of care at Dartmouth Hitchcock Medical Centre. And from the everyday life of White River Junction and Lebanon; of Hanover and Rutland; of Quechee and Woodstock; of Lyme and Andover; of Enfield and New London; and all the other communities I have savoured. My afternoon rambles bring me face to face with the richness and diversity to be found in the ordinary intercourse of everyday life, the America Walt Whitman so memorably described in Song of Myself. This experience has truly humbled me: reminding me of the deep current of humanity that runs swift and true, far beneath the inchoate political battles and media furor.

My weeks in the Upper Valley have connected me with Gandhi's truth, for strangers have understood our suffering, opened their arms and hearts, welcomed us as though we were their own.

Hanover, New Hampshire, USA, September 2018

Midnight has come and gone at Maynard House, as has the seventh week of my precious nephew's arduous journey through a catastrophic illness. It is scant days since the doctors at Dartmouth declared that Prateek has crossed from "uncharted territory" to familiar ground, mightily easing the sorrow of his loved ones who have taken refuge at Maynard: his toddler daughter, wife, parents, mother-in-law, cousins, brother, friends.

Maynard House is a most Gandhian sanctuary: a hostel begun by two dozen volunteers some 40 years ago, as a refuge for patients and their families far from home. And supported by volunteers still, the refrigerator stocked with their home-cooked meat loaves and casseroles, and a communal table where our lives intertwine.

This is a stellar example of how you can make an extraordinary difference in the lives of others, through the consequences of small kindnesses that will alter lives in ways you may not be able to imagine.

I am sitting alone in the dark in the corner drawing room, TV long extinguished, finding solace in the storm lashing the windows. At times the wind retreats to a susurrus through the ample foliage, with a hiss of rain on gravel and mulch; before it picks up pace as the rain grows heavier, hurtling like cavalry against the unyielding glass. It is as Whitman described in a perfectly weighted line of *Song of Myself:* "The youth lies awake in the cedar roofed garrett and harks to the musical rain."

This is the solitude I enjoy most when sleep is far away: it is my time of healing, of connecting with the calmness within, gathering the resolve I need to navigate the clamorous emotions of the family as we wait for our loved one to emerge from darkness to the first gleam of hope.

Maynard is refuge and sanctuary, a place to be alone and be together: not just with friends, but with the ever-changing gathering around the table: where in sharing our cares, we find communion and companionship in the comfort of newfound friends who were strangers only moments ago.

We trudge weary and drained after another trying day at Dartmouth, to be greeted by house director Elizabeth Clarke's caring queries, her unceasingly thoughtful ways to lighten our burden with outings and visits, the relaxation of every house rule to accommodate the caprices of my 18-month-old grandniece.

I am often the last to retreat to my hostel bed, and am always rewarded by a chat with Darcy, who lives in the staff quarters upstairs. She comes down for a nightly ritual of running the dishwasher, tidying up, setting the windows or the air conditioning just so. Our words might be a few exchanges, yet in the course of our conversations, I discover the compassion of one who has overcome the hurt and sorrow of life's difficult journey with the redemptive power of forgiveness.

Maynard has meant the world to us, my nephew's far-flung family brought to Dartmouth Hitchcock Medical Centre from Canada and India and Florida in a time of calamity. It is here where we meet people we might never have encountered, learn of lives so far removed from the America portrayed in media and mythology as to evoke a bygone age. People who have bears and deer for neighbours. Folks who seldom visit a supermarket because they take a moose to last them the winter and fish all summer long. People who open their hearts to us, as we open ours to them.

We are grateful beneficiaries of the kindness of the volunteers who support Maynard, of founder Ann James whose weekly cookie delivery swiftly disappears, of the community's cooks who always have a hearty and wholesome meal waiting in the refrigerator.

This is the intersection of lives of dignity and purpose far removed from the toxic swirl of politics and the hard-voiced delirium of cable news. Here is the true greatness of the American spirit, forgotten or even dismissed by so much of its elite: the impulse to welcome and shelter strangers in need.

And this too is the journey of *Us*.

Us, as in you and me.

And all the people we know.

And all the people they know.

And their circles: both the intimate and the professional.

And their spheres of influence, from the vividly public ones to the deeply personal ones.

Us. Inspired with the blessing of Gandhi: to explore how we move beyond a culture of violence, a culture infected by greed; to rediscover how we can live together, free of fear and free of want.

Us will not dwell on Gandhi the man and his human follies. Nor on those of King and Mandela after him.

Our journey will take the power of Gandhi's ideas and example, the examples of King and Mandela, and use them as route-markers to illuminate the way. We will consider how they used populism as an instrument for change (even while others harnessed populism to the spread of resentment, hatred and violence).

In our journey, we will use Gandhi and King and Mandela as guides and even trailblazers, but the journey is ours to make: to find answers for our time and our challenges, drawing from the lessons of those who strode before us.

It will take just a few hours to take this journey, yet I hope it will inspire you to make a difference.

And how will we know the rules of the road for the travels ahead? We will know when we demand nothing more or less of each other than honesty, integrity, transparency, accountability and wisdom. Once that is reflected by us and within us, nearly everything else is detail. For this is how we take the honest measure of our worth, and showcase the inherent value of these values.

We will travel through history, through time, through the fog of atavistic memory, through the present, to the many versions of the future that await. I do not know what you will take away, as we travel together.

I hope that as we explore, you will be free and frank in examining both my provocations and your own provocations, and through it all come to a clearer understanding of the possibilities that await *Us*.

Shall we begin?

Chapter Two

Awaking with Dr. King

Nashville, Tennessee, USA, November 1963

By today's standards, the image on the bulging cathode ray tube is primitive indeed: black and white, flickering. Barely in focus. Yet we are riveted to it, my classmates and I, at a spectacle we have never seen: the state funeral of an assassinated American president.

I am standing among my Grade 3 classmates who have become friends; near flaxen-haired Prudy, who had put her arm beside mine to marvel at the difference in pigmentation before declaring she liked me. We are in the company of teachers with moist eyes and glistening faces as the cortege advances and the sonorous tones of Walter Cronkite fill the room.

Childhood memories are so shimmery that only the indelible details remain. Nonetheless, I vividly recall my gasp at the sight of three-year-old John F. Kennedy Jr. saluting his father's coffin. It is my first recollection of shock since Ma, the maternal grandmother who raised me, died when I was almost five.

I am the only person with dark skin in this pale-pigmented assembly in the Demonstration School of the George Peabody College for Teachers, an exception to the carefully-constructed skein of laws and customs which kept differently-shaded skin separate and apart. An exception, and also the vanguard of the changes that are about to sweep the American south.

Seeing that little boy brings home the enormity of what is happening. I still cannot articulate what I felt: it was certainly an echo of the inexpressible feelings that consumed me when cancer claimed Ma. I turn to catch Prudy's tearful eyes: children bonded in a loss we do not fully comprehend.

My first two months at Peabody are in every way a delight. A new world, a new school, the exotic cadence of southern American English, sparking a sense of wonder and discovery.

Our teachers were fully invested in opening young minds to the benefits of camaraderie and common purpose. Our chairs were arranged in a circle more frequently than rows of desks. A visit to the library inevitably ended with a glass of fruit punch from the teacher-librarian. As befitting a demonstration school of a college for teachers, this was indeed the foundation of the progressive education which unleashed creativity and built confidence.

The Kennedy presidency was both embodiment and catalyst for the enduring American optimism that the Republic's best days are still to come: a bred-in-the-bone belief that was made all the stronger by the fierce hope evoked by Dr. King in his leadership of the civil rights movement. Each was a soaring orator, Kennedy with his patrician roots in American nobility, and King with the atavistic power of prophecy; each able to stir and inspire the deepest impulses for good in the human heart.

Even before we came to America, the Kennedy name was magic in our house. It was a byword for optimism, hope, a future of endless bounty. More than that, the Kennedy family literally brought us to Nashville. In 1962, The Joseph P. Kennedy Jr. Foundation established visiting professorships to advance research into children with developmental disabilities. My father was one of the first three Kennedy professors appointed in 1963.

And now, as the Kennedy cortege makes its way to Arlington National Cemetery, our teachers have the bewildered look of adults who really do not know what comes next.

Looking back after the passage of decades, it is the moment of my political awakening. It comes at a particularly consequential time in America's life.

The Sixties brought a remaking of the old order, hastened by the campaign for civil rights and social justice where Martin Luther King Jr. is the first among equals. It is scarcely three months since he rallied light skinned and dark skinned Americans alike on the National Mall in Washington, with what history would come to know as his "I Have a Dream" speech.

Dr. King has awakened not just a quest for justice. His embrace of non-violence, his fearless advocacy, his conviction that the hatred of others must be answered with forbearance and love, give him moral supremacy. For the many pale skinned Americans who do indeed wish to give full measure to the noble words of their constitution — that all are created equal — support of Dr. King's movement becomes a moral obligation.

Our family are not only disruptors, we are a catalyst for change: I have come to understand, in my few fortnights in Nashville, that as invited guests to the United States of America, we are accommodated in ways far beyond the expectations of any Americans with similar pigmentation. Looking back over the span of many years, I marvel today at the bubble created for our family by the open heart of our American hosts. It is a generosity that is remarkable, and particularly courageous in the context of the times.

And I realise now, after many decades, that King's stirring leadership, his fearless activism, gave impetus to the many decent Americans of the ruling elites who wanted a different, more just, and more inclusive future for their country. In our own way, our family is part of that change.

The immense kindness of our family's hosts cocoons us in a special place, shelters us from the separate worlds only just beginning an uneasy intersection. The ample welcome offered by my teachers and classmates, their embrace of someone from a distant land, is remarkable by the societal norms of the American South in the 1960s.

Peabody College itself is part of that moral leadership. Dr. Nicholas Hobbs, the child psychologist who leads the college's teaching of human development, is seeking an inclusion that few adults have thought about in 1963: teaching developmentally disabled children, and bringing them into the mainstream of society. In a few months, Peabody would become one of the first elite schools in the south to abolish pigmentation-based entrance standards.

Indeed, our American hosts go out of their way to treat us as honoured guests, and to shelter us from the tribal storms that govern their own society.

Professor H. Carl Haywood, who would form a lifelong friendship with my parents, is exceptionally welcoming in his role as facilitator for the three Kennedy Foundation visiting professors recruited by Dr. Hobbs: my father, Bill Lynch and Len Ross. We are invited for cookouts in his backyard, socialise with other American academics. Dr. Hobbs plays a personal role in securing our accommodation, making sure we would not fall into the "whites" and "coloured" segregation of their society.

And even when apartheid applies its exclusion, and my Dad is refused service at an Atlanta restaurant during a conference, there is support and solidarity from his pale-pigmented colleagues, who refuse to grant their custom to a "whites only" restaurant.

Indeed, at the time of my enrolment in September 1963, the Peabody Board of Trustees voted to open the demonstration school to all qualified students regardless of race, creed and colour: 1964 brought the first full desegregation in all the classes.

The world beyond our sheltered sphere was frightening and violent indeed. All over the American south, pale-skinned people, infuriated at an uprising against the established social order, resorted to unbridled violence to preserve a pigmentation-based hierarchy. On September 15, 1963, the week after my term at Peabody began, white supremacists blew up the 16th Street Baptist Church in Birmingham, Alabama; murdering children gathered to worship. The bombers were finally convicted in 2001.

On June 15, 1963, President John F. Kennedy, goaded to action by Dr. King and impelled at last by a bomb attack on Dr. King's home on May 12, delivered a report to the nation on civil rights. The speech promised that dark-skinned Americans would at last enjoy the civil rights implicit in the emancipation of slaves a century earlier — and explicit in the United States Constitution.

For white supremacists, this was an absolute betrayal — even as Dr. King and civil rights activists deplored Kennedy for being too slow and too cautious. Despite all the hesitancy of his early presidency, Kennedy finally took action when the governor of Alabama, George Corley Wallace, stood at an auditorium door to prevent dark-pigmented students from enrolling — directly defying a court order. Kennedy framed his response as a moral obligation:

> We are confronted primarily with a moral issue. It is as old as the scriptures and is as clear as the American Constitution.
>
> The heart of the question is whether all Americans are to be afforded equal rights and equal opportunities, whether we are going to treat our fellow Americans as we want to be treated. If an American, because his skin is dark, cannot eat lunch in a restaurant open to the public, if he cannot send his children to the best public school available, if he cannot vote for the public officials who represent him, if, in short, he cannot enjoy the full and free life which all of us want, then who among us would be content to have the color of his skin changed and stand in his place?
>
> Who among us would then be content with the counsels of patience and delay? One hundred years of delay have passed

since President Lincoln freed the slaves, yet their heirs, their grandsons, are not fully free. They are not yet freed from the bonds of injustice. They are not yet freed from social and economic oppression. And this Nation, for all its hopes and all its boasts, will not be fully free until all its citizens are free.

We preach freedom around the world, and we mean it, and we cherish our freedom here at home, but are we to say to the world, and much more importantly, to each other that this is a land of the free except for the Negroes; that we have no second-class citizens except Negroes; that we have no class or caste system, no ghettoes, no master race except with respect to Negroes?

Now the time has come for this Nation to fulfill its promise. The events in Birmingham and elsewhere have so increased the cries for equality that no city or State or legislative body can prudently choose to ignore them.

The fires of frustration and discord are burning in every city, North and South, where legal remedies are not at hand. Redress is sought in the streets, in demonstrations, parades, and protests which create tensions and threaten violence and threaten lives.

We face, therefore, a moral crisis as a country and as a people. It cannot be met by repressive police action. It cannot be left to increased demonstrations in the streets.

It cannot be quieted by token moves or talk. It is a time to act in the Congress, in your State and local legislative body and, above all, in all of our daily lives. It is not enough to pin the blame on others, to say this is a problem of one section of the country or another, or deplore the fact that we face. A great change is at hand, and our task, our obligation, is to make that revolution, that change, peaceful and constructive for all.

Those who do nothing are inviting shame as well as violence. Those who act boldly are recognising right as well as reality. Next week I shall ask the Congress of the United States to act, to make a commitment it has not fully made in this century to the proposition that race has no place in American life or law.

That evening in Jackson, Mississippi, a pale-skinned fertiliser salesman named Byron de la Beckwith — himself raised by a dark-skinned nanny after both parents died in his childhood — lay in wait for a quarry.

His target was a decorated American soldier, Medgar Wiley Evers, a veteran of the D-Day landings in Normandy which hastened the Allied victory in the Second World War. After the war, Sgt. Evers became a civil rights leader, and famously declared, "You can kill a man, but you can't kill an idea."

Beckwith lay in wait with a rifle across the street from the Evers home, and shot Sgt. Evers in the back. Twice acquitted by similarly-pigmented hung juries, Beckwith was finally convicted of his crime in 1984 — a generation after the murder, and two years after the City of Jackson erected a statue of Evers. Two decades later, the airport was renamed in Evers' honour.

These tumultuous events in the summer of 1963 set the stage for the most remarkable appeal, perhaps the finest political oration of the 20th century, delivered by Dr. King on the steps of the Lincoln Memorial in Washington on August 28, 1963. (If you are not already familiar with it, it is widely available online and well worth listening to in its entirety in King's own voice.)

The power of his argument evoked a moral obligation:

> Five score years ago, a great American, in whose symbolic shadow we stand today, signed the Emancipation Proclamation. This momentous decree came as a great beacon light of hope to millions of Negro slaves who had been seared in the flames of withering injustice. It came as a joyous daybreak to end the long night of their captivity.
>
> But one hundred years later, the Negro still is not free. One hundred years later, the life of the Negro is still sadly crippled by the manacles of segregation and the chains of discrimination. One hundred years later, the Negro lives on a lonely island of poverty in the midst of a vast ocean of material prosperity. One hundred years later, the Negro is still languishing in the corners of American society and finds himself an exile in his own land. So we have come here today to dramatise a shameful condition.
>
> In a sense we have come to our nation's capital to cash a check. When the architects of our republic wrote the magnificent words of the Constitution and the Declaration of Independence, they were signing a promissory note to which every American was to fall heir. This note was a promise that all men, yes, black men as well as white men, would be guaranteed the unalienable rights of life, liberty, and the pursuit of happiness.
>
> ...

So we have come to cash this check — a check that will give us upon demand the riches of freedom and the security of justice. We have also come to this hallowed spot to remind America of the fierce urgency of now.

Then, Dr. King made an unprecedented declaration. Revolt, he said, cannot mean violence. Indeed, in his explicit call for non-violence as the only available moral instrument, he gave a full throated echo of Gandhi, especially in evoking the courage to face martyrdom.

But there is something that I must say to my people who stand on the warm threshold which leads into the palace of justice. In the process of gaining our rightful place we must not be guilty of wrongful deeds. Let us not seek to satisfy our thirst for freedom by drinking from the cup of bitterness and hatred.

We must forever conduct our struggle on the high plane of dignity and discipline. We must not allow our creative protest to degenerate into physical violence.

Again and again we must rise to the majestic heights of meeting physical force with soul force.

The marvelous new militancy which has engulfed the Negro community must not lead us to a distrust of all white people, for many of our white brothers, as evidenced by their presence here today, have come to realise that their destiny is tied up with our destiny. They have come to realise that their freedom is inextricably bound to our freedom. We cannot walk alone.

...

I am not unmindful that some of you have come here out of great trials and tribulations. Some of you have come fresh from narrow jail cells. Some of you have come from areas where your quest for freedom left you battered by the storms of persecution and staggered by the winds of police brutality. You have been the veterans of creative suffering.

Continue to work with the faith that unearned suffering is redemptive.

Dr. King offered a social contract. A means of being and belonging to and with one another. It may remain forever a work in progress, yet it is a blueprint that can be adopted by any society, and adapted to fit the needs of any society.

If there is only one principal learning in your own quest to become an even more effective agent of change, it is to be found in Dr. King's words, which have as great an urgency today as they did then.

I say to you today, my friends, so even though we face the difficulties of today and tomorrow, I still have a dream. It is a dream deeply rooted in the American dream.

I have a dream that one day this nation will rise up and live out the true meaning of its creed: "We hold these truths to be self-evident: that all men are created equal."

I have a dream that one day on the red hills of Georgia the sons of former slaves and the sons of former slave owners will be able to sit down together at the table of brotherhood.

I have a dream that one day even the state of Mississippi, a state sweltering with the heat of injustice, sweltering with the heat of oppression, will be transformed into an oasis of freedom and justice.

I have a dream that my four little children will one day live in a nation where they will not be judged by the colour of their skin but by the content of their character.

I have a dream today.

I have a dream that one day, down in Alabama, with its vicious racists, with its governor having his lips dripping with the words of interposition and nullification; one day right there in Alabama, little black boys and black girls will be able to join hands with little white boys and white girls as sisters and brothers.

I have a dream today.

I have a dream that one day every valley shall be exalted, every hill and mountain shall be made low, the rough places will be made plain, and the crooked places will be made straight, and the glory of the Lord shall be revealed, and all flesh shall see it together.

Then, in a stirring conclusion that still has no parallel in public discourse during my lifetime, Dr. King turned the dream into a call for action that could not be negated.

This is our hope. This is the faith that I go back to the South with.

With this faith we will be able to hew out of the mountain of despair a stone of hope.

With this faith we will be able to transform the jangling discords of our nation into a beautiful symphony of brotherhood.

With this faith we will be able to work together, to pray together, to struggle together, to go to jail together, to stand up for freedom together, knowing that we will be free one day

This will be the day when all of God's children will be able to sing with a new meaning, "My country, 'tis of thee, sweet land of liberty, of thee I sing. Land where my fathers died, land of the pilgrim's pride, from every mountainside, let freedom ring."

And if America is to be a great nation this must become true. So let freedom ring from the prodigious hilltops of New Hampshire.
Let freedom ring from the mighty mountains of New York.
Let freedom ring from the heightening Alleghenies of Pennsylvania!
Let freedom ring from the snow capped Rockies of Colorado!
Let freedom ring from the curvaceous slopes of California!
But not only that; let freedom ring from Stone Mountain of Georgia!
Let freedom ring from Lookout Mountain of Tennessee!
Let freedom ring from every hill and molehill of Mississippi.
From every mountainside, let freedom ring.

And when this happens, when we allow freedom to ring, when we let it ring from every village and every hamlet, from every state and every city, we will be able to speed up that day when all of God's children, black men and white men, Jews and Gentiles, Protestants and Catholics, will be able to join hands and sing in the words of the old Negro spiritual, "Free at last! free at last! thank God Almighty, we are free at last!"

Reading these words today, I hear his voice, his cadence, his unmistakable and inimitable way of infusing his statements into one's deepest consciousness. Above all, in this age of "African-Americans", I recall how King despised the term, rejected its implied divisiveness and its attempt to dilute the American identity promised by the Constitution. He insisted that dark-pigmented Americans be accepted as Americans, without hyphens, arguing that "America must be made a nation in which its multiracial people are partners in power."

Even so, it might have been difficult for King to imagine that the seeds of that future already were sown. There were portents of change in America in 1963 that even King's most ardent followers may not have been able to foresee in their time. In a two-bedroom apartment on Alexander Street in Honolulu, a two-storey edifice around a swimming pool with a courtyard, a single mother barely out of her teens was organising a life for herself and her son in her parents' home. She had separated from her husband, who turned out to be a bigamist with another family in his native land. So Stanley Ann Dunham enrolled at the University of Hawaii in an academic career that would lead to a PhD; and a life journey that would take her to Indonesia for field research: all the while providing a stimulating life for her son, Barack Hussein Obama Jr.

Barack Obama raised eyebrows, headlines, and expectations when he won the Democratic party nomination for the presidency in 2008, leaving Dr. King's companions from the "I Have a Dream" rally replete with disbelief.

"I will be on the platform, and I'm going to try to keep my balance and not have what I call an out-of-body experience," Congressman John Lewis said before Obama's presidential inauguration.

"I want to be able to see down the Mall and past the Washington Monument and get a glimpse of the Lincoln Memorial, where we stood 45 years ago.

"When we were organising voter-registration drives, going on the Freedom Rides, sitting in, coming here to Washington for the first time, getting arrested, going to jail, being beaten, I never thought — I never dreamed — of the possibility that an African American would one day be elected President of the United States," said Lewis, whom police bludgeoned into unconsciousness during the Selma voting rights march in the spring of 1965.

And as King spoke of his dream from the steps of the Lincoln Memorial, another foundation of the future was about to unfold. On the west coast of the United States. At the University of California at Berkeley, Shyamala Gopalan, a brilliant scientist from Madras in southern India, had recently married Donald Harris, a fellow graduate student, from the Caribbean island of Jamaica. In a few weeks she would be pregnant with her first daughter, whom she would name after the Great Goddess manifested in the beauty of a lotus blossom, Kamala Devi Harris.

Consider that only one election cycle after the Obama presidency, when Kamala Harris announced her own candidacy for the White House in 2019, the loudest media turmoil was whether she had been too rigorous or too lenient in her administration of criminal justice while Attorney General of California. There was only a secondary reference to what might have been the dominant headline a decade earlier: that a woman of Indo-Caribbean ancestry is credibly seeking the presidency of the United States.

As Dr. King foresaw, the day has come when leaders are judged not by the colour of their skin, but by the content of their character.

Santa Monica, California, USA, August 1964

I have just arrived with my family in Los Angeles, for the second chapter of our American adventure. After completing his year at Nashville, my father accepted a post as a visiting professor at the University of California at Los Angeles. It is already understood that he can make a career here, with the potential for tenure and a full professorship by the time he turns 35, in January 1966. It has been an exhilarating summer. After saying goodbye to our newfound friends in Nashville, we came west in a roundabout way: stopping in Washington DC and New York, finally boarding a train in Chicago for the leisurely overland trip to the west coast.

My political awakening surging, I have followed and cheered the transformative events of a tumultuous summer. On May 28, President Lyndon Baines Johnson signed into law the Civil Rights Act, banning discrimination based on race, colour, religion, sex, or national origin. And handed the pen to Dr. King. This is the moment of legal triumph minorities awaited for a century, since President Abraham Lincoln signed the Emancipation Proclamation in January 1863, ending slavery.

Chapter Three

Mandela's truth

Cambridge, United Kingdom, February 1987

Tendayi Nyakunu pulls up the collar of his overcoat as we lean into the relentless wind driving the dampness of the Cambridgeshire fens deep into the bone, already shivering even though we are only a few hundred metres from the house we share on Barton Road. We catch one another's eye and nod in unison, dipping into the embracing heat of our local pub, the Hat and Feathers, and its warming array of whisky.

Ours is a pleasing companionship. We are among the three holders of a media fellowship funded by the Nuffield Foundation, and with our Singaporean colleague Tan Wang Joo, we have full run of the considerable delights Cambridge offers a curious mind. Indeed, both Wolfson College and the university as a whole evoke a feeling of belonging.

For the first time in my adult life, I feel free to be who I am. Everyone is clever. There is no need for pretension or egotism, because all are capable of deflating the slightest sign of posturing and preening.

In fact, I have already come to understand that people of genuine accomplishment embrace humility as a cardinal virtue.

We three Nuffield journalists, products of a once far-flung empire who make their living writing in English, give truth to the collaborative possibilities of diverse nations bound by a common tongue. The warmth of the welcome offered me by Cambridge, and my instinctive sense of seamlessly belonging, is a comforting evocation of the sentiment Derek Walcott offered about Wystan Auden's poetry in his *Eulogy to W.H. Auden:*

> *in treachery and in union,*
> *despite your Empire's wrong,*
> *I made my first communion*
> *there, with the English tongue.*

Despite my feelings of communion with what I have come to consider as the very best of English culture and civilisation, Tendayi and I are en route to oppose a particularly nasty imperial legacy: the race-based power structure in South Africa.

My country, Canada, led the expulsion of South Africa from the Commonwealth, and was a leader in an international campaign of divestment and sanctions against a racialist regime. Nonetheless, I have my own misgivings about the daily evidence that violence begets violence, and wonder if there ever can be a relatively peaceful transition to majority rule. The necessity of emancipation does not quell a legitimate and abiding fear that the brutality of apartheid will bring an equally brutal reckoning.

In Britain, the divestment and sanctions programme does not carry the support of the British government of Margaret Thatcher, because of the primacy of British business interests. Moreover, the view is far from universal in Britain, where Nelson Mandela is an icon of liberation. So much so that in Britain's second city of Glasgow, the municipal politicians have renamed the gathering place in their city's heart as Nelson Mandela Square.

Yet as I take an ample mouthful of whisky beside Tendayi, Mandela is more an icon and an image than a person of flesh and blood. We have no idea what he looks like, save a handful of grainy photographs: as a huge, burly, immensely handsome boxer; his defiance in the dock as he was sentenced to life imprisonment in 1964 for sabotage. He has been out of sight, but absolutely not out of mind; and the South African resistance led in his name has made those old pictures a symbol of their fight.

Even so, the future of South Africa is uncharted territory. Unlike Gandhi, unlike Martin Luther King Jr., Mandela went to prison for life in 1964 with an open embrace of violence as the only remaining course to oppose the injustice of apartheid. As he declared in his opening statement at the Rivonia Trial:

> I came to the conclusion that as violence in this country was inevitable, it would be unrealistic to continue preaching peace and non-violence. This conclusion was not easily arrived at. It was only when all else had failed, when all channels of peaceful protest had been barred to us, that the decision was made to embark on violent forms of political struggle. I can only say that I felt morally obliged to do what I did.

What Mandela took to be his moral obligation was quite the opposite of the martyrdom-inflected journeys of Gandhi and King. Nonetheless, there is power and logic in Mandela's reasoning:

> Four forms of violence were possible. There is sabotage, there is guerrilla warfare, there is terrorism, and there is open revolution. We chose to adopt the first. Sabotage did not involve loss of life, and it offered the best hope for future race relations. Bitterness would be kept to a minimum and, if the policy bore fruit, democratic government could become a reality.

There is a parallel to the vision and teachings of both Gandhi and King. Mandela foresaw a shared future where people could transcend hatred, rise above divisions of race and economic injustice, and flourish together. In his final public declaration before he was jailed, Mandela laid out his aspiration in compelling words:

> I have fought against white domination and I have fought against black domination. I have cherished the ideal of a democratic and free society in which all persons live together in harmony and with equal opportunities. It is an ideal which I hope to live for and to achieve. But if needs be, it is an ideal for which I am prepared to die.

Tonight, as we venture into the bleak midwinter, Mandela's vision is in the realm of improbability. Street resistors in South Africa are fighting the organised brutality of the state with rocks and petrol bombs, even as Tendayi and I sit in the comfort of a

Cambridgeshire pub, in the agreeable company of others seeking a haven of warmth and welcome.

The fortifying whisky within us, we step out of the Hat and Feathers back into an East Anglian winter's night, pulling our scarves tighter. We come upon the open playing fields and feel the full force of the wind lashing the fens, as we complete the bracing trek across Sheep's Green. And by the time we reach the slippery stones of the Silver Street bridge we are ready for respite. Heads down, we trudge on. Another stop would make us late for the event none wanted to miss: the concert at Cambridge's Corn Exchange by the exiled South African trumpeter Hugh Masekela, who has just written and released the evocative anthem "Bring Him Back Home."

That evocation of home is a far remove indeed from these windy fens. For Harare-bred Tendayi, this is a bittersweet moment. As a journalist in Zimbabwe, he has experienced the elation of independence turn into the dour cynicism of a revolution that has consumed its own. He knows all too well from his own experience, that national liberation can quickly devolve into despotism.

In scant months, Tendayi will go home to face the desolate prospect of decades of rule by Robert Gabriel Mugabe, the Jesuit trained revolutionary who has crushed all rivals, slaughtered political opponents, and now styles himself as the champion of "scientific Marxism" as he prepares to convert his prime ministership into a presidency for life.

Masekela carries the promise of South African liberation: and the distant hope that after Zimbabwe, South Africa will get it right.

There already is a swirling eddy of sweater-and-jacket clad humanity in the cavernous hall, once a medieval granary, repurposed into an entertainment venue. A soaring note stills the crowd, and all attention switches to the stage.

Masekela's trumpet fills the warm and smoky hall with the lyricism of loss, a declaration that exile is a fruitless ramble in the darkest caverns of the soul, where your lost homeland calls to you with a longing that is beyond the experience of those of us who left our hearths by choice.

After exploring nearly every emotion a horn can conjure, Masekela unleashes his voice in that in-between land that is neither tenor nor baritone:

> *Bring back Nelson Mandela*
> *Bring him back home to Soweto*
> *I want to see him walking down the streets*
> *Of South Africa, tomorrow*

It is a melody so infectious that in another circumstance it might have carried the calypso exuberance of The Mighty Sparrow, or even the rough-hewn slyness of Chester Arthur Burnett, who styled himself the Howlin' Wolf. There is much more to it than lyricism, much more than protest and defiance. In that close-pressed intimacy of the Cambridge Corn Exchange, as the audience takes up the anthem, a spark of hope swells into an outpouring of conviction that Nelson Mandela soon will be free to walk in Soweto.

Within weeks of that performance in the Corn Exchange, Masekela's work would become the global anthem of the movement to liberate Mandela and emancipate South Africa. Indeed, it was a moment of *ubuntu*, the articulation of deep empathy with the other; a revelation of the connective energies that transcend origin and cultures to bind humankind as one.

Three years later, on Feb. 11 1990, Mandela walked out of prison after reaching an agreement with President F.W. de Klerk, whom he called a "man of integrity." There was no agreement on emancipation, only to "normalise" the political climate in South Africa.

And a fortnight later, in Durban, to the dismay of armed militants and those who believed violence as a necessary weapon against oppression, Mandela called on his compatriots to abandon arms.

> Friends, comrades, and the people of Natal, I greet you all. I do so in the name of peace, the peace that is so desperately and urgently needed in this region.
>
> In Natal, apartheid is a deadly cancer in our midst, setting house against house, and eating away at the precious ties that bound us together. This strife among ourselves wastes our energy and destroys our unity. My message to those of you involved in this battle of brother against brother is this: take your guns, your knives, and your pangas, and throw them into the sea. Close down the death factories. End this war now!
>
> We also come together today to renew the ties that make us one people, and to reaffirm a single united stand against the oppression of apartheid. We have gathered here to find a way of building even greater unity than we already have. Unity is the pillar and foundation of our struggle to end the misery which is caused by the oppression which is our greatest enemy. This

repression and the violence it creates cannot be ended if we fight and attack each other.

He drew a direct line from Gandhi's first campaign for equality in South Africa to the choices facing his country today, and evoked a unity wherein all could live with dignity.

> Another strand in the struggle against oppression began with the formation, right here in Natal, of the first black political organisation in Africa. The Natal Indian Congress, founded in 1894, began a tradition of extra-parliamentary protest that continues into the present. The next decade saw the increasing radicalisation of Indian politics under the leadership of Mahatma Gandhi.
>
> In 1906, at the time when Bambatha led sections of Africans in a war to destroy the Poll Tax, our brothers who originated from India, led by Mahatma Gandhi, fought against the oppression of the British Government. In 1913, we see Indian workers striking in the sugar-cane plantations and in the coal mines. These actions show the oppressed of South Africa waging a struggle to end exploitation and oppression, mounting an important challenge to the repressive British rule.
>
> In the passive resistance campaign of 1946, over 2,000 Indians went to jail, many for occupying land reserved for whites. The campaign made clear the common nature of Indian and African oppression and the necessity of united resistance. . . We remind the people of Natal of this long and proud tradition of cooperation between Africans and Indians against racial discrimination and other forms of injustice and oppression.

Months after his release from prison, when Nelson Mandela walked into the House of Commons in Ottawa on 18 June 1990, I found it difficult to resist a swell of pride as he said:

> I would like to take this opportunity to salute the great Canadian people whom you represent, and with whom we believe you are in full accord on the question of South Africa. They have proved themselves not only to be steadfast friends of our struggling people but great defenders of human rights and the idea of democracy itself. They are to us like brothers and sisters from whose warm embrace we shall never be parted...

> In this context, I would also like to pay special tribute to the Prime Minister of this country, Brian Mulroney, who has continued along the path charted by Prime Minister Diefenbaker who acted against apartheid because he knew that no person of conscience could stand aside as a crime against humanity was being committed... We are certain that you will, together with the rest of the Canadian people, stay the course with us, not only as we battle on to end the apartheid system but also as we work to build a happy, peaceful and prosperous future for all the people of South and Southern Africa.

The events leading up to Mandela's speech in the Canadian Parliament were nearly four decades in the making, beginning at a time when apartheid still pervaded both the southern United States and South Africa.

The struggle for civil rights within the United States far overshadowed South Africa's anti-apartheid movement in the world's consciousness in 1960, when Canada's Prime Minister John Diefenbaker led South Africa's expulsion from the Commonwealth.

By 1964, when I was a boy in Nashville confronting water fountains and washrooms marked "white" and "coloured," all eyes were on Martin Luther King Jr., whose soaring oratory led freedom marchers to confront police dogs and police bullets in the United States. Relatively few in the outside world paid attention when a lawyer turned defiant saboteur named Nelson Mandela was sentenced to life imprisonment by a South African court, proclaiming that he was willing to give his life in the quest for a free, democratic and inclusive society.

Due to the Progressive Conservative Prime Minister Diefenbaker's leadership, Canada was one of the few countries that kept South Africa's struggle for emancipation front and centre in the 1960s, particularly within the Commonwealth.

By the time Mandela walked out of prison, the firebrand in the apartheid dock had evolved into an ardent champion of non-violence, imbued with the healing and empowering force called forgiveness.

By unleashing the power of forgiving his oppressors, Mandela had fully embraced the principles of Mohandas Karamchand Gandhi. The arc of history did indeed bend to justice: Mahatma Gandhi was part of the liberation movement that led to the founding of the African National Congress in 1912, six years before Mandela's birth. Gandhi used his South African experience to bolster the Indian National Congress, which led to the emancipation of India in 1947. In 1990, the newly freed Mandela led the African National Congress in the negotiation of a post-apartheid constitution that would at last bring the emancipation of South Africa.

Gandhi's dream of emancipation was shattered by the partition of India, and the million slaughtered in the ensuing riots of 1947, along the arbitrary lines drawn by the British colonial administration. That lesson was not lost on Mandela, who faced and succeeded in the enormous challenge of a peaceful transition to inclusive governance because of his own example of forgiveness, and his embrace of non-violence as a way of being in the world.

Indeed, as a remedy to the culture of war and violence, Mandela called on the world to embrace a new political culture based on human rights as a way of life: this is the unrealised dream he leaves us as his legacy.

Chapter Four

Learning to embrace Gandhi

Ahmedabad, India, December 2011

I have arrived at the moment of truth, but I cannot bring myself to do what I need to do.

I have walked in circles, hesitated, stared, circled some more. Listened to the surging crescendo of evening birds coming home to roost in the neem tree he planted, beneath whose branches he meditated and held court. I have circled the neem more than once, looked askance at the maze of concrete well-meaning civic authorities built on the banks of the Sabarmati river which once flowed past serene and uncontrolled, and returned to the moment of indecision.

I sense the next act will accomplish a pilgrimage that began with my first sentience; bring me to a connection that might offer succour for my soul, solace after the restlessness of exile. Still I hesitate, hovering above the fading ochre paint of the verandah, and the simple whitewash of the cottage it serves.

I cannot escape the feeling that what I am about to do amounts to sacrilege: a ridiculous thought to be sure, but one I cannot shake.

I close my eyes, draw in my deepest breath, and as the neem resounds with birdsong, I do it. I lower my bulky frame to the verandah, lean my back to the wall, and sit where he sat. My eyes still shut, feeling the same hard surfaces he felt, I imagine the weight of his slight body on this very spot, the company he welcomed, the spinning wheel which became a universal symbol of self-reliance, the passions he kindled and the change he embodied.

I am deep in the moment, mindful of the birds and the thunder of Ahmedabad traffic beyond the ashram gates, yet feeling the pacifying flow that comes from meditation. Feeling his presence, on the weathered cement floor in his dwelling at the Sabarmati Ashram he established in 1917. And when at last I exhale and open my eyes, I slowly bring the horizon into focus, seeing at least a semblance of what he would have seen, all those decades ago.

Rooted to the very spot whence he tried to wean us from the seductive allure of might and domination, animated by his embrace of the power of truth, coming to full reckoning with the very meaning of my name and its burden of identity, I at last accept communion with Mohandas Karamchand Gandhi.

It is at once overwhelming, exhilarating, liberating.

And a moment of absolute clarity; I feel a tingle that starts in my scalp, suffuses my face and runs down into my shoulders and finally reaches my heart: the sensation of blessing hands being laid upon my head.

That benediction weighs upon me then, as it does now.

It did not come easily, that act of Communion. Since my earliest memories, Gandhi has been everywhere, even more in my private life than in the public sphere. All my grandparents followed the Vaishnava tradition of Gandhi's Hindu faith, its belief in finding bliss through devotion remarkably reminiscent of evangelical Christianity and Sufi Islam.

My paternal grandfather Biswanath and my grandmother Nilamani expected their descendants to live lives of humility and grace, favouring homespun cotton and sandals (my father wore long pants for the first time when he left home for graduate studies at the University of Patna).

I have endearing memories of both my grandfathers taking me to the Gaudiya ashram on the Grand Road in Puri, just down the street from the Jagannatha (lord of the universe) temple which is one of the required pilgrimages of every Hindu life, for a delicious vegetarian lunch and the blessings of their unfailingly kind and welcoming *gurubhais* (those who have been initiated by the same guru).

Indeed, my maternal grandfather Ramchandra's *gurubhai,* who took the name Prabhupada, would bring the Vaishnava tradition outside India by preaching devotion to Krishna. He did so by establishing a worldwide network of temples through the International Society for Krishna Consciousness, popularly known as the Hare Krishna movement with its exuberant devotees of every culture, gender, and ethnic origin.

In my grandparents' teaching, the highest aspiration is to be a kind and loving person, causing neither hurt nor harm through speech and deed; freeing yourself of attachment to material things, focusing on the divinity that resides within each individual.

This catalogue of shared values is an ideal foundation for a culture of love. These are the building blocks in living human rights as a way of life, and claiming the right to be human.

This is the tradition captured in one of Gandhi's favourite hymns, describing the duty of a Vaishnava: feel the pain of others, selflessly help the afflicted, respect all, disparage none, welcome and celebrate the world entire, utter no untruth, respect all women as though they were your mother, forsake greed and avarice, reject worldly attachments, yield to neither lust nor anger.

In my own experience, I have always felt this to be an impossibly high standard, which is why it was so difficult for me to sit in Gandhi's spot at the Sabarmati ashram. I am an epicure. I enjoy drink, live a gregarious life, have a fondness for bawdy humour, weep during sentimental films. I have a weakness for French cologne, distinctive wines, and a well-tailored suit. I lack entirely the discipline to renounce all the things that bring me pleasure. And despite long flirtations with vegetarianism (the Vaishnava diet is so restrained it bans even onions and garlic as foods that ignite the passions), I always relapse to the lure of the omnivore.

And yet, there is a bond.

I have at last come to believe, since the Sabarmati epiphany, that perhaps one need not subscribe to the puritanical standards Gandhi preached and practised — and indeed, rituals that many modern people would believe patriarchal if not downright creepy — in order to embrace the ideas and principles Gandhi forged into his moral weapons:

- *satyagraha* (literally adherence to truth; more philosophically the pursuit of imbuing truth with moral force to improve one's own soul and bring change in the larger world),

- *sarvodaya* (serving the well-being of all) and

- *ahimsa* (the absence of violence).

In this sesquicentennial year there are many volumes written about Gandhi the man: already, there are tomes delving into his complexity, and his persona of a saintly but flawed man, a patriarch par excellence who nonetheless empowered women to emerge from the stifling cloisters of family and social convention. The journey of *Us* does not take that diversion.

The clarity that followed my Sabarmati communion brought me to this: the clearest possible understanding that there can be no human dignity so long as fear prevails. As the poet Seferis put it, if pain is human we are not human beings merely to suffer pain. And this: while Gandhi's Vaishnava philosophy asks you not to covet, it also imbues with the duty to ensure none are without the necessities of life.

Freedom from fear. Freedom from want. This is the basis on which we build lives of meaning and purpose.

Gandhi was murdered in January 1948, and it is astonishing to think that his entire life's work unfolded against a backdrop where the mighty trampled the weak with impunity.

This was long before the rise of human rights as a secular religion, with its own institutions and high priests and rituals. Even so, Gandhi's work deeply informed the evolution of our societal thinking: it became a foundation for the Universal Declaration of Human Rights adopted by the newly-formed United Nations on the 10th of December 1948, and all that flowed therefrom.

It was here in this cottage, on this verandah, that Gandhi defined the seven public sins he believed must be overcome; to move the arc of civilisation towards justice. He named these in 1925:

· Wealth without Work

· Pleasure without Conscience

· Knowledge without Character

· Commerce without Morality

· Science without Humanity

· Worship without Sacrifice

· Politics without Principle

Stop and think about this diagnosis.

Look at the world around you, your community, your workplace; take stock of the people you know. If you maintain a clear-eyed gaze, you will find examples of each one of these public sins.

Now think about the historic context. Gandhi's diagnosis came at the height of the colonial era, when much of Europe and North America was prospering in the years that followed the First World War.

It came only seven years after the Russian Revolution, before Stalin killed off his rivals and began his reign of terror. It came only four years after the Shanghai meeting that established the Communist Party of China, at a time of feuding warlords, when Mao Zedong was still an idealistic revolutionary in his twenties. It came four years before the Great Depression, when the fruits of "commerce without morality" plunged the world economy into the abyss.

The "if only" of hindsight is all too tempting when one looks at the two decades that followed Gandhi's assessment of what ails the world.

Consider the barbaric folly of the Georgian tyrant Iosif Vissarionovich Dzhugashvili (who took the *nom de guerre* Stalin); and the catastrophe his leadership brought to the Union of Soviet Socialist Republics: twenty million residents dead in the Second World War, millions more perishing in his purges and in labour-camp exile to the frozen barren lands of Siberia.

Consider the cynical fascism of Benito Mussolini, the iron-fisted rule of Francisco Franco in Spain and Antonio Salazar in Portugal.

Consider the arc of the brooding Austrian painter Adolf Hitler, whose ability to mesmerise masses with his dreams of uniting the German speaking peoples into a blood-and-soil nationalism forged the ideology of National Socialism and the industrial slaughter of 11 million humans in concentration camps, including the calculated and relentless genocide (by the historian Martin Gilbert's reckoning) of at least 5,758,720 Jewish people.

It is all too easy now to look back at history and understand how these public sins unleashed a paroxysm of violence that engulfed the world. But it is not just a question of history.

As they did in Gandhi's time, these public sins continue to afflict humankind and the species with whom we share this biosphere.

Each of us can look within our community, our polity, our nation, and our state to find myriad examples. Indeed, there are entire cadres of leadership — in the public, private and even philanthropic spheres — who openly and ardently embrace these sins as markers on the path to "success", or as a necessary means to secure their own ambitions.

And we see all too clearly that these public sins bolster a culture of might, dominance and subjugation — especially in the Gandhian construct, which holds poverty as the most debilitating form of violence.

Mandela, who himself took inspiration from Gandhi during his long incarceration, concluded that the world needs an entirely new political culture. One based on our common humanity. On collaboration and cooperation. One in which the right to a fulfilled, meaningful human life is paramount: a culture of human rights.

As you and I continue the journey of *Us,* we will explore how we can be the agents of change. We have at our disposal the astonishing connectivity of the digital world, ways to intermingle that were not imagined in the last century, or even when the new millennium began.

Even now, it is worth recalling Gandhi's methods, and how he became a peerless agent of change. He believed in the power of example. Specifically, the power of sacrifice. In Gandhi's view, the glue of social cohesion was to be selfless.

Rather than the pursuit of individual liberty, he believed in the fulfilment of individual obligations. Our obligations to our family, our friends. The responsibility to care for one another, to believe in one another, to build the bonds of love and trust and fellowship and companionship.

Gandhi had no illusions about the chicanery of politics, about the corrosive power of greed and inequality. Giving of yourself, in the service of those in your family and your community, took precedence over gratifying your personal desires and the exclusive pursuit of your personal happiness. And above all, to make these sacrifices without expecting anything in return. This in itself is the polar opposite of transactional relationships. He believed that this willingness to sacrifice makes you fearless.

His second method was to walk in the shoes of the dispossessed, the forgotten, those at the fringes of society. Gandhi believed that the only democracy worthy of the name would put human dignity far ahead of accumulated wealth. Once the poorest enjoyed the same respect accorded to the wealthiest, when the human dignity of the poorest in a society mattered above all, then we could rightly claim that the arc of history would bend toward justice.

Poverty, in Gandhi's view, was the worst and most pervasive form of violence. Thus he evoked a concept he called *sarvodaya* — a Sanskrit word roughly translating as the welfare of all. It can be more clearly expressed in English as a philosophy that nurtures the common good and enhances the common wealth.

Thus, the twin concepts of *satyagraha* and *sarvodaya* become the radiant principles of Gandhi's goal of societal transformation.

Gandhi thought economic inequality was a tyranny with a sugar coating: that the interests of the rich and powerful would always prevail until we all recognised our obligation to uplift the weakest and powerless. Thus, he eschewed his privileged background — his merchant family, after all, had been prosperous enough to send him to the University of London, despite the perpetuated myth that Gandhi came from an impoverished home — to live, eat and dress as simply as possible.

(This is the Gandhian image that led the British wartime leader and long-time prime minister Winston Spencer Churchill to tartly observe, after Gandhi met with the British viceroy Lord Irwin in February 1931 to negotiate a timetable for autonomy, that: "It is alarming and nauseating to see Mr Gandhi, a seditious Middle Temple lawyer, now posing as a fakir of a type well known in the east, striding half naked up the steps of the viceregal palace, while he is still organising and conducting a campaign of civil disobedience, to parlay on equal terms with the representative of the Emperor-King.")

Gandhi's self-generated humility, and identification with the poorest of the poor, gave him the ability to build from the ground up: in utter contrast to the post-colonial politicians who often imposed top-down, centralised "solutions" for inequity in their efforts to abet societal development.

The willingness to sacrifice, and to shed privilege to empathise with the poor, was the ardent core of *satyagraha:* to use the power of selflessness and sacrifice to shame the powerful and privileged to dilute their advantages for the betterment of the common good.

His simplest organising principle was the power of 10. Find ten people who will spread your message. Task each with finding ten more. And watch it multiply. This is how he was able to motivate tens of thousands of people to join his cause, across a country with dozens of languages and ethnicities in a vast geography, long before there was any facility and ease in mass communications.

Imagine how much more that power is amplified in the digital era, and what you can do with this organising principle.

Underlying this principle was the cheerful commitment to face the consequences of your actions, even if you knew you were breaking the law. This is civil disobedience: standing up to an unjust law, and being perfectly willing to face imprisonment — which made you a martyr, drew attention to your cause, and gave it much more prominence than it might otherwise have gained. A principle used to great effect by Dr. King and his contemporaries.

Gandhi learned this technique while he was a law student at University College, London. He had arrived in 1888 at the dawn of the women's suffrage movement: the campaign to empower women to vote in elections. The International Council of Women (ICW) was founded in that year, the very first women's rights organisation. Its members took to the streets to demand equality and justice, courting imprisonment and arrest.

Having been formed in a rigid patriarchy — and educated in one, during his London years — Gandhi did not necessarily agree with the ICW or the suffrage movements which began in the mid-19th century as a movement striving for gender equality. Rather, he learned how a movement can win the battle for moral superiority by disrupting an unjust social order, and how this sustained civil disobedience can shame even a powerful patriarchy into making concessions.

We will walk along these pathways as we continue. We can learn anew the essence of what Gandhi gave us, adapt his ideas to the reality of our world, bring thinking shaped by the events and currents of the early 20th century into relevance for the life we live today.

In doing so, we will establish new ways to move away from the culture of violence and the politics of division. We will explore what we can do, as true communitarians working in community with collaboration and cooperation, to advance the common good and nurture our common wealth.

Chapter Five

Being and Becoming

New York City, USA, July 1964

We are about to enter the newly-built United Nations headquarters on the East River, my parents and I, when I feel a frisson that comes from nowhere.

It is a feeling one sometimes has, logically absurd but emotionally resonant, that one belongs to a particular spot on the planet: although you are here for the first time, it is somehow familiar, calling to you with a connection you cannot quite understand. For the first time since leaving India a year before, the sensation of belonging ripples through me, on the plaza of the United Nations building. It's a confusing feeling, one I really can't articulate. Somehow, being here just feels right.

Forty years later, I would be meeting inside with the secretary-general's staff, discussing my proposal to levy a global tax on military spending to pay for peacebuilding and peacekeeping. And the book with the chapter that sparked the consultation would be in a prominent display in the United Nations bookstore.

That future is completely beyond the imagination of my eight-year-old self. Even so, my political awakening taking its first toddler steps, entering the UN is a thrill — even more than the 1964 World's Fair in Queens, which offered the flavours and displayed the cultures of the countries represented in the UN.

Our tour takes us into the General Assembly, the Security Council, the translators' booths, the meeting rooms where the six committees of the United Nations developed policies and proposals. (Decades later, as part of my work with Shulamith Koenig, who in 2003 was awarded the United Nations Prize in the Field of Human Rights, I would be sitting behind a microphone in one of those rooms, addressing the Third Committee — which deals with human rights, humanitarian affairs and social matters — on enabling people to know their human rights so they can claim their human rights).

For me, each door opens into a place of wonder. I have never seen such a diversity of people, and it fires my imagination to think that they are trying to work together to find better answers for how we might all live together.

Bhubaneswar, India, November 1966

Harris steps up to the blackboard. He draws a circle. Bisects it vertically. And draws a chevron in the bottom half.

Does anyone know what this is, he asks?

None of us do.

Harris is new, a teacher sent to Stewart School in Bhubaneswar for an overseas teaching assignment, funded by the British Council. I never did learn his first name. He is supposed to teach

English, but he is really in the business of awakening our minds and connecting us with the universe opened by a command of the English tongue.

So he tells us about the British Committee for Nuclear Disarmament, and the emblem designed for it by the artist Gerald Holtom in 1958. And proceeds to teach us about the bombing of Hiroshima and Nagasaki, the nuclear tensions fuelling the Cold War, and — scant months after India and Pakistan have fought a war that forced us into blackouts for nights on end in 1965 and 1966 — the realisation that there is no return from a nuclear strike. He spoke of the peace movement gathering throughout England, demanding an end to weapons that have the power to eradicate humankind.

Looking back after decades, Harris was among a handful of teachers who stirred my intellect and set me on the path that made me a writer. Three of them — Harris, Fernandes, and Mishra — were at Stewart School during my time there from 1965 to 1968.

When I first enrolled in 1961, Stewart was a brand new school, the second campus of the school established in neighbouring Kataka in 1882 by Dr. William Day Stewart, a senior official (called the civil surgeon) in the Imperial civil service's department of health. The Bhubaneswar school was just finding its feet under the guidance of a stern but kindly disciplinarian, its first Principal, Rev. E.G. Collins. We were mostly boys, with only a few girls. The school followed the ancient maxim of a healthy mind in a healthy body. At morning recess we would line up for mugs of sweet lemonade. Mid-day brought a hot lunch; and the half-day Saturdays ended with a delicious mutton curry to send the day scholars on their way and the boarders to their leisure. Part of teachers' duties at the Kataka school was campus patrol — sometimes extending to the railway platform on Saturday nights — to ensure the ethnic Chinese boarding-school students didn't run back home to Kolkata.

Returning in 1965 from Los Angeles, it is quickly evident that my former classmates thrive and revel in the atmosphere, welcoming me back with a flurry of questions.

My mates defend me from the predations of the Hindi teacher, a stern chap from the brook-no-nonsense stream of education. He begins each morning with a snap quiz: we hold out our hands palm up as he strides down the rows, a wrong answer bringing a sharp thwack with the metal edge of the ruler. After a few stings do nothing to improve my non-existent grasp of a language I have yet to learn, he takes to giving me a backhanded slap when I reply in English, then in Odia, that I do not understand. One of my classmates — a native Hindi speaker from a merchant family — says I am just returned from the United States and don't know the language. I am left alone after that, but receive no help in catching up.

The Hindi master is the exception.

In the two years following my return, I am the beneficiary of outstanding teachers who not only instil knowledge, but a way of being and belonging in the world that shaped and guided the course of my life. Humility. Loyalty. Teamwork. Fair play. Service above self. Fidelity to the common good.

The best teachers don't beat children. Yet the experience of corporal punishment teaches us the difference between inspired leadership, and the crutch of brute force. About people who use the power at their disposal to exercise control and dominion, and people who use their ability to inspire and motivate, to impel you to reach within yourself and be your best. More than that, it quickly forces children to either submit or defy. Along with a handful of friends, I am among the defiant ones. This early separation of leaders and followers, those who would chart their own course and those who would submit to authority, was in its own way a means of shaping character. As for the few girls in our classes, patriarchal norms protect them from any form of corporal punishment, a barked "incorrect" replacing the strikes reserved for boys.

And it must be admitted: it isn't as though we don't deserve the occasional chastisement. Part of the process of moulding character and leadership is to empower us to find our own voice — which comes with our own rebellion. We have a nickname for every teacher. And some of the natural-born leaders among us compete to see who can actually slip the teacher's nickname into class interaction, without the victim being any the wiser. For reasons I no longer recall, our art teacher, a recent arrival from Kerala, is tagged with the nickname "dope."

He is a reticent chap finding his feet in a new school, a new city, a new local language, and a new state. Which of course makes him an easy target for our malice. I draw a police jeep with DOPE on the side.

"What is this?" the art teacher asks.

"Sir, it is to welcome you," I reply. "It is Department of Police, Ernakulam."

"Oh!" he says, beaming. "I belong to Ernakulam itself!"

Needless to say, "I belong to Ernakulam itself!" becomes the playground meme for the afternoon recess: mimicked, complete with side-to-side head shake, by the boys who came up to give me my winnings. This is the day I go home with pockets bulging with hard candies.

I fall in readily and easily with the quarter or so among the boys who challenge the unjust application of authority, and bear the resulting physical punishment with equanimity. It becomes something of a badge of honour to provoke a disciplinarian teacher's simmering anger into an act of gratuitous violence, which proves him the lesser man. Philips, the maths teacher, is a most frequent target. He prefers that one memorise formulas without knowing why: he simply doesn't have it in him to teach mathematics as a symbolic language, with an elegance of its own. Philips likes to pinch and twist one's upper arm to the point of bruising, and there are days when we compare the aftermath to see whose punishment has left the most visible mark.

Stoicism in the face of a teacher's violence is the expected response. I take it further one day by locking eyes with Philips, staring him down with a half-mocking smile even as he pinched harder, then asking once again if he could explain the logic of quadratic equations. This is the day he draws blood.

The few power-drunk dullards among the teachers bring an even greater appreciation of the good ones.

Harris' earliest gift is to open my life to Homer and Shakespeare. The Odyssey captivates me. The parallels between the heroic tales from Indian epics — my grandparents and parents told me stories from the *Mahabharata* and the *Ramayana,* and I became addicted to the graphic novel renditions of the epics in the publications collected as *Amar Chitra Katha* — and the travails of Odysseus fascinate me.

Harris not only sees me, he hears my voice. "Das, you are like the Bard of Avon. You are the Bhubaneswar Bard," he tells me after reading my essay on Odysseus and the Sirens. He steers and subtly shapes my use of language, encourages the use of precise imagery, shows me how to illuminate a thought. Harris awakens in me a deeper consciousness: the power of language and art to transcend the limits of convention, to provoke deep reflections on being and belonging to something larger than oneself.

We perform scenes from the Merchant of Venice and Julius Caesar. With Harris' tutelage, I learn the rhythms of Shakespeare's English, much as I learnt the rhythms of the Sanskrit tongue through the hymns of praise to the Mother Goddess that have infused my life since childhood. As with Sanskrit metre, learning to sound out Shakespeare changes one forever: you can no longer "read" the words without hearing their articulated power. And you look for connections. I find a resonance of our family tradition of praising the Mother Goddess in Ben Jonson's Hymn to Diana, one of the poems in *Palgrave's Golden Treasury*. And Portia's speech on the quality of mercy in the Merchant of Venice carries an echo of King's belief in the redemptive power of forgiveness. Harris asks me how I know about King, so I tell him of my American sojourn and share that I still keenly follow the civil rights movement in the United States. Whereupon he gives me a second great gift: teaching me to appreciate the power of words to influence minds and open hearts.

The passage of decades makes it possible to understand the mutuality that informed my explorations with Harris. He needed someone like me to teach. And I needed someone like him to teach me. I embrace every target he sets to expand my horizons, and he keeps pushing me farther. By Grade Seven I have absorbed The Odyssey and The Iliad. I know passages of Julius Caesar by heart, and indeed, day-dream about upbraiding Philips with:

> And Caesar's spirit, ranging for revenge,
> With Ate by his side come hot from hell,
> Shall in these confines with a monarch's voice
> Cry 'Havoc,' and let slip the dogs of war;
> That this foul deed shall smell above the earth
> With carrion men, groaning for burial.

I feel the full-blooded call of Harry's address on the eve of Agincourt in Henry V, one of the excerpts that constituted my extra reading, and understand the allure of being one of the happy few bound in brotherhood against hopeless odds.

I find a special resonance in The Odyssey when Odysseus, come home in disguise after years of war, questions Penelope's fidelity even while massacring the suitors who sought to take his place on the marital bed. There are striking parallels with the Ramayana as Rama similarly doubted Sita, abducted by the king of Sri Lanka. And in Odysseus' test of prowess before the suitors, bending the unbendable bow and thrumming its arrow through the rings of arrayed axe-handles, there is an echo of Karna besting Arjuna in marksmanship to pursue Draupadi's hand in the Mahabharata.

Now, in describing the journey of *Us*, I find the Homeric and Shakespearian lyricism Harris wove into me still informs my prose, despite the succinct phrasing imparted by a quarter century in journalism. Harris gives me 110 in English when the maximum mark is 100 (and securing 65 is considered a first-division threshold), which proves rather disruptive within the school's protocols.

Captain Fernandes, responsible for both physical and moral education, blending philosophy both on the playing field and in the lessons of history, distils a memorable blueprint for life. Three things to remember, he says. Trust begets trust. Treat others as you yourself wish to be treated. And remember that there are some rules. Follow the first two, and the third will become self-evident.

The Captain's third principle is particularly helpful in quelling roiling hormones.

My first crush is lovely Ava, who takes my breath away with her reading of Portia's "quality of mercy" speech. After we declaim scenes from The Tempest (I have taken to naming Philips "Caliban"), I find the resolve to tell her she is lovelier than Miranda. Which makes her blush and look away.

Some days later, she asks me if I can stay behind at recess to work on her recitation of Ariel's song:

> *Full fathom five thy father lies;*
> *Of his bones are coral made;*
> *Those are pearls that were his eyes:*
> *Nothing of him that doth fade,*
> *But doth suffer a sea–change*

Into something rich and strange.
Sea-nymphs hourly ring his knell:
Hark! now I hear them,—ding-dong, bell.

At that moment, I would have gone to the ends of the earth for her. And like an utter fool, I choose to run off and play gilli-danda with the boys.

At daily assembly, where we recite the Lord's Prayer as befitting an Anglican school (though most of the students are Hindu, with a sprinkling of Buddhists and Muslims, this is in fact the best English-language education to be found in the region), both Collins and his successor Frank Wells instil the maxim that leadership begins with character. Indeed, much is to be gleaned from the school's rather ominous motto: *Domini Timor Prima Sapientia* (Fear of the Lord is the First Wisdom). The fear or "timor" is in fact a reverence and a respect for the higher power, an affirmation that there is a commonality beyond your individual self, that you are just one manifestation of a unity beyond human understanding. In this, it meshes neatly with the Hindu Vaishnava traditions that shaped me at home, and the foundations of faith (albeit in different faith traditions) that anchored both Gandhi and King.

The positive influence of Harris and Fernandes, and my maturing perspective, does not go unrewarded by my family. My uncle Kuna, my mom's elder brother, introduces me to Jean-Paul Sartre and Albert Camus, and the evolution of democratic socialist thought, on an autumn vacation in my mom's village when I am about to turn twelve. Kuna, who had been studying law in Kolkata when he was called prematurely home to assume his feudal responsibilities after his mother's demise, leads me through Sartre, verses me in the essential point of existential-ist philosophy — that we have the ability and the responsibility to make our own future — and offers me *Pride and Prejudice* to better appreciate the customs and culture of the English. Our village, Jamirapal, is seven kilometres from the nearest railhead at Dantan; requiring us to make part of the journey by bullock cart and boat across the Subarnarekha (the Golden Divide) River. I lie belly-down on the straw and bamboo deck of the bullock cart as we ford the shallows of the Subarnarekha, absorbed in the final few pages of Sartre's *Iron in the Soul*.

On the same trip, my mother's younger brother Kanu — who himself had been a student of Captain Fernandes in Kataka — catches me up on maths. He teaches me the FOIL (first, outer, inner, last) mnemonic for multiplying binomials. On the ce-mented rooftop of our feudal mansion, Kanu employs chalk to teach me the rudiments of algebra, by the light of a lantern in those days before electricity. Kanu also explains, as Philips could not, that quadratic equations are useful for describing the arc of an object from the moment it is launched or thrown into the sky until it approaches its destination — which he demon-strates by taking me into our forecourt and firing an arrow from a bamboo bow.

It is also my last idyll in my mother's village. Within months, we will leave India behind for good, to follow my father to a new job as a research professor at a Canadian university, in a place I had never heard of: Edmonton.

Vancouver, Canada, April 1968

We step into the arrivals hall at Vancouver airport, my mother and I with my nine-month old sister Sheela, and look for my father. He had left for Canada the previous January, just before his 37th birthday.

I am filled with the excitement of starting a new life in an unknown country.

The long journey here brought us from Kolkata to Tokyo, my maternal grandfather Ramchandra standing stiff as a board in his white dhoti and kurta, silent tears streaming down his stoic face, as I lost sight of him from the Kolkata departure gate.

My mother spent her meagre stock of foreign currency (one was allowed to carry only eight dollars upon exiting India) during our stopover in Tokyo so I could take a city tour while she stayed in the airline-supplied New Otani hotel with Sheela. The funds my father wired to us in Tokyo hadn't arrived, so we had no money as we boarded the Canadian Pacific Airlines Douglas DC-8 for my first trans-Pacific flight.

We were at the very back of the plane, where there was space for baby bassinets to be hung from the overhead luggage racks. This was long before the age of in-flight entertainment, with ample seats and sumptuous meals as compensation.

Prepared for the adventure ahead as we finally land and clear immigration formalities, I greet my father with delight. And as we are about to catch our propeller-driven Air Canada Vickers Viscount for the connecting flight to Edmonton, I learn in one devastating moment the news that plunges me from joy to shock: Dr. Martin Luther King is dead, felled by a fatal bullet on a balcony of the Lorraine Motel in Memphis, Tennessee; fired by the assassin James Earl Ray.

Edmonton, Canada, April 1968

"Do you know what a boner is?" asks little Peter, one of my brand new classmates at King Edward Junior High School in Edmonton, where I have joined the last few weeks of Grade Seven in the Canadian school term. We are just walking out of our home room, where the teacher introduces me and asks the class to give me a proper welcome.

Which is precisely what Peter is doing.

When I confess that I do not, he proceeds to enlighten me, and mirthfully explains to other boys the profundity of my ignorance. Within a week I am well settled, having been through the boys' welcoming challenge of an after school fight. I strike with an open palm instead of a fist, and after I have felled two boys they declare me their friend.

When I become a target of a bully, my classmates side with me: one of them, an Anglican preacher's son, tells the bully he will have to fight us all.

There is such little immigration from the Indian subcontinent that I am viewed as an exotic; in a school where the derided immigrants are of German ancestry. The memories of the Second World War still carry force, and the German kids are taunted during field sports and in the locker room with the marching songs of the Canadian soldiers who came home to Edmonton after the war. (*Hitler has only one right ball/The other is hanging on the wall/His mother, his dirty mother/Cut it off when he was small*).

I find school a breeze. I have already learned, at Stewart School, all the material being taught in Canada. By the time I enter Grade 8 in September, I surprise the science teacher with my detailed knowledge of the periodic table — learned in sixth grade at Stewart — and the social studies teacher with my ability to name most of the world's countries and capital cities, drilled into us in the fifth and sixth grade in India. The only exception is maths, where I am unable to grasp "the new math" learning which is the trend of the day.

And I am about to discover that being shaped by Harris isn't entirely beneficial. Our English class is studying W.O. Mitchell's novel *Who has Seen the Wind?* and asked to write a book report. I quite like the work. I cite the Homeric allure of Mitchell's description of the Canadian prairies, as poetically described as the seas Odysseus sailed; allude to the eponymous poem by Christina Rossetti, which conveys that we are shaped by forces we cannot see, and, drawing on my experience of my grandmother's agony, how difficult it is for a boy to cope with an unjust and untimely death.

The well-meaning teacher impresses upon me the importance of attributing sources; and explains that the purpose of the assignment isn't to lift ideas from university books, but to find my own words and express my own thoughts. I am too young, and too new to the country, to stand my ground. So I spurn the Homeric allusion and the evocation of Rossetti, strip my essay of insight, and use the teacher-prescribed structure to dash out a few glib observations about the friendship between Brian and Fat, and the vastness of the Canadian prairies, so different from forested India. I am given an A+ for this effort hastily cobbled in my anger and my shame. I have never been able to read Mitchell since. Having drowned my voice aged 12, it would take me the better part of a decade to bring it back to life.

The relative ease of the welcome at King Edward becomes rather more challenging when I begin high school: where I am one of only two dark-skinned people in a school of 2,200 pupils. The usual turmoil of adolescence thus assumes another dimension of obstacles and barriers, from a handful of deeply insecure students who use racism and xenophobia to compensate for the deficiencies in their own lives. But Harry Ainlay High School offers many paths for the pursuit of excellence, and I know that if I am to thrive rather than survive, I must rise above the fray. To my great fortune, I find two teachers who see me as clearly as Harris did: Jim Jenks and Mike Demaine. They push me to explore every dimension of my abilities. And fully support me in the extracurricular activities that shape my path: the debating team, the school newspaper, a knowledge quiz show called Reach for the Top that put competing high schools on television.

By the time I get to university, I am so immersed in writing that I stop going to classes after November to work full time on The Gateway, the student newspaper at the University of Alberta.

After the inevitable rustication, and the spasms of parental anguish (a professor's son expelled, quel scandale!) I find my way to a small-city newspaper called The Red Deer Advocate on the strength of my clippings, where in the fall of 1974 I embark on a path that would lead me to a life as a writer.

Edmonton, Canada, June 2015

The black tomato bore fruit today, two little green globes bursting from a promising canopy of flowers. It is morning in my dappled garden in suburban Edmonton, the sun already mounting the June sky even though it's barely 730 a.m. The black tomato is from heirloom seeds, its origins in the Russian steppes: like me a transplant into the rich soil of northwestern Canada. It will be weeks before these first fruits grow and ripen, readied for table with a drizzle of mustard oil and a sprinkling of shallots. I am unreasonably happy to see them.

Mita and I have just returned from our younger daughter Somya's convocation at the University of Victoria, embracing her in silence so I could hold back my tears, visiting the lovely Vancouver flat whence she is launching her life.

On the long drive through the most gorgeous mountainscapes in North America, I am filled with a giddy sense of *duty done:* the children grown and settled, in a country I came to as a stranger and now embrace as home. Now we step anew into the unknown, a life beyond family obligations. The black tomato affirms that I am at the age where these small pleasures will carry more weight than any momentous achievements in my life.

It has been a good life as far as exiles go, because fate brought me to the province of Alberta, a place where the world is still being made, and offered me a role in the making. The task is not done, and perhaps never will be: yet I feel ever more able to shape this part of the world with the values and principles left to us by M.K. Gandhi, and the many prophets of peace who came before him.

This has been my life's work, though it did not always seem so: to instil my corner of the world with freedom from fear and freedom from want, so that all of us can live together with dignity, in community, in harmony with one another and the natural world.

Today's Canada is the beginning of an answer to the late Nelson Mandela's call for a new political culture founded on human rights and human dignity, as a counterpoint to the politics of power and violence that has consumed humankind for millennia. But it is more than that.

The journey from charity to dignity, from powerlessness to the true enjoyment of freedom from fear and freedom from want, is really the foundation for a sustainable life that can be an exemplar to simply show that it can be done. That one country accommodating more than 200 streams of the human experience, with its myriad languages and cultures, can indeed evolve a collective future where we all belong. Where "us" is the rightful heart of "sustainability." And oddly enough, this quest for a sustainability where "us" carries a genuinely inclusive meaning, is taking root in a petro-state.

Alberta is host to the largest hydrocarbon deposit on the planet, a vast repository of fossil fuels in a world addicted to them. This addiction is eroding the very capacity of the planet to bear the consequences of a rapidly changing climate that is transmuting the very foundations of earthly life.

In many ways, Alberta is an island: made insular by its singular hydrocarbon wealth, which sets it apart from every other state or province in North America. While it is unique in having stewardship — seldom well-exercised, with far too much oversight in the hands of tenants whose primary motive is profit — the transparency that accompanies democracy makes it a particularly tempting target in the gallery of carbon-emitting rogues.

My Alberta is more than an island of oil wealth in the vast land-mass of North America. It is also bound to its country, Canada, by the societal consensus that has emerged since Canada adopted human rights as its constitutional foundation in 1982: a startling ambition to move beyond a corrosive history of indigenous genocide, imperialist wrongs and divisive colonial legacies to evoke a society where all of "us" can belong.

As we shall explore in much fuller detail as we progress, transforming these ambitions into sustainable actions is a challenge that must engage as many of us as possible.

We already have seen that it is never good enough to declare "mission accomplished." Certainly not after a far-right university student, having been radicalised online, shot six worshippers dead and injured 19 others in a mosque in Quebec City. Nor when we see, as we did in 2014, ceremonial soldier Cpl. Nathan Cirillo shot dead by a mixed-origin child of Canadian parents, who then tried to shoot his way into Parliament in a confused and murderous effort to become a terrorist, before he himself was killed. Nor when we see Canadians setting off to fight for fanatics in a faraway civil war in the Balkans; among them Gojko Susak, a pizzaman from Ottawa who ended up as Croatia's defense minister.

And on this sunny morning in my Edmonton garden, birdsong rising beyond the traffic noise and feral hares savaging the unfenced flowers in the neighbours' yards, I recall a momentous event on a faraway island that changed all of our lives for the better.

It's the 15th day of June 2015 today, eight hundred years to the day since England's barons rose in revolt against the capricious and arbitrary reign of King John, demanding through the guarantees and assurances of a "Great Charter" that none is above the law. This is the day the Magna Carta was signed, laying the foundation and sowing the promise for the rule of law, the foundation of what would one become a system of governance that includes us all.

It is also a day when we in Alberta see the first tangible fruits of a decision we took on the 5th of May, when we broke 44 years of one-party rule to elect a new government. In a few hours, I will be in the Members Gallery of the Legislative Assembly of Alberta as the province's newly appointed vicereine reads the Speech from the Throne crafted by Her Majesty's Government, particularly resonant on this anniversary, with opening words that acknowledge a truth no previous Alberta government ever has uttered:

> Friends, Alberta is a province of indigenous peoples whose roots in this land go back thousands of years, and who will be stewards of this land for thousands of years to come. Together, we are learning to respect that.

Against great odds, we have included many streams of the human experience in building the communities we call home.

For those of us born outside of Canada, there is still a sense of wonder in this our adopted home, where we have set down roots seasoned and tempered with the passing of winters, made a life in this vast and empty land in a cluster of cities scattered across the immensity of our geography.

Most of the world will never know the value and privilege of a life made in Canada. Whether we came here by choice or compulsion, to pursue work and careers or merely to take a risk on chasing a dream, we have made a country where the word "Canadian" encompasses every race, colour, gender, language, and faith.

I am ever mindful that we are here because of treaties signed more than a century ago with the original inhabitants of the land, whom we promised to honour as landlords, with due dignity and respect, "as long as the sun shines and the rivers flow." All of us newcomers, all who have come here from my ancestral India and elsewhere, are people of the treaty: more specifically, Treaty 6, which enables us to build our present and our future on the traditional lands of the First Nations leased from them in perpetuity.

In our Edmonton home, we are the latest occupants of one of the oldest continuous human habitations on the planet, first settled more than 12,000 years ago.

As I celebrate the birth of modern Canada under that big prairie sky, I thank the many generations who lived on this land and bound us all as people of treaty; renew my vows to the country that welcomed us.

And come to realise that we too have moral obligation: to share what we have learned in shaping an inclusive life in Canada, and to invite meaningful engagement in return.

And above all, we have the moral obligation to atone and make amends for Canada's original and never-ending sin: the appalling violence and carnage wrought by the government policies that resulted in the cultural genocide of the First Nations, the original inhabitants of this land.

Chapter Six

Our roads to reconciliation

Amiskwaciy-wâskahikan, April 2016

We are seated in a circle in a brick and stone building, some two dozen of us. The colonisers who came to Amiskwaciy-wâskahikan claimed there was such a thing as "owning" the land that kisemanito, the creator, gave us to share. They put this building here. They called it the Prince of Wales Armoury. They gave their young men guns and helmets, and sent them off by the thousands, from this very spot, to die on foreign shores. All to serve the delusion that people can "own" the Mother Earth which all are meant to share.

This is the circle in which we the people have met in Amiskwaciy-wâskahikan for more than 10,000 years, as the colonisers reckon time. This is where we are gathered today, newcomers and the descendants of the first people to live along this river and these hills, as the people of Treaty Six. This is the sacred agreement, sealed with a bundle, that enables first peoples and newcomers to share this land, to care for the land and water and sky — and for each other — as long as the sun shines and the rivers flow.

And today in this circle, we are coming to grips with the great wrong the colonisers wrought, the terror they visited on those who had shared Amiskwaciy-wâskahikan — Beaver Hills House, in the language in which the colonists govern — and what can be done to reconcile the future with the never-ending sin of what was done in the past. This is land once shared by the Cree and Dene, by the Lacotah and the Métis, the Siksika and the Pikani. Today it is dominated by newcomers. The colonisers who divided up "ownership" of this land named the territory after a princess from a faraway land across the sea. They called it Alberta.

The colonists came here for the pelts of the beavers after whom first peoples named this place. And their first leader, a Hudson's Bay Company factor, gave Amiskwaciy-wâskahikan the name of the place he came from. Edmonton.

I have convened this circle, in my role as chair of the Edmonton Heritage Council. In the centre of the circle is a pile of books, a catalogue of pain, dripping with the unhealed wounds of those of our brothers and sisters who were plucked up by their roots, sent to state detention, forced to abandon everything that defined their being and belonging: names, languages, family, culture, heritage, spirit, and the absolute freedom to roam these lands.

This stack of books is the report of the Truth and Reconciliation Commission which travelled the country called Canada for six years, to understand the pain of the first peoples so brutally wrenched from all we have and are, and to find a path towards mutual healing. Beginning with the recognition of the wrongs committed in the never-ending sin.

We are listening to one of the Commissioners, Wilton Littlechild, as our circle evokes the paths to reconciliation the Edmonton Heritage Council can pursue. I knew Chief Littlechild during the many years he represented Maskwacis and surrounding coloniser communities: as a Progressive Conservative member of Parliament in the House of Commons of Canada; and as regional chief of Alberta, representing the people of Treaties Six, Seven and Eight in the Assembly of First Nations. He has agreed to come to this circle, to help we keepers of shared heritage navigate a new way of being and belonging together.

Canada is the name the colonisers applied to the entire land they claimed from sea to sea to sea, even though its origin, *kanata,* is the word for a pristine settlement on Turtle Island, in the language of the Haudenosaunee people who lived along the Kaniatarowanenneh, the great river-sea, which the first colonisers named le Saint-Laurent. These colonists called the people the Iroquois, but knew the Haudenosaunee comprised six distinct indigenous nations.

The mighty river did not change, nor did the people, as the English colonists who defeated the French ones called the river St. Lawrence, and named the people "savages."

The official practice, among the English colonists, was to call all the people who lived on Turtle Island "Indians." All because of a foolish explorer named Cristobal Colon (Christopher Columbus in English), who set sail from faraway Barcelona. Leading a flotilla of three sailing ships, Colon reached the cluster of south-eastern islands off these shores in year 1492 of the Christian calendar — many millennia after the first people's ancestors spread throughout these lands. Colon thought he had found the western route to the country his peers knew as India, thus the people he encountered must be "Indians."

In fact the first people's ancestors already had made contact with people from northern Europe called Viking, who left a settlement in the land of the Beothuk, the Mi'kmaq, and the Inuit five hundred years before Colon. Unlike Colon, they had no deranged notion that kisemanito's bounty to the people actually belonged to anyone who could take "ownership" by violence.

Colon and the colonists who arrived with him claimed ownership of the land in the name of their king and queen. These monarchs were two genetically inbred individuals named Ferdinand and Isabella: who called themselves "their most Catholic Majesties" and believed that kisemanito was in fact incarnated as a bearded man nailed to a cross. And that this nailed god gave them the divine power to take "ownership" of any part of Turtle Island reached by their mariners and voyagers.

In the name of their god, the French colonisers led by Jacques Cartier, and Samuel de Champlain after him, took tracts of kisemanito's land, and claimed all of it should be called New France. They were defeated in battles by English colonists. These English brought diseases which took the lives of many people who lived along the great river. And for those who survived, the fate of their descendants was even worse: to lose their very identity and being as their "government" snatched children away from their families, determined that there should be "no trace of the savage left" in any "Indian" once the prison-schools in which they confined the children had finished in their task of erasing who and what the children once were.

These are the stories of the traduced first people and their descendants, in the pile of books in the centre of our circle. Chief Littlechild's voice is even, his tone restrained, as he continues to describe the indescribable. And insists we are here to find a path forward in the mutuality of being and belonging. His calmness is overwhelming, and for those of us who have read the report, the dignified timbre of his voice is unbearable. A shouted reproach would have been easier to understand; his demeanour merely emphasises the enormity of the sin unredeemed.

Pomona, California, USA, September 1964

My parents and I are invited to visit the suburban home of one of my father's colleagues in the psychology department of the University of California at Los Angeles. We arrive in our family's first car, a 1953 Oldsmobile, having driven from our apartment in Brentwood.

When we pull up, we find their children have climbed up the tree in the front yard, scampering up to the highest limbs that will bear their weight, trembling in terror.

They were told by their father that Indians are coming to their home.

Amiskwaciy-wâskahikan, April 2016

Wilton Littlechild, Grand Chief of the Confederacy of Treaty Six First Nations, speaks in our circle about the chronicles of injustice and grief in his commission's report, takes measure of our burdened faces. He passes me the sacred object which entitles the bearer to speak in circle. My heart is so laden that no words come. I pass.

I understand why Chief Littlechild has spoken the way he has, how he has stayed so composed in describing the commission's work: page after harrowing page, churning the emotions of all who learn the experiences captured in the testimony gathered by the Truth and Reconciliation researchers.

Describing another catalogue of brutality, the Second World War, whose terrors unfolded in a different continent at a different time, the Greek poet Yiorgos Seferis observed in *The Last Stop:*

> *Ki' a sou mílo me paramýthia kai paravolés*
> *eínai giatí to' akoús glykótera, ki i friki*
> *de kouventiázetai giatí eínai zontaní*
> *giatí eínai amíliti kai prochoráei*
> *Stásei ti méra stásei ston ýpno*
> *mnisipímon pónos*

Which in my rough-hewn translation becomes:

> *If I speak to you in myths and parables*
> *it is gentler for you that way, because horror*
> *really can't be described, because it's living*
> *because it multiplies without speaking*
> *a pain that wounds memory*
> *drip by drip, by day by night*

All the justifications used by the government of Canada: the need to "civilise" cultures they did not understand, to violently coerce "savages" into a "superior" culture, are echoed in modern China's reasons for the mass detention and "re-education" of Uygur Muslims in Xinjiang since 2016. The difference is this: Canada had no intention, as China does, of bringing economic development and a higher standard of living to the first peoples. Nor did Canada face violent, armed resistance to their governance. Nearly all who were detained by Canada, with the aim to have their roots and their identity destroyed, were people of treaty who were promised mutually beneficial coexistence with the colonists and the newcomers.

The Truth and Reconciliation Commission arose from the settlement the government of Canada reached in 2007 with the survivors of the residential schools. It was launched after a historic apology delivered in the House of Commons by Prime Minister Stephen Harper on June 10, 2008:

> For more than a century, Indian Residential Schools separated over 150,000 Aboriginal children from their families and communities. In the 1870s, the federal government, partly in order to meet its obligation to educate Aboriginal children, began to play a role in the development and administration of these schools. Two primary objectives of the Residential Schools system were to remove and isolate children from the influence of their homes, families, traditions and cultures, and to assimilate them into the dominant culture. These objectives were based on the assumption Aboriginal cultures and spiritual beliefs were inferior and unequal. Indeed, some sought, as it was infamously said, "to kill the Indian in the child." Today, we recognise that this policy of assimilation was wrong, has caused great harm, and has no place in our country.

> One hundred and thirty-two federally-supported schools were located in every province and territory, except Newfoundland,

New Brunswick and Prince Edward Island. Most schools were operated as "joint ventures" with Anglican, Catholic, Presbyterian or United Churches. The Government of Canada built an educational system in which very young children were often forcibly removed from their homes, often taken far from their communities. Many were inadequately fed, clothed and housed. All were deprived of the care and nurturing of their parents, grandparents and communities. First Nations, Inuit and Métis languages and cultural practices were prohibited in these schools. Tragically, some of these children died while attending residential schools and others never returned home.

...

To the approximately 80,000 living former students, and all family members and communities, the Government of Canada now recognises that it was wrong to forcibly remove children from their homes and we apologise for having done this. We now recognise that it was wrong to separate children from rich and vibrant cultures and traditions that it created a void in many lives and communities, and we apologise for having done this. We now recognise that, in separating children from their families, we undermined the ability of many to adequately parent their own children and sowed the seeds for generations to follow, and we apologise for having done this. We now recognise that, far too often, these institutions gave rise to abuse or neglect and were inadequately controlled, and we apologise for failing to protect you. Not only did you suffer these abuses as children, but as you became parents, you were powerless to protect your own children from suffering the same experience, and for this we are sorry.

> The burden of this experience has been on your shoulders for far too long. The burden is properly ours as a Government, and as a country. There is no place in Canada for the attitudes that inspired the Indian Residential Schools system to ever prevail again. You have been working on recovering from this experience for a long time and in a very real sense, we are now joining you on this journey. The Government of Canada sincerely apologises and asks the forgiveness of the Aboriginal peoples of this country for failing them so profoundly.

The apology acknowledges the fate foreseen by the two prominent chiefs who did not sign Treaty Six: Mistahi-maskwa (called Big Bear in English) and Pihtokahanapiwiyin (known to the colonisers as Poundmaker). Each thought the promises made to their people under treaty would not go far enough to protect their heritage, their ability to be and to belong.

Pihtokahanapiwiyin and Mistahi-maskwa were persecuted by the Canadian government as traitors after the North-West Rebellion of 1885. Mistahi-maskwa tried to stop his followers from attacking a settlement at Frog Lake, but was convicted by Canadian courts for the death of nine colonists that became known as the "Frog Lake massacre" in colonial history.

Pihtokahanapiwiyin in fact renounced violence, a fact finally acknowledged by Prime Minister Justin Trudeau on 23 May 2019: "In 2019, we recognise the truth in his words that he — as a leader, statesman and peacemaker — did everything he could to ensure that lives were not needlessly lost. It has taken us 134 years to reach today's milestone — the exoneration of Chief Poundmaker."

And yet, from the ashes of betrayal and deracination, new leadership arises. We learn from the leadership of Autumn Peltier that wisdom is not confined to elders. As an 11-year-old she met with Justin Trudeau, and elicited from him a tearful promise that he would indeed ensure safe water for indigenous Canadians. The Trudeau government allocated billions of dollars to do so, but the money set aside is slow to be delivered, and in early 2019 there is little to show as tangible progress in terms of building the modern sewage and water treatment that would bring First Nations communities the civic infrastructure that prevails across Canada.

Autumn's great-aunt was Water Walker Josephine Mandamin, who walked around all of the Great Lakes, and the entire length of the St. Lawrence River, starting in 2003. Autumn inherited her mantle. Aged eight, she participated in a water ceremony at Serpent River First Nation. As she described it at a mid-February 2019 meeting of Nishnawbe Aski Nation (NAN) Oshkaatisak Youth Council gathering in Thunder Bay:

"I noticed there were signs on the walls that said: 'Don't drink this water, not for consumption, it's toxic'. I asked my mom, 'what does that mean?' and she told me they were on a boil water advisory — they can't drink their water. So after hearing that it became one of my biggest concerns, so I started public speaking about it."

Her advocacy did not go unnoticed. Aged 13, Autumn was invited to address the United Nations General Assembly on World

Water Day, March 22, 2018. She wore the mantle of leadership with a natural comfort, a girl barely into her teens, standing up before the assembled delegates of the world. And her words carried the clarity of uncompromised and undiluted belief: "Our water deserves to be treated as human with human rights. We need to acknowledge our waters with personhood so we can protect our waters."

The notion of giving one of the elements essential to all life on earth the role of a person, is indeed a wrenching shift in thinking. Autumn and other keepers of the water know they have to care for this life-giving force because the adult world hasn't. Autumn's courage in speaking truth to power is a living example of *satyagraha*.

Her advocacy includes a guide for others who wish to become guardians of water. After her UN speech, she set out the path in an interview with CBC News:

- Learn as much as you can from your elders
  and your teachers.

- Learn your history. Learn your language.
  Listen and ask questions.

- Pay attention to the climate and the animals.
  Have respect for all living things.

- Talk with Mother Earth, sit with her and thank her.
  Make offerings of tobacco, pray and give thanks.

- Have fun and be a kid as much as you can. Get your school
  or class involved in a type of activity to help the land.

- Talk to your friends and share ideas.
  Inspire and encourage others.

- If you have an idea, act and make it happen. Don't be shy,
  there are no rights or wrongs — anyone can do this work.

- Just do it!!!

The way Autumn and her generation perceive and approach Canada's cultural genocide of indigenous communities is so strikingly different from the skein of prejudices which prompted residential schools — prejudices which persist in an adult population conditioned and shaped to regard indigenous Canadians as the Other. The classical perspective of a colonising population that has displaced the original inhabitants of the land is giving way to a new worldview, empowered by truth-telling and shaped by pluralism.

The children of Autumn's generation are the first batch of schoolchildren to come to grips with the report of the Truth and Reconciliation Commission: the catalogue of pain Chief Littlechild brought to our circle. In a Grade 9 classroom in southeast Edmonton, a raucous, passionate, occasionally insightful band of 14- and 15-year-olds come face to face with truth long suppressed. They are a diverse classroom typical of today's urban Canada. They are first- and second-generation immigrants, the descendants of settlers from long ago and of the original people of Turtle Island. Their ethnic origins include Punjabi and Filipino, Somali and Colombian, Jamaican and German, Albanian and Canadian, Métis and Cree.

Many of them are being raised by single parents, adoptive parents, step-parents, and grandparents. They all face challenges, including those brought on by the pervasive violence of poverty, but these young people know that they are safe at school and that they have adults in their lives who love them fiercely. Today, they are uncharacteristically quiet. They are reading about residential school experiences, collected by the Truth and Reconciliation Commission and told in the survivors' own words.

This is what the children have to say in response.

> "What happened to these kids shouldn't have started in the first place. I see no reason as to why they treated kids that way just to assimilate them and make them act like white people. I hope the nuns and people who ran the school at least felt sorry after the schools shut down."
>
> ...
>
> "It's ironic that the nuns and priests beat them to the extremes when they were supposed to be people of 'God'. Why were they strapped for playing and talking? Expecting a child not to be a child is impossible."
>
> ...
>
> "Kids were severely punished for stupid reasons like talking, going pee at night, laughing, playing, and talking in their language. I knew kids were getting beat but I didn't know what the reasons were until now. When I first learned about these schools I was curious about them, and now that I know more I feel absolutely sickened by how no one stood up for these kids at the start. Just thinking about it makes me want to go back in time and give those teachers a piece of my mind."
>
> ...

"People shouldn't be forcibly separated from your loved ones, especially if they're properly caring for you. ... Being beaten won't change a person, it only builds up anger and hatred, especially for something like wanting to keep your language and culture when your roots are all you have."

...

"The nuns beating kids challenged my thinking because nuns are supposed to be like helpful loving people. I could never imagine being whipped by some random person when my parents don't even hit me, the most they do is yell at me."

...

"If I was in this position I would feel so helpless and lost and upset. I would probably try to run away, too."

...

"I assumed that these kids would at least have some freedom but it turns out every minute was monitored. I felt surprised and sad that these schools treated kids with neglect and fear and pain so they could control and change them. The public didn't even know about this for the longest time and the public just assumed that the schools was a safe space for these children when in reality they're getting abused."

...

"I thought these people were messed up but still had some shred of humanity, but my thinking changed after reading this. I felt disappointed that the people doing these things could have quite possibly been my ancestors. I feel empathy for those who survived and realise how much I've taken for granted."

…

"I knew the people working there would say ruthless things to the kids, but my perspective changed when I found out the kids would say such bad things about their own race and language. They felt being Aboriginal was a bad thing and felt ashamed for their families and the skin they had. I feel honestly disgusted by how they treated the children and if I were in their position, I would feel so upset and terrible."

…

"I felt understanding when they expressed their pain and anger and how small they felt. After reading these experiences from other people, I realise how lucky I am. It really makes you wonder how the government thought they were in the right to send kids to these schools that were 90% abuse."

…

"I believe that the First Nations were scammed and tortured for nothing but selfish and stupid reasons. The Europeans could've shown what they wanted in different ways that didn't involve torture and harm to others. No one deserved to go through that torture. What they did goes against human rights, and just isn't human in general."

…

"What I took to heart was the amount of children who hated themselves and their parents and that is really sad because they didn't get to live their lives like we do. Their whole lives got affected. … I would go back and make a difference if I could."

…

"How can you learn to love or care about others when you don't know how to love yourself? When you're used to being treated badly you think it's okay, but it's not."

…

"I was surprised by how little the government cared about these kids and how they didn't see that they were humans too. Reading this gave me more respect for First Nations and helped me understand the impact residential schools have had on First Nations today. I feel that this is the most racist thing Canada has done and hope that people see that white supremacy holds humans back as a species to this day."

…

"They took their lands, language, rights, children… I feel an immense amount of sadness because I cannot even imagine going through this. I don't know how people could be so cruel."

After these insights from a group of junior high school students learning about residential schools and exploring reconciliation, I can only add: Children, teach your parents well.

Amiskwaciy-wâskahikan May 2019

I am seated at my kitchen table with George Stanley and his brother Ernest. And although I do not know it, this is the day I am about to cross a threshold of trust and intimacy which is so deeply meaningful that it warms me to my core.

George is the fifth generation of hereditary chiefs in the Frog Lake First Nation. The hereditary system gave way to elections, but the heredity still carries an obligation to service. George calls me his brother, and enlists my support in seeking for his people all the benefits of modern life enjoyed by other Canadians. George has been an elected chief for his nation and a regional chief for Alberta in the Assembly of First Nations. He is the seventh of nine children and the youngest among the boys, yet his grandfather marked him as the hereditary chief: because the youngest sibling, not the oldest, is the one formed to lead.

George remembers sitting around the family dinner table before he was 10, when his father, Chief Jean-Baptiste Stanley, told him he would one day be the hereditary chief of his people: and schooled him thereafter in the art of leadership. George is my age. Luckily, he was spared the gauntlet of residential school education. His mother, Mary, was not so fortunate. She was torn away from her family on the Onion Lake First Nation when she was five, and did not return home until she had completed Grade Nine. George remembers the hole between the bones in the forefinger where she was injured in a teacher's beating, the fracture never properly set or healed.

Today at my table, George seated in his familiar place, looking out the French doors to the garden, we are joined by George's elder brother, Ernest. Ernie, as the family knows him, has met me perhaps a half a dozen times. And said very little. George is the voluble one, the born politician. Ernie has always been reserved, keeping his thoughts and emotions to himself. There has been a time or two when George — his mobile phone gone awry — uses his siblings' phones instead, so I am used to calls from numbers I do not recognise. The most Ernie has ever said to me, when I answer the phone is, "This is Ernie. Your brother wants to talk to you," as he passes George the phone.

Ernie is the bundle holder, the keeper of the sacred relic that validates and sanctifies Treaty Six. Today, at my kitchen table, George tells me that Ernie has something to say. Ernie produces a filter tipped cigarette. The gift of tobacco. He asks me to place it at the base of a tree. I step outside into the yard, break the cigarette apart, and place the blessed tobacco in a little hollow I carve at the roots of our rhododendron.

Then Ernie speaks. I listen, rapt, for ten minutes as he articulates a profound emotion, not daring to interrupt. He and his fellow elders are deeply concerned by the corruption they perceive in the government-sanctioned elections on their nation. They have come through a recent exercise where candidates distributed ballots, and recounts that changed the results were held with only half the scrutineers present.

"We respect the Indian Act, the laws of the Crown," Ernie says, "because we have followed it for so many years. I want to make that clear. But for many years now, we have seen how the laws of the Crown lead to corruption. This time, we elders want to step in. We have been the guardians of our people. Before elections, we were the ones responsible to make sure our people were wisely led. But now, we have to step in. The Crown laws bring us leaders who are corrupt. We have to keep the trust of the people."

Ernie asks my help as a scribe in gathering his thoughts into a letter he and his fellow Elders will send to Her Majesty the Queen in Right of Canada. And invites me to a sacred gathering to share a pipe with the elders to commemorate treaty, where the bundle may be opened for the first time in many years.

I am still coming to grips with what Ernie has just said, the blessing he has conferred on me and my family with the gift of tobacco, the door he has opened as keeper of the Treaty Six bundle. This is the moment I go beyond my passport identity, my legal status of citizenship, to become fully and wholly Canadian: a child of kisemanito's bounty, at last in the full embrace of the first peoples who welcomed newcomers to this land.

The corruption Ernie speaks of, George's continuing efforts to secure clean water and proper sanitation for his nation, are part of the failures for which Canada must atone.

At the bookends of generations, Autumn and George are leading the same human right: the right to clean water. Very much a part of the right to health, and to the security of the person. George, the veteran politician. Autumn, the vanguard of the children who will cope with the toxic legacy we are leaving them.

Frog Lake First Nation has its very own oil company, but the community itself has open sewage lagoons between the high school and the hospital. The government of Canada, which has overarching control of infrastructure on reserves, has determined that these lagoons are the most cost-efficient way of treating cess and effluents. The civil servants who designed and emplaced these cesspits do not have to live next to them.

Safe water, a given for nearly every Canadian living off-reserve in a municipality, is denied to thousands of Indigenous people. In April 2019, there were 57 Indigenous communities where residents were asked to boil water before consuming it. The

Government of Canada aims to provide safe water to all affected communities by March 2021.

For George, this is just another deferred promise: a pattern of the broken or unfulfilled commitments made by the politicians of the Crown, only to be thwarted in execution and delivery by the structure of governance.

As George and I engage in meaningful conversation week by week, we wonder where we have gone wrong: at the end of the day, we as leaders, we as a country, have failed utterly to provide the basics of a clement life to indigenous Canadians. And we know that we cannot look Autumn in the eye without feeling a measure of failure and shame. We are passing her the torch, yet the light is anything but pure and bright.

Which is why we Canadians cannot even afford a hint of smugness or sanctimony as we lecture others on human rights. Until we have atoned for the never-ending sin, until we have fulfilled the birthright of indigenous Canadians to live a life of meaning and purpose in the full expression of human dignity, with freedom from fear and freedom from want, we have no lesson to teach anyone.

If we are all people of Treaty, if we are all the fruit of the creation animated by kisemanito, why do we find it so hard to ensure that all Canadians enjoy clean water, clean air, and life-bearing land?

The answer lies, perhaps, in what Gandhi taught. Our continuing journey through the story of *Us* brings an understanding that we must each, in our own way, become the change we want to see. And find our own path, our own way of being and becoming, as we pursue a better world than the one we inherited.

Chapter Seven

Finding your Path

The Danforth, Toronto, Canada, May 2019

The amiable host of the lovely bistro Soulas pours out gold-hued glasses of fragrant Moschofilero in the heart of the Greek Village on The Danforth, one of those iconic Canadian neighbourhoods where a host of cultural streams mingle to delightful effect. Further east on the avenue, the Mediterranean dominion cedes to Ethiopian and East African shops and restaurants, interspersed with Irish pubs, coffee shops, and bars. A community church and a Bangladeshi restaurant with a tandoori chef stand across the road from the Medina masjid. Beside the mosque a string of storefronts offers: a halal grocery; a garment shop of Indian and Pakistani apparel that sports a Union Jack on its sign; and an Islamic fashion specialist with hijabs in its window which sits easily beside a sports bar licenced for both alcohol and off-track betting.

I feel elated because my nephew Prateek was able to join me on a two kilometre ramble down The Danforth without tiring. This is gratifying progress in his recovery, and it already is clear that he has reclaimed a meaningful life as his brain continues to re-cover its higher functions. His brave wife Swati, my remarkable daughter-in-law who has borne his illness with breathtaking fortitude, found that he is one of only two known cases of people afflicted in the last half century, anywhere in the world, with the particular brain infection and inflammation he sustained. My nephew is the only known survivor. I have spent the past days with him and his family: my grandniece Arya aged two years and her two month old sister Moksha, who was in her mother's womb when her dad was stricken. These scenes make it difficult to deny the existence of miracles.

Cuddling Arya and Moksha on either knee recalls that indelible first memory of meeting Prateek, who was 15 months old when Mita and I agreed to build a life together. He nestled into my lap, climbed into my heart, and never left.

Our Greek host takes the lunch order at Soulas after the delicious wine from Mantinela is well settled in our glasses, as I join my editors Linda and Beno in a toast to the journey of *Us*. I have been coming to the spot Soulas occupies for decades, since it was first known as Pan on the Danforth, where our affable master of the house was a fixture for years. Linda and Beno are meeting for the first time. As I observe their easy camaraderie, I feel a pang of regret at never having brought them together from the compartments of my friendships. I have known each of them since the beginning of my adulthood; drawn to each by feelings never really examined in any depth: an instinctive coalescing, with a complete absence of romantic attraction, with a boundless supply of unconditional love.

They are the people I trust most to offer me an honest appraisal of my work, and to remedy the missteps they might find.

Linda offers both reproach and regret as she recalls our years on The Edmonton Journal's editorial board, the intense discussions we shared daily, without really knowing much of the experiences that shaped us before we met. It is, we agree, part of the masks we wear, the facades we use as armour, in those formative years when we are finding our paths in life.

As a toothsome lunch comes and goes — our aging host is hard of hearing these days, but the Pan signature dessert of fig-and-port-wine ice cream is as heavenly as ever — the afternoon settles into the comfortable rhythm of formative friendships resumed after years. Beno and I agree that now that we are in our sixties, we no longer care about what people think of us: a liberation that took far too long in a life moulded to solicit the approval of what we believed others wanted to see in us.

We talk about the choices we made in our lives, about the paths we chose to follow and the paths we left unexplored. Beno and I share a fondness for the poetry of Seferis, and are reminded of his insight in *Argonauts:*

> *kai psychí*
> *eí méllei gnósesthai aftín*
> *eis psychín*
> *aftí vlépete:*
> *ton xéno kai ton echthró ton eídame ston kathréfti*

In my rough translation:

And if the soul
is to know itself
It must look into your soul:
The stranger and the enemy, we see him in our mirror

Perhaps you are at an age, dear companion, where you have made a range of choices, looking back with regret at what was left undone. As Beno and Linda offer their counsel on how I might better calibrate the journey, I am once again reminded that our most fateful choices are guided by chance.

After I was required to leave university, I put in two years of "journalism school" in Red Deer before returning to the University of Alberta to read economics, political science and French. And to enrol in the creative writing class that brought Beno and I to one another. And the subsequent summer internship at The Edmonton Journal where Linda and I met.

Those choices eventually opened the door in 1987 to a fellowship for journalists underwritten by the Nuffield Foundation, for a programme of open-ended research and study at the University of Cambridge. And the best chance so far to fulfil the quest that remained with me: to find Harris.

London, United Kingdom, January 1987

I am more than a little downcast as I step into El Vino, and find a corner table in the afternoon lull. The place is a Fleet Street legend, a 19th century bar captured in literature (as Pomeroy's, the favourite respite of barrister Horace Rumpole in John Mortimer's delightful books); one of the habitual gathering places for lawyers from the nearby Inns of the Court, and hacks and scribes during the golden age of newspapers. The server, an older gent, asks, "Where in Canada?" as he takes my order for a glass of claret and a Ploughman's Lunch. Edmonton, I reply, which he correctly locates in the northwest: evidently having been at El Vino since the days Canadian was widely spoken on Fleet Street.

I have walked down the Strand for nearly a half hour on this damp and gloomy January afternoon, having spent a fruitless two hours in the British Council offices trying to find any trace of Harris. All I had was a surname and the years he had been in Bhubaneswar with funding from the council. Perhaps somewhere in the archival files, I was finally told by a not unsympathetic senior administrator after traversing three administrative levels. But even if they did find a record, they would need a more compelling reason than "a former student" to even make the effort to locate him. An earlier stop at the High Commission of India elicited a firm answer that visa records are entirely confidential, and unless I had a proper juridical request, there was nothing to be done.

With a classic London drizzle outside, with barely a separation between the roiling grey of the sky and the swirling tide of the Thames, I settle into the bone-warming heat and comfort of this welcoming haven. I begin to think about my journey from Harris to here — a term at Cambridge for mid-career journalists, supported by funding from the Nuffield Foundation — and wonder where I might find not just Harris, but the just and fair England he evoked.

The England I have come to is a society about to fracture, into a ruling elite and a permanent underclass. By early 1987, poverty has deepened to Dickensian levels, a downward spiral from which the government's prescription of economic austerity offers no rescue. Even though North Americans like me could afford the modest delights of El Vino, this is a world beyond the reach of East London and North London, where a second generation of families is condemned to life on state support: having neither the skills nor the education to survive the demise of coal mining, steel manufacturing and hands-on labour.

Tribalism and racial feelings ran deep, as it became ever more evident that people from Britain's former colonies would endure a generation of hardship to flourish, while the government did nothing to address the mass unemployment provoked by the death of traditional industries whose jobs had moved offshore. The government of the day spent billions of pounds on maintaining Britain's nuclear arsenal and conventional armed forces, yet seemed entirely oblivious to the serious internal divisions developing within Britain.

Surely security in the broadest sense included a vigorous and stable society that could be happy and productive? Investment in health, learning, retraining, skills upgrading, affordable housing, and the other cross-bracing of a viable society was nowhere on the horizon.

Between the nostalgic yearning of Neil Kinnock's Labour party towards an England of societal equity where there would be good factory jobs and social security for the salt of the earth; and the by-your-bootstraps self-reliance of Margaret Thatcher's Conservatives; there was a viable middle ground that none claimed.

If social stability were considered essential for national security, then it made sense to invest in programmes that would enable every Briton to lead a healthy and secure life: freedom from fear, and freedom from want were surely the fundamental human rights that this mother democracy could achieve? From such a climate, sustainable economic growth would be well within reach. Nonetheless, during the 1980s, obvious disparities broadened.

Large numbers of idle people without any hope of a productive future had already filled the streets of Britain's inner cities with riot and mayhem. Indeed, the displacement of the British people, the evolution of an impoverished north and a relatively prosperous south, seemed as momentous a change as the permanent fractures wrought by the partition of the Indian subcontinent, that last reckless act by colonial masters whose descendants were now presiding over the ruination of their own country.

The polarity between rich and poor, the imminent impoverishment of what had been Britain's middle class, only hardened tribal resolve between the haves and have-nots. This change brought the waning of hope among good people, the passing of a way of a communitarian life no longer valued in a wealth-oriented system, and a ruling ideology that reduced human beings to commodities: measuring human lives and human worth by productive capacity.

The displacement spread from the ever-poorer middle class and consumed the powerless in a society where wealth was increasingly the only measure of human worth. Even as the power of economics and trade was erasing boundaries between nation-states, cultures and societies were erecting new ones — not just around their nations, but around their tribes.

Even El Vino's London was caught in the turmoil. The year before, Fleet Street with its raucous parade of journalists and newspapers ranging from wildly populist to stoically conservative, had been shaken to its core.

The Australian scoundrel Rupert Murdoch, who would one day go on to poison the health of American politics by creating a noxious propaganda organ called Fox News, began to mute the democratic clamour of journalism and transform it into a lucrative means of elite enrichment. He shut down his newspapering operations on Fleet Street and moved them to Wapping in the London Docklands — where development land was plentiful.

With the Thatcher government's ready assent, Murdoch broke the back of the Fleet Street press unions. Ever since the move a year previous, there had been ugly confrontations, heavy limits on pickets at the plant, and a climate of bitterness which amounted to tribal warfare. Around the anniversary of the move, there was a major altercation one night just outside the Wapping gates, hand to hand combat between strikers and police: a stark evocation of peasants storming the gates of the baronial castle.

If Murdoch represented the bleakest face of capitalism, then the unions represented the lengths to which people will go when their very survival is at stake. Shortly after the riot, the union gave up. Murdoch had won his battle to put profit ahead of people, but at what human cost? What had happened to civility? To consensus? To negotiating in good faith? Or had it, in this case, come down to a tribal clash for survival?

After this, it became impossible for me to look upon England as a country that had once dominated the two cultures that bred me. I could in no way understand how the society I was experiencing could ever, ever have ruled over India and Canada. I began to see the society, as a literature student put it one night, as "the honest island people we were before this aberration of empire."

And they were a people I could look upon with affection. My own colonial hangups vanished; I began to like England and the English much more than I thought I would. I began to see the paradoxes not merely as indications of an approaching social catastrophe, but as the inevitable byproducts of a civilisation in decline. There was little but the past to cling on to, and no matter how diminished it became, it would always claim its dignity as best it could.

It was very much like the first big revelation of adulthood: when you begin to see your mother and father not as parents but for the people they are, and begin to deal with them as friends.

Even so, there was ample scope for a young journalist — I was only 31 at the time, with more than a decade already invested in journalism — to speak truth to power amid England's devolution. And the opportunity was there. Already, my academic tutors at Cambridge had asked if I wished to pursue a Master's degree — a two-year MPhil with a thesis that could be expanded into a PhD — that would surely lead to permanent residence and a life built in England.

My marriage was still new and we had no children. Europe, and England's membership in the European Union, offered its own allure. I already was a Francophile by then, having made more than half a dozen trips to France before my marriage: and England offered an ample stage for a flourishing career in journalism, particularly if my entry came with a Cambridge pedigree.

I had wonderful mentors in Cambridge, ones who evoked the very best of the England Harris represented. My academic advisor, David Fieldhouse, revelled in the title of Vere Harmsworth Professor of Imperial and Naval History, and was widely recognised as the foremost authority on colonial economics. I was offered expansive warmth and kindness at my home college, Wolfson, by the college president Sir David Williams (later to be Cambridge's first full-time vice chancellor), in whom I found a kindred spirit. And there was a particularly supportive welcome from Bill Kirkman, a one time foreign correspondent for the Times of London, who looked after the programmes for press fellows.

I particularly enjoyed the weekly tutorials with David Fieldhouse. He would light the gas fire in his bitterly cold rooms in the stone-walled precincts of Jesus College, pour us each a glass of sherry, and elegantly dissect whatever I'd written that week ("Might it be useful to elaborate a bit on these data?").

David Williams took pains to introduce me widely at the reception preceding formal dinners. And to share a bottle of champagne whenever the occasion warranted. One evening he advised me on the ideal way to consume haggis — the Scottish steamed pudding of oatmeal and sheep's offal — at the college's celebration on Robbie Burns night. "You'll need three drams of The Balvenie in you, and another three drams in the haggis after it's addressed: I'm quite certain you'll find it more palatable than one might expect."

Even so, I was all too keenly aware of the vast chasm between my coddled life in Cambridge and the harshness of government austerity programs that inflicted misery as a public policy choice on the most vulnerable Britons.

Bill Kirkman took me around to London charities he helped, where good-hearted people on shoestring budgets were doing the best they could to cope with the government-planned decline in living standards.

I spent time in London at the Pimlico home of old family friends: Prafulla, an Odia artist and writer who had been a classmate of my uncle Jadunath; and his husband Derek, a Cambridge-trained barrister. In that bitter winter of 1987, Derek would tell me of the homes he visited in the course of his work with the rent control tribunal: homes where elderly people could afford to heat only one room. And even then, it was clear they had turned on the heat only to accommodate Derek's visit. A bedroom or two; and the space that served as living room, dining room, and parlour: all feebly warmed on a rationed fire and the leftover heat from the stove. Every room would be damp and clammy once you moved away from the one fire they could afford, Derek noted, and people wore layers of sweaters and coats.

A few centimetres of snow, and a never-ending dampness, had thrown the country into chaos. There were many debates in the House of Commons about a five-pound monthly heating subsidy for freezing pensioners. At that time, five pounds bought you a pint and a sandwich in a pub. The government led by Prime Minister Margaret Thatcher worked out some sort of formula for the gradient of temperatures that would trigger the payment for heating in different parts of the country. An earnest government minister, well leashed and brought to heel by the permanent bureaucracy, explained his department was developing a new brochure that would set out how pensioners could apply for the subsidy.

At last, the government capitulated and authorised an emergency heating subsidy regardless of temperature. This was all mitigation, because the government had privatised state-owned British Gas, which had kept rates affordable for all. Gas rates were jacked up just before privatisation, to make revenue forecasts more attractive to investors. Now that pensioners were freezing, the government finally offered a rebate. The government wouldn't even entertain any thought that perhaps it was a bad idea to privatise critical national infrastructure which literally kept people safe and warm.

The untreated mentally ill were everywhere. In much of London, especially the neighbourhoods east of St. Paul's Cathedral, people wandered the streets speaking to themselves or shouting at passers-by. Some slept in subway cars and stations, slugging a self-medicating beer on the District Line.

Standards of health care were changing. Private insurance was allowed to compete with the National Health Service. Those who could afford to pay received much better and swifter medical care than working Britons. There were no queues for those who could pay. Even as affluent patients moved out of the public system, the government told health authorities that costs were rising "too fast" because doctors were seeing "too many" patients.

The proposed solution was to reduce the number of consultations, and to close hospital beds, so fewer people would be treated. Many doctors thought this absurd. (Across the channel in France, illness was treated as an emergency response, like firefighting, with abundant capacity to meet demand). Moreover, health authorities were told that unless they cut budgets by treating fewer patients, they would be replaced.

It appeared obvious to all but government that economic deprivation only increased the demand for health services. To achieve a healthier population — surely the most effective way of reducing costs in the medium term — people would need security and stability in their lives, and guidance in healthier eating to reduce some of the world's highest instances of preventable coronary disease. The absurdity of treating fewer patients, leaving larger numbers of the sick uncared for, did not seem to provoke compassion: let alone evoke a sensible or even an agreeable solution from the government of the day.

An election was coming sometime in 1987, and the political manoeuvring was well under way. The Labour Party leader Neil Kinnock took the bold position that Britain should abolish its nuclear arsenal — the much larger American nuclear capability already was dedicated to the defence of Western Europe — and use the money to alleviate poverty and restore a viable life to the millions of Britons in the bottom 40 percent of income.

Rupert Murdoch's scurrilous newspapers led the charge against Kinnock, accusing him of "running up the white flag of surrender" to the Soviet Union — which was engaged in reordering its economy and society under the leadership of Mikhail Gorbachev, whose plans of glasnost and perestroika (openness and restructuring) soon would devolve the Soviet Union into its constituent republics.

In the absence of any prospect of opposition victory, the field was left open to Prime Minister Thatcher and her cabinet to reshape Britain in the small-government dogma that further afflicted the afflicted and further comforted the comfortable.

The fact that misery was inflicted as a policy choice, in a country that wrapped itself in a self-image of decency, fair play, and shared community, made this pervasive erosion of human rights all the more difficult to bear.

In 1931, Gandhi was invited to visit a textile mill in Darwen, Lancashire, to see the economic turmoil imposed by the Indian nationalist boycott of imported milled cotton in favour of indigenous home-spun cotton. Instead of being greeted by the hostility authorities expected, he was welcomed with incredible warmth by the mill workers. They understood, far better than the ruling elite, that their own plight was not so different from the plight of the Indians Gandhi wished to emancipate. "They treated me as one of their own. I shall never forget that," Gandhi said of the mill workers.

I wondered whether the cruelties of the Thatcher government might have been lessened, if Britain had its own Gandhi or King or Mandela in the 1980s. Once the foundation of suffering was laid, it was there to stay.

In the decades that followed, leader after leader chose austerity over community, culminating in the debacle of a ginned referendum on leaving Europe: replete with false promises such as hundreds of millions more pounds for national health and the common good.

Now, in July 2019, the Tory party has chosen a particularly duplicitous leader of the "leave Europe" movement to be prime minister. This tow-headed flamethrower readily brings to mind the novelist P.G. Wodehouse's portrayal (*Mulliner Nights*) of another well-born boulevardier as a "vapid and irreflective guffin, totally lacking in character and purpose."

At the time of writing, this feckless choice truly seems the nadir of what was once responsible governance. And it affirms my belief that I chose the path that was right for me, at that formative moment in 1987.

My choice might have been shaped differently, despite Britain's travails, had I been able to find Harris. Rather than settle in England, I chose to return to Canada: to make a difference in a world that was still being built, to shape a society still open to being shaped, in a land of abundant resources.

Looking back, that choice was the second important evolution of my own life in the 1980s. The first great life-changing moment arrived in May of 1983.

Having unsuccessfully navigated the labyrinths of love in a handful of relationships, I agreed with my parents that perhaps I might be introduced to a woman known to our extended family. Thus it was that I found myself on a first solo date — after two visits amidst family — under the arcades of Connaught Circus in New Delhi, in a grand air-conditioned café called the *Volga*. After the opening rounds of an amiable conversation, I at last held her eyes. And was stricken: suffused in the absolute, compelling clarity that this is my life companion.

I thought of that moment on a joyous Saturday morning in March 2019: our toddler grandson Krishan awoke between us and launched himself into Mita with a ferocious nuzzle, demanding to be changed and fed, flashing me an infectious smile from his grandmother's shoulder as she carried him away.

Chapter Eight

Finding freedom from fear

Alappuzha, Kerala, India, March 2014

A soft wake laps against the side of our houseboat in the gloam-ing, as passengers nimbly step off the boat-bus at the nearby jetty. Their farewells float across the hot, damp air; as night comes to the backwaters of Kerala. Mosquito curtains shroud the foredeck of dozens of tourist houseboats moored for the night. A snatch of evensong wafts from an unseen church down the other shore, a sweet balm of faith from the heart.

Aboard our gently-rocking craft, the cook and boatman are attacking our gin bottle with gusto, the fizz of tonic quelled as the glasses fill and they withdraw with a conspiratorial grin to the privacy of their afterdeck.

On our shore and across the channel, the life of the village falls into the routine of homecoming: fish fry mingles with the eve-ning smell of ripening fields, the vivid green of the day now more aroma than a vision. Televisions flicker here and there, homework at a kitchen table; a sliver of moonlight plays across the waters, a lone paddler pulls up to a village shop, as I look up to a blazing canopy of stars.

This should be an invitation to serenity, to the calmness and stillness so lacking in urban life. Yet I am overcome by an unbearable sense of loss, a sensation so vital that I can see and hear and feel that village of a bygone age, the first and only place where I ever understood the meaning of home: an exile's yearning, the unrequited longing for being and belonging in the intimacy of one's rightful place on earth.

It is the wound that has never healed, no matter how much I consign it to the past, no matter how much rationality I bring to dampen the memory of a land that calls to me: for now and in time to be, as Yeats might have said, whenever green is borne.

Nestled in a rattan chair on the bobbing deck, feeling the velvet heat of the night above the cool water, I wish I could weave my life into the fabric of this village, take ease and comfort in this parade of brightly-hued homes with their tiled roofs and cosy verandahs, a rustic charm spiced every now and then with a mega mansion fuelled by remittance money from the Persian Gulf. Strong though the pull may be, even if I wished to set down what roots I could in this tropical tip of southern India, I know that the exile's trudge would call me away: to another river, another boat, another set of lights, another Grail quest for the earth that speaks my name.

Home. How did it come to be? How was it that one piece of earth, on the ample banks of the broad Subarnarekha River in eastern India, claimed me for itself, for now and for time to be?

In post-independence India, my parents met and married at the intersection of the falling aristocracy and the rising middle class. And in keeping with the emergence of a new nation, where education and the universal availability of knowledge would erode the old feudal power structures more quickly than anyone might have imagined, my parents were the vanguard generation.

Indeed, my mother Gita was among the first women who travelled to London for their education; and her feudal family was open to the idea that she should leave her newborn son with them, while she broadened and expanded her already remarkable intellectual horizons. From a sprawling family estate, where her father held dominion over 45 neighbouring villages (a historic title, last confirmed in 1803 following a decree enacted by Lord Cornwallis some years before in his time as Governor General of India), my mother eschewed the prospect of an arranged marriage and chose a life with a young academic from an impoverished family with a handful of siblings to support.

From a household with a legion of servants to answer her every beck and call, she moved to a single room in London with my father Jagannath Prasad (JP) Das, sharing one heavy woollen dressing gown between them for warmth. He left weeks before I was born, and six months after my birth, my mother joined him, leaving her baby in her family's care: Me.

In my first recollection of coherence, those tesserae of cognition that filter the realm of earliest childhood memory, I always come back to the village that infused my life. Sometimes it is the sound of crickets, the aroma of ripening gourds atop roofs of bamboo and thatch, the thud of a zinc bucket against a well. Or the tannic purple stain of ripe rose-apples, the surging sweetness of custard apples, the waft of mangos on an afternoon breeze. Home.

Invariably, I return to the arcaded upstairs veranda of my maternal grandparents' estate, in the arms of my uncles Kuna and Kanu, or my mother's youngest sister Timi, as much a sibling as an aunt. There were the sturdier grasps of my nanny Ishwarmani or our butler Rama: a work-worn adult finger pointing beyond the courtyard, beyond the fish ponds, beyond the crossroads temple, to the rammed-earth path running between huts and groves and paddy fields, always with a whispered declaration that we are nearly at the end of the wait for my father to reclaim me, that the day of reunion is nearly here.

The Wait carries meaning and conviction only while I am nestled in the grandmother whom I call Ma, and who does nothing to disabuse me of the illusion that I am her son. Time and again, as though preparing me for catastrophe, she tells me that one day I would leave her doting bosom, to be with a father I have never seen: known only from a toothy picture in a glass-fronted *al-mira* beside my grandparents' hunting rifle and shotgun. Home.

There is absolute clarity about the end of The Wait. A slight figure comes through the gate of the estate, with a crowd gathered to meet him as he crosses the outer courtyard to the walls of the mansion. And in my clearest flash of childhood memory, we are at the arcaded veranda where my grandfather Ramchandra held court for the 45 villages in his domain, when Ma declares, "This is your father."

And thus begins a life's bond, informed with such warmth and compassion that for years to come I thought all fathers were that loving. And although I could not know it then, it also means the end of Home, and the start of Exile. And a journey that brings me to a houseboat in Kerala in the spring of 2014, a life and an age away from where I began.

Asi es la vida, Neruda might say, and he would be right: this is how life is. The cook ends my reverie by announcing dinner, and graciously accepts another tot of gin. I reflect on why I feel so unsettled, so consumed by foreboding, so mindful of being disconnected from Home.

I admit to myself the apprehension I have all day denied: tomorrow morning I will return, after an absence of 17 years, to another village that shaped and informed my journey. I will return to the place that taught me, with startling clarity, two of the three essential foundations of a meaningful human life: freedom from fear and freedom from want.

Above all, I am to see the woman who infused the lives of her children with the third essential element, the bounty of unconditional love: Vijayamma. In all these years, I have wondered what became of her and the forsaken children she raised as her own. I never dared to find out, for fear that all might have turned out badly in the end. To be sure it is an exile's cowardice. But it is more.

My recollection of Vijayamma is entwined with my own sense of self, a central source of my own commitment to human dignity and the human right to a meaningful life. That fateful meeting in the course of my work as a foreign correspondent came to affirm the very purpose of my public life and its mission to make a difference in the world.

The experience of Vijayamma and her village became a compelling narrative in my advocacy of human rights as a way of life. It illuminated the why and how of seeking to evolve societies where all humans can live together with dignity, in community, in harmony with one another and with the natural world.

My commitment to sustainability, to a new way of being and belonging in the world with dignity as its hallmark, always found new energy when I thought of her, and the hundreds of other mothers serving in SOS Children's Villages all over the world.

Coming back to Aluva, to a village that left such a mark on my life's journey, I cannot bear the thought that the inspiration I took there might be shattered by disillusion. Now that the path is set, I know I must be prepared to accept with equanimity whatever I may find.

They are immense now, the spreading shade trees that announce the village: her village, Vijayamma's village. Trees that seemed little more than striplings all those years ago, bursting with birdsong in the blistering noonday heat of the humid Kerala coast, giving shelter to the ample homes ringing the village amphitheatre.

Without the trees that signal the imminence of the village, one would have been lost in the busy sprawl of Kochi, in a neighbourhood so transformed in 17 years as to bewilder and bedazzle. What was once a village distant from the bustle of the city is now surrounded by the thudding din of construction. The Kochi Metro line, apartment blocks, office towers, rising from a dusty haze of cranes and sweat and heat: the cement dust itself the new incense for the deity of newfound wealth.

It has been a long morning's drive indeed, from the bucolic houseboat jetty in Alappuzha to the emerging megapolis of Kochi, every kilometre moving us from serenity to chaos.

My day began before the light, as I arose at the first brightening of the night sky, evoking the presence of the Mother Goddess in timeless Sanskrit verse while I waited for the water and the village to awaken. I completed my ablutions, my first pre-dawn bath in many years, and emerged on deck to immerse myself in the stirring of a new day. During my dawn prayers and meditation I tried my best to quell the unease that always overtakes me during trips to India: knowing that I have returned to the country of my birth, but cannot ever go Home.

I snap my tablet shut, and look to the lightening horizon. A cargo-laden longboat, piled with gunny sacks, breaks the stillness of the day with the whirr of its engine, as the horizon brightens above the eastern banks. My traveling companion Woody Johnson — a Canadian friend of Swedish ancestry who has chosen to give himself a 70th birthday trip to India although he has not been to Sweden — emerges from his cabin.

We watch the flotilla of school-boats pass by over a leisurely breakfast, sail by bathers on the ghats, a sari-draped woman pouring a brass jug of lake-water over herself with a sinuous grace, a school-bound boy being fussed over by a mother tucking in his shirt and handing him his tiffin-box before sending him off to the jetty with a little guiding shove. The morning light carries the hues of well-polished brass, as all around us the world comes alive. Soon the charms of waterborne life are left far behind, as we dock, drive through rural roads, and lunge into the thundering, never-ending churn of highway traffic.

I have learned with my years to value the apprehension that crackles through every anticipation of reunion, for it is the simplest prophylactic against disappointment. After two hours in which our driver Dilip displayed a remarkable calm and patience, going past turns which exist in theory but turn out to be blocked by construction, finally making our way through the half-formed concrete and relentless dust, we at last found our way to Aluva, and the village gate.

The hazy memory of yesteryear takes on new shape and clarity, as the eye confirms what the mind recalls. I know I have arrived when I see the garlanded bust of the village's visionary founder, Hermann Gmeiner, in the plaza, and step out of the car into the breezy arcade of the visitors' reception.

I step into the open verandah, and there she is, with Daliya, a colleague who has kindly agreed to interpret from Malayalam to English. And the warmth of Vijayamma's greeting needs no translation. She is radiant. From the first look I can see that her life has unfolded in grace, that the selfless commitment she made all those years ago has brought her the fulfilment and satisfaction that comes from making a difference in the lives of others.

Vijayamma had only been a few years at the SOS Children's Village in Aluva when we met in 1996. She was a young widow in her 30s who, giving up any chance of remaking a life with another partner, set out to devote the rest of her life to being a mother to children with nowhere to go. Back then, I could sense the anxiety that seeped to the surface: the anxieties that every parent has, multiplied tenfold: the constant vigil to be the best you can be in infusing these young lives with dignity, confidence, meaning and purpose. Now, as we walk across the grounds to Vijayamma's house, she carries the ease of years of accomplishment.

Vijayamma is one of 15 mothers at SOS Children's Village in Aluva, women who dedicate themselves to providing four critical support of a child's life: a home, a mother, siblings, and a shared and supportive community. This is the practical, hands on means to achieve the two foundational human rights: freedom from fear, and freedom from want.

Like the Universal Declaration of Human Rights, SOS Children's Villages were born from the ashes of the Second World War. If the Universal Declaration made compelling promises of how human life ought to be lived, the SOS Children's Villages actually enabled that life to be lived.

The experience of a life lived within the context of human rights and human dignity is deeply empowering and enabling, a way of life that in itself is a vaccination against the corrosive impetus to violence.

Indeed, as Gandhi reminded us time and again, non-violence is nothing more and nothing less than the absence of fear. The village itself provides freedom from want: shelter, clothing, food, education, a supportive family, the companionship of a community. And a mother's love.

Timi and I tussle for that mother's love, one on each side of Ma in her large four-poster bed, as she gazes directly to the ceiling rather than turning towards either of us. There are only five years between Timi and me, and before I came along she had had the privileged love always showered on the youngest and last of the children.

For my twice-widowed grandfather Ramchandra, who had lost two wives and two children to illness before marrying Ma, his children and grandson are objects of unrestrained indulgence. Ma gives us firmness with her ample love, and in every unspoken gesture she imparts to us the willpower and discipline that makes leaders.

We do not have her for long. Cancer takes Ma before Timi's tenth birthday, before my fifth, when I still think her my mother. The medicine of 1959 can do little more than manage her agony.

The hospital room in Kataka is enormous, in the full clarity of indelible memory. Ma is lying on her side, facing me as I stand by her head. It is nearly evening and the shade tree outside her room — a spreading banyan, under which nothing grows — is raucous with a parliament of homecoming birds.

Ma looks at me, a searching look, her pain-dimmed eyes carrying a stoic serenity. "Take Silu away from here," she said at last, using my pet-name. And rolls over, turning her back.

I am ushered outside by adult hands, to stand beneath the tree. Wisps of cloud drift across the evening sky, carried ever more swiftly in a gathering breeze. The chorus of birds grows louder and louder, until it is the only sound in my head. She was 45.

Ma was born Tilottoma Patnaik. She learned civil disobedience as a teenage volunteer in Gandhi's independence movement. She knew how to read Sanskrit, shoot a rifle, rule men, ride a horse, govern a feudal estate, use a camera, argue philosophy. And hold a family together, which she did through her marriage to Ramchandra Dasmohapatra, the birth of four children, and the first of her grandchildren: me.

She was our centre, and after her, things fell apart. Mere anarchy was indeed loosed upon our world, with a Maoist insurgency driving the family off our land a scant decade after Ma's death. Exile. For now, and in time to be.

Vijayamma, and hundreds of other SOS mothers like her, are the indispensable healers of a motherless world. For every child who has lost a mother, for children discarded and abandoned before they could even think, for children born into cruelty and deprivation, Vijayamma and her legion are a beacon of hope. They fulfill a child's human right to love, to dignity, to security, to respect, to be valued and cherished.

These mothers do more than build families and hold them together. They shape, nurture, guide a family that is ever evolving and ever growing.

These mothers forego their own choice to seek a life partner: there are no fathers in SOS villages. Just mothers, who have made a commitment to raising a village full of children within a safe, secure and supportive cradle of familial love.

The Austrian-born Gmeiner, a soldier on the Russian front during the Second World War, understood that the shattered lives of children in war and conflict could not be rebuilt without a home of their own. His singular determination, beginning with $40, created the first SOS home in the Tyrol in 1949. The movement he inspired is making a signal difference in the world.

My 1996 introduction to SOS Children's Villages, personified in my meeting with Vijayamma and her family, became a catalyst in my own personal development. At the turn of the millennium, I walked away from journalism at the pinnacle of my career, stepping off the platform of security and esteem to make a genuine difference in the world — as who I am, rather than what I am. Without official position, without a bully pulpit, I determined to come down from the tower to the street. And I have never looked back.

Providing children with the love and community they deserve is not an act of charity: there is an inherent recognition that this is a child's birth right. Thus, it is an act of enabling the human dignity with which each of us is born.

The SOS approach is not a "one size fits all." Indeed, in the experience of Vijayamma and her fellow mothers in Aluva, it evolves from within the community, accommodating its unique cultural norms and behaviours, and its own approaches to consensus and coalition building.

The commonality in each SOS Children's Village is to enable freedom from fear and freedom from want within their own communities. In very practical terms, their practice of human dignity illustrates how the children they nurture are achieving, and can achieve, both of those foundational freedoms.

We are walking across the gravel yard to Vijayamma's house with its shaded flower-garden. In 1996, Vijayamma had just brought a newborn into the house, Ponnu, whose arrival provoked sulking and jealousy in some of the newfound siblings. Her toddler Mallu clung especially fiercely to Vijayamma's sari, wondering when the new baby would return whence it came.

Mallu's birth mother had abandoned her on a bus, asking the lady in the next seat to hold Mallu while she went to the washroom. Vijayamma's children included a school-age girl and her younger brother, whose mother had been driven to take her own life. And there was Rani, eight or nine at the time, trying to distract Mallu, understanding then and there that being a big sister to the new arrivals would be a definition of her life.

Vijayamma is a grandmother now. She last became a mother aged 45, and with just a few years of active child-rearing lying ahead, takes a merited satisfaction in the well-formed lives of the children she has already raised. Most of the children are at university or beyond, including two working in the Middle East which brings a level of affluence their siblings could scarcely have expected.

It is early 2014. Ponnu will finish high school later this year, and pursue a polytechnic course. Mallu has three years of engineering college behind her, with more to come. Hima, scarcely older than Mallu, is pursuing an MBA in Chennai. Vijayamma's oldest, Unni, is proprietor of a photography studio in Aluva, not far from where Vijayamma raised her.

Murugan came to Vijayamma after his parents died from drinking counterfeit liquor from a government-run store. Dozens more were blinded apart from the six dozen dead, and more than 600 families were left orphaned and bereft. Today Murugan is an engineer in Chennai, married with a child. Salu, Murugan's sister, finished her MBA and went to work for a prestigious international bank. Children once discarded, bereft of home and parents, with even the prospect of survival in doubt.

We walk into the ample front room, with its play area for the younger children, and space enough for the family to gather. Most of the village children are away at school, this is the time the mothers have to get everything ready for their arrival: snacks, dinner, organising the routines.

Vijayamma invites us in for lunch. We begin with water boiled with cumin — the habit of purifying the municipal water supply brings a delectable bonus in flavour. The freshness of the greens and vegetables, the simplicity of the cooking, amplifies and enhances the natural flavours of every ingredient.

Vijayamma rejects every compliment with a little smile of dismissal that endeared her to me all those years ago. And when I inquire about what became of the children, she replies by pulling out a book and opening it on the living room table.

It is Rani's wedding book, photos and text printed and bound into a commemorative volume. Rani is a stunningly beautiful bride, and Vijayamma a justly proud mother. Rani studied hotel management, won an internship in the Taj group's hotel on Kerala's famed Kovalam Beach, and met her husband, a financial officer in the hotel. I am overwhelmed as I reconcile my memory of Rani the child with these images of a poised and assured young woman on her wedding day. (Months after my March 2014 visit, her newborn son became the latest addition to Vijayamma's flock of grandchildren). Here are all the trappings of a middle-class Indian wedding. A plenitude of guests, flower-bedecked car for the bride and groom, the newlyweds touching Vijayamma's feet in a gesture of respect, the suits and sparkly saris and laden tables of food and refreshment. Vijayamma raised two sons, Anish and Rajesh, who sent their mother money from their jobs in the Persian Gulf to ensure Rani enjoyed a grand wedding.

Here is the flowering of a human life.

The arc of Rani's life is what we can multiply tenfold, hundred-fold, thousand-fold, when we establish and nurture freedom from fear and freedom from want. Not as an act of charity, but as the fulfilment of human dignity.

There should be no piety nor sanctimony nor indeed the seductive corruption of giving to the "less fortunate." What the SOS Village and Vijayamma's love gave Rani was nothing more and nothing less than her birthright: the possibility to live a life of dignity. This journey, from charity to dignity, is a transformation from "giver and receiver", and the power relationship implicit therein, to the shared consciousness of being and belonging with and to one another.

This is the very act of overcoming "otherness," of embracing pluralism, affirming that many streams of human experience and of the human condition can live together in dignity, under the rule of law, with diversity seen as a source of strength and resiliency. Freedom from fear, freedom from want. Moving from charity to dignity. This is the radiant heart of sustainability.

Sitting beside Vijayamma, drinking in the images of Rani's wedding book, I begin to weave together the thoughts I have just shared with you. And I see past my restive exile, past the rootlessness and sense of drift that has consumed me for all these decades, and come to a kernel of truth.

When we free ourselves enough to embrace human rights as a way of life, when we approach one another with the abundance of unconditional love, when we see ourselves in the Other, we can indeed find a communion that transcends origin, geography, race and societal place.

And if our journey of *Us* will provoke you to look within yourself, to know yourself, and to act upon what you find, your world and our world will be transformed. And when that happens, sisters and brothers, I will be Home.

A postscript, 2017:

Vijayamma retired at the prescribed age, about a year after this vignette. Rather than live in a hostel for retired SOS mothers, she moved into a house her children bought for her, one ample enough to accommodate regular visits by her children and grandchildren. When she fell seriously ill in 2016, the hospital was overwhelmed by nearly three dozen visitors come to abet her recovery: her children and their families. The hospital administrators, recalls Mallu (now a software engineer with Hewlett Packard), wondered what sort of celebrity or VIP they had in their midst.

Chapter Nine

In search of a civil society

Arima, Trinidad and Tobago, October 2013

From the colonial-bungalow verandah of the Asa Wright Nature Centre, all we can see on this autumn day is a canopy of foliage, undulating waves of forest following the contours of the hills and hillocks, suffused with the melodious buzz of humming-birds swarming the feeders below. Mita and I are atop the Arima Valley in the rugged hills of Trinidad. All morning we have kept our eyes on these distant hills, making our way past the pleasing ruckus of life on the seashore and the plains, stopping at the stalls lining the parking lot of a supermarket for a street-food snack of aloo pie and doubles, the lilt of island English as lyrical to the ear as a calypso tune.

Leaving behind the highway with its gleaming new malls, I zig-zag our tiny rented Toyota up the steepest paved road I have ever seen, hoping that the little engine will power us to the plateau. It does, and we are soon on a narrow and twisty mountain road in the searing midday heat, heading toward the high hills above Blanchisseuses Bay, into the heart of Trinidad's rain forest. Our morning has been like a Buddhist pilgrimage, ascending from the swarm and chaos of daily life to a place of serenity: *sunyata* with the sky above and forest below, and a gust of breeze mimicking the distant susurrus of the sea.

On the forest floor there is no sun, the light blocked and filtered by the dense canopy, vines and mosses nourished only by clouds, and all around us the thrilling sounds of dozens of avian languages, amid fleeting glimpses of birds of all sizes and colours. We watch in wonder as column after column of ants streams across the forest floor, each insect bearing a leaf-cutting many times its body weight, to feed a colony of 10,000 or more under the dominion of a single queen. A human misstep merely diverts the enfilade around the obstacle, the disruption acknowledged and avoided. On and on it goes, stretching hundreds of metres across the valley floor, and its fragrant mass of decaying forest debris that feeds the roots of the enormous cloud forest. It is an awe-inspiring demonstration: the manifestation of a hard-wired genetic instinct of being and belonging that bears no relation to human notions of morality, sympathy, empathy, or any of the other attributes we evoke to justify our gregarious lives.

Protecting what remains of this natural patrimony is a point of pride in Trinidad. The Arima valley, endpoint of the Andean cordillera which forms the spine of South America, is one such reserve. Another is the sprawling Caroni swamp. You emerge by boat from mangrove forests full of tree-hugging boa constrictors overhead; to an open lagoon with the wondrous spectacle of thousands of scarlet ibis and white egrets, spread against the evening sky, coming home to roost on a vivid green island.

We city dwellers are little more than witless slabs of protein amid the astonishing biodiversity of the island rainforest. We haven't a clue which of the many spiders are poisonous, or which misstep might rouse a *fer de lance,* deadliest of Trinidad's venomous snakes. Even as we thrill to the song of hundreds of tiny hummingbirds, we know this is the solace one yearns for in the headlong rush of urban life: a moment of stillness, the absent noise of artifice.

The ceaseless parade of ants, so ordered, so synchronised, is indeed a wonder of nature, a visible manifestation of what is within us, but invisible to our eyes and even our minds. I have seen the hard-wiring that drives the ants to work in such precise collaboration, because it is the way we ourselves are programmed.

Shortly after the turn of the millennium, over a pleasant Italian lunch on a summer patio, the pioneering crystallographer Michael James showed me a video taken from an immensely detailed microscope at Canada's National Institute of Nanotechnology in Edmonton. A molecule of polystyrene loomed large as a football. Round it, subatomic particles organised themselves into a nano-motor, to move the polystyrene across a surface. The impulse to work together is in our very chemistry, in every essence of our being. What the nano-motor showed is precisely what we observe in the long parade of ants across the floor of Arima's cloud forest. It is mesmerising to see the ants enacting the very rhythms and patterns embedded in each and every one of our cells.

As we all know from the most cursory examination of the world we have made, that hard-wiring from our very nature is lost and subsumed in the complexity of the societies humans have built.

This brief interlude within the Arima cloud forest is a temptation to look beyond the world we made, to the world we left behind in our headlong impetus to dominate the planet and all the species who call it home. In this cloud forest, slowing to the pace and the rhythms of the wild, is an invitation to the contemplation and recognition of who we are, to know ourselves with clarity of heart and mind.

And it invites us to think of what sustainability truly means. If even subatomic particles are programmed for common purpose and work, then working in community is ingrained in every part of us. If the Arima ants know by instinct that individualism and isolation cannot be sustained, why is it so difficult for humans to admit the impulse quite literally contained in every fibre of their being?

On the next stop of the journey, we will explore the paths to connect the better angels of our nature. By creating and nurturing shared values. By looking beyond our superficial differences to find what united us, to rediscover the merits of cooperation and collaboration and shared purpose: to foster the common wealth and the common good.

One of the very first myths we need to re-examine is the notion that agreement and consensus are necessary at every step for a sustainable future — that the "common purpose" essential to the common good and the common wealth must carry an implicit unanimity. In fact, just as you can find multiple paths to the same destination, common purpose can be achieved by diverse means.

As one illustration, all Canadian politicians agree on the "common purpose" of government-funded health care, and that this health care should be comprehensive, universal, publicly-administered, portable, and accessible.

Within this common purpose, there is ample room for debate and disagreement: on the relative role of a purely public sector provision of health care, or on whether the private sector should play a greater or lesser role. Indeed, the Canadian system is predicated upon a choice for physicians: the option to be a salaried employee, or work as an independent contractor providing services through contracts with the publicly-administered system.

When we focus on common purpose and the common good, it becomes apparent that sustainability is about accommodating differences. It is about finding the compromises necessary so that people from very different backgrounds, raised with divergent experiences, each one's version of "truth" shaded by the perceptions that have made them, can find a way to share a society.

This is the difference between a sustainable social cohesion and "winner take all" attitude in democratic elections, where the dominant political party or tribe rules to the exclusion of all other interests, until it is duly removed from office by another political tribe — or by armed force.

The model of sustainable coexistence among many realities is really one of pluralism: a harmonious co-mingling that acknowledges and accommodates disagreement, and a continuous search for the trade-offs we are willing to make, until we emerge with shared values.

This has been the great virtue of modern Canada, our ability and capacity to mingle many streams of the human experience into a rich and dynamic national identity. It did not occur by chance. It is a continuing effort, one that allows for our definition of being and belonging to evolve over time.

This notion is beautifully distilled by a religious leader, the Aga Khan, who ardently believes the Canadian experience can serve as a model for the world. So much so that he has created a Global Centre for Pluralism to study and perpetuate inclusion. The real aim is not democracy per se, as a tribal competition of ideas with winners and losers. Rather, it is meaningful participation in the shared life of one's community and society. In the charged climate of the times, the vision of the Aga Khan, spiritual leader of the world's 15 million Ismaili Muslims, drives the centre's advocacy of pluralism. As the centre sees its mandate:

> Defined simply, pluralism is an ethic of respect for diversity. Whereas diversity is a fact, pluralism is a choice. Pluralism results from the daily decisions taken by state institutions, by civil society actors and associations and by individuals to recognise and value human differences.

> Pluralist societies are not accidents of history. They require continuous investment and decision-making across many different sectors — economic, political and social. Although every society must define its own path, comparative experiences can be studied to better understand different possible outcomes.

As the Aga Khan himself put it in the 2010 Lafontaine-Baldwin lecture where he set out the case for building a pluralism centre in Canada:

Clearly, the challenges posed by diversity are mounting. New technologies mean that people mix and mingle more than ever before. Massive human migrations are part of the story — two-thirds of recent population growth in the 30 largest OECD countries has resulted from highly diverse migrations. Meanwhile, communications technology means that even those who live on the other side of the world are as near to us as those who live on the other side of the street. The variety of the world is not only more available, it is nearly inescapable. Human difference is more proximate — and more intense. What was once beyond our view is now at our side — and, indeed, to use the popular expression, "in our face." Almost everything now seems to "flow" globally — people and images, money and credit, goods and services, microbes and viruses, pollution and armaments, crime and terror. But let us remember, too, that constructive impulses can also flow more readily, as they do when international organisations join hands across dividing lines.

The challenge of diversity is now a global challenge — and how we address it will have global consequences. Economic stress and new environmental fragilities have further intensified the difficulties, and so has the fading of the bi-polar political order. It was once said that the end of the Cold War meant "the end of history." In fact, just the reverse was true. History resumed in earnest in the 1990's — as old tribal passions resurfaced.

Think for a moment that this is the perspective of a Muslim spiritual leader: if only to dispel the stereotypes and prejudices that are attached to Islam in popular discourse, especially in the inflammatory attitudes of the demagogue who holds the presidency of the United States in 2019.

The Aga Khan went on to warn of ways disinformation — "fake news," if you will — threatens social order.

> Meanwhile, the way we communicate with one another has been revolutionised. But more communication has not meant more cooperation. More information has also meant more mis-information — more superficial snapshots, more shards of stray information taken out of context. And it has also meant more willful dis-information — not only differences of opinion, but distortions of fact. A wide-open internet allows divisive information to travel as far and as fast as reliable information. There are virtually no barriers to entry — and anyone, responsible or irresponsible — can play the game. New digital technologies mean more access, but less accountability. The advent of the internet and the omnipresence of mobile telephony seem to promise so much! But so, once, did television and radio — and the telegraph before that — and, even earlier, the invention of the printing press. Yet each of these breakthroughs, while connecting so many, was also used to widen cultural gulfs. Technologies, after all, are merely instruments — they can be used for good or ill. How we use them will depend — in every age and in every culture — not on what sits on our desktops, but on what is in our heads — and in our hearts.

And at this point in the journey, we come to the most compelling reason for building inclusive societies, and finding strength in diversity. The Aga Khan was prescient in his 2010 remarks, and they carry an even greater urgency today:

Let me warn, first, against a naïve hope that simply advancing the concept of democracy will achieve our goals. Not so. The high count of failed democracies — including some 40 percent of the member states of the United Nations — should disabuse us of this notion. Too often, democracy is understood to be only about elections — momentary majorities. But effective governance is much more than that.

What happens before and after elections?
How are choices framed and explained?
How is decision-making shared so that leaders of different backgrounds can interactively govern, rather than small cliques who rule autocratically?

We must go beyond the simple word "democracy" if we are to build a framework for effective pluralism.

This will mean writing more effective constitutions — informed by more sophisticated understandings of comparative political systems. It will mean explaining those arrangements more adequately — and adjusting and amending them. It will mean separating and balancing powers, structuring multi-tiered — and often asymmetrical — systems of federalism, and defining rights and freedoms — as Canada has learned to do. I would also point here to the experience of the largest democracy, India, which defines specific Constitutional rights for eight distinctive cultural groups, an approach which has been echoed in Malaysia. And we have seen how Kenya and Kyrgyzstan are moving now to decentralise power.

All of these institutional arrangements can help resolve political deadlock, build social coherence and avoid the dangers of "winner take all." They can provide multiple levers of social influence, allowing individuals of every background to feel that they have "a stake in society" — that they can influence the forces that shape their lives.

In this vision, real sustainability comes from enabling all to participate meaningfully in their societies. By transcending division so that differences can be discussed, and accommodated. In order to do so, we need to embed societal foundations that are both flexible and durable. In our next stop, we will look at how we can do just that.

Edmonton, Canada, March 2019

Gurcharan Singh Bhatia really can't hear any more, so he sits facing me squarely at the neighbourhood café, so he can read my lips and hear at least an echo of my voice, which has been in his ear for nearly 40 years.

We are catching up on his recent travel to India at the age of 88, his first trip back since being widowed. Gurcharan takes a long sip of black oolong tea, then shares his memories of the two deeply meaningful celebrations of life organised in Jiti's memory by the extended family in Delhi and Kolkata; and his pilgrimage to the Golden temple in Amritsar.

This ought to be a time of relaxation, of peace, of ease: but for Gurcharan, it is an evocation of how much remains undone in easing the injustices of the world. His always lively mind is in hyperdrive as he reflects on the latest tensions between India and Pakistan, and wonders if we can bring people from both countries together in a friendly third territory like Canada, for a people-to-people exchange of ideas that would bypass governments, military establishments and the shadow-play posturing of two nuclear-armed nations. This, he feels, is the only means to build a sustainable relationship between two nations that were once one. "There is so much I could get done, if I didn't have this problem," he says, tapping his turbaned ears with the heels of his palms.

Despite what Seferis called the "justified shipwreck of age," Gurcharan squeezes out and claims every milligram of joy life has on offer. Indeed, he has a reputation as someone who cannot be refused, who refuses to take "impossible" as an answer. Envisioning a 1998 conference to mark the 50th anniversary of the Universal Declaration of Human Rights, Gurcharan determined that a leading figure in ending South African apartheid, the Anglican archbishop Desmond Tutu, ought to come to Edmonton to deliver the keynote address. Gurcharan would not accept Archbishop Tutu's "no" for an answer.

He spent weeks flying the short-haul between Edmonton and Calgary, meeting friends for lunch or just having a same-day ramble, until he accumulated enough frequent flyer points to cover a trip to South Africa. There — after the initial "it's just not possible" — he sat in Archbishop Tutu's anteroom for eight days, respectfully requesting even a five minute audience.

When the 50th anniversary conference finally unfolded in Edmonton in December 1998, the headliner was none other than Desmond Tutu.

For that act of chutzpah, Gurcharan was inducted into the Order of Canada.

Gurcharan's determination was forged early in his life. As recounted in Alexis Kienlen's excellent 2014 biography, Gurcharan faced a choice when an imbecile British administration sanctioned a move that would ultimately uproot and displace 15 million people: the partition of pre-independence India, executed by a civil servant who had never even visited the subcontinent. (In 2018 and 2019, their descendants comprehensively fornicated an ill-intentioned effort to break Britain out of the European Union, thus one need not say more).

In the ensuing civil unrest, Gurcharan's father, a senior police official and a turban-wearing Sikh, thrust himself into a melee to calm tensions between Hindus and Muslims bent on mayhem.

Gurcharan's father was killed. And Gurcharan, thrust into being the senior male of the family aged 16, had a choice: vengeance, or non-violence. He chose the Gandhian path, and it informed his life from that day forth.

In the 1980s, Gurcharan veered from a career in real estate development to make a significant difference in civic discourse. He and I developed the notion of "Canadian values" to unite the tesserae of multiculturalism, a "separate but equal" construct embraced by community leaders who sought a power base among monocultural — and sadly, monolingual—immigrant enclaves. The whole notion of multiculturalism was greatly abetted by the government of Premier Peter Lougheed in Alberta.

In 1974, a Bavarian immigrant, Horst Schmid, introduced the first legislation in the western world to enshrine multiculturalism as a foundational tenet of society. Gurcharan, seeking to transcend cultural ghettos, laughed a newspaper in 1980 and called it The Canadian Link. It advocated a Canada built on the values common to all Canadians, regardless of their origin or place in the cultural matrix. He and I felt that in order to emerge from a history of bigotry, we would have to discover our shared humanity and common purpose

Edmonton, Canada, November 1975

I have joined the Press Gallery of the Legislative Assembly of Alberta scant days after my 20th birthday, as the parliamentary correspondent of the Red Deer Advocate. Despite a façade of bravado, I am terrified. I am the only dark-skinned person — indeed, the first — to join the press gallery. The only other minority, joining about the same time, is a Canadian journalist of Chinese ethnicity, Joe Ma of the Canadian Press.

Even though the very definition of my role is adversarial, I have nonetheless benefited from a subtle yet warm welcome. Premier Peter Lougheed always ensures that I am one of the first three questioners he entertains at his media briefings. And I strike an instant connection with Horst Schmid — the beginning of a lifetime bond — who is already an admirer and disciple of Mahatma Gandhi.

The Alberta of this era is slowly beginning to emerge from a racist past: one which classified indigenous Canadians as lesser. Until this year, and the closing of Alberta's last government-sanctioned residential school, Canada perpetuated a programme of severing its original inhabitants of their ancestral roots and assimilating them into "civilised" culture.

(The building that was once St. Mary's Residential School, which was given back to the Blood First Nation in 1975, would go on to house Canada's first tribal community college. It was destroyed by an arsonist in 2015, evoking mixed emotions within the community.)

Even though I have been here for less than a month, Horst has conveyed that he will do everything he can to abet my career (at the time of writing in 2019, I am serving my eighth year on the board of a listed company of which he is Chair).

On this November day, Alberta is flexing a more prominent role on the national stage. Premier Lougheed has just returned from Quebec, where he has just cemented an alliance with the government of Canada's francophone province to resist the federal government's encroachment on provincial rights. He presents this as a moment of triumph, applauded even by the leader of the opposition, Grant Notley (whose daughter Rachel would in 2015 become the 17th Premier of Alberta).

And although none expected it, we are about to finally understand the concept of ice-cold rage. One of the members of the legislative assembly rises to ask a question. Like Premier Lougheed, he is a Progressive Conservative. (The government owned a bank and an airline, and you can connect the dots thereafter on the seeming contradiction of a party at once progressive and conservative.) His name is Allison Ira "Mick" Fluker, the representative from St. Paul — the oldest and largest vestige of the francophones who led the European settlement of the province.

Quite incredibly, Mick asks whether every other seat in Montreal's Olympic Stadium is being replaced "with lily pads for frogs."

He chuckles in self-appreciative humour.

We in the press gallery look down at the assembly floor in horror and fascination as Lougheed stands rigid, even catatonic, scarcely believing his ears.

All colour drains from his face, a visage as devoid of pity as a marble bust, as he turns to Fluker, lances a finger at him, and mouths: "You. Out."

We scribes rush down to the anteroom behind the government benches just before Mick enters. "Hey guys, it was just a joke. Jeez!"

The premier enters. We take one look at his fury, and are already heading for the exit as he says in a voice of terrifying calm, "Gentlemen, you will excuse us."

We are stunned as we listen, behind a closed door, to Lougheed's quiet rage, never rising to even the decibel level of normal speech.

When the still-ashen Premier resumes his place in the Chamber, he finds the opposition already has moved to have Mick's remarks stricken from the record, with the unanimous consent of the house.

Mick's next job was selling vacuum cleaners.

Edmonton, Canada, October 2014

Having retired from the Court of Canadian Citizenship, Gurcharan comes roaring into his eighties with a new vision. A culture of peace and human rights is not enough, he says. One needs to build and nurture a civil society to offer a context wherein human rights and peace can flourish and grow.

To add intellectual heft to my meagre capacity, and to comingle a voice I respect to its core, I have induced my friend David Evans to join Gurcharan's dream. And today, we wait in some trepidation until Gurchuran declares himself satisfied with the vision we have wrought of his recently formed group, Canadians for a Civil Society.

He doesn't want an academic essay or theories, he says. What we need is a manifesto. A Civil Society manifesto. Setting out five principles — pillars, he called them — that would provoke people to rethink their comfort and complacency.

David and I tried to argue that there are other "pillars," other building blocks for civil society. Nonetheless, these were the pillars Gurcharan envisioned, his own approach to our common purpose, and so we set out to write our manifesto.

This is the thinking David and I distilled. Today, it serves as the guiding principles and rationale of Canadians for a Civil Society, which becomes ever more robust as it completes its first decade of existence (in July 2019, I retired from the CCS board, having served three full terms as a director).

Rereading these lines in 2019, recalling the memories we shared, I feel David's absence deeply. He is my fellow navigator on this journey, although he is no longer in the physical world.

As you read what we wrought, you will surely appreciate how his thinking and mine intertwined. I am only sorry that you did not meet him leaning back in a Bistro Praha chair, in cotton shirt and fleece vest, arms folded, Mozart flowing from the restaurant's sound system, a keen and piercing look in his eyes, venturing that our evocation of civil society "is somewhat short of being a *complete* disaster."

So for better or worse, dear companion, here is our Civil Society manifesto.

A Civil Society: A habit of the heart
By David Evans and Satya Das

In ages to come, the dawn of the Common Era's third millennium will be remembered as the watershed moment of transition from Government for the People to genuine Government by the People.

And a Civil Society — a state of mind built on five pillars of respect, literacy, rights, the rule of law and meaningful economic opportunity — will be the essence, the lifeblood that makes this new era truly human.

Already, all around us, we can see progress toward a civilisation that no longer accepts that some must lose for others to win in the sense of reaching their full human potential. We have charters of rights and freedoms; we have international criminal courts; we have laws that embody a growing revulsion against discrimination on the basis of gender, ethnicity, sexual orientation and economic background.

We see progress toward a world in which both governments and private individuals feel guided and constrained by the mass of ordinary people whose only power is the certain knowledge that they share common values. Today in Alberta we have a public health system our leaders wanted to change but couldn't, we have peace policies where leaders wanted war, we have constitutional "notwithstanding clauses" governments fear to use.

We see progress toward a world in which citizens do not wait for government, but rather take it upon themselves to organise events like Daughter's Day to encourage new ways to ensure an equitable, respectful society — and to send out signals that old dispensations must change.

But in a world still willing to live with the marginalisation and death of too many aboriginal women, and that still struggles to accept same-sex relationships — even in a land of diversity and inclusion such as Canada — we are still many, many bricks from the finished human home. What are these five pillars on which it must stand?

Respect:

Canadians for a Civil Society believes that the respect we once demanded for ourselves must now become the Respect we willingly and actively give to all other living human beings. That is to say, we believe that grudging tolerance, while better than intolerance, must mature into instinctive, automatic, colour-blind, gender-blind inclusion. This Respect would have made the Holocaust, the India's communal violence in 1947 and the Rwandan genocide unthinkable, because people would no longer have been capable of so grossly exaggerating difference.

Literacy:

We believe the literacy we once saw as the doorway for our own advancement and intellectual fulfilment, and our own ability to compete for the heights, must become the Literacy that allows everyone to learn and understand and think for themselves. Literacy is a prerequisite for education, and education fuels understanding. Literacy makes possible the communication with which people link up across town and around the world to bypass government and create new consensus.

Law:

We believe the law we once saw dictated by rulers — be they absolute monarchs, republican oligarchs or bullying democratic majorities — must become subsumed in the Rule of Law that stands higher than both the government of the day and the sometimes over-mighty citizens of the private sector. We believe that no government, however wise and effective in reducing evil, can be truly just if its freedom is not limited by a higher law it cannot readily change.

Rights:

We believe the rights that individuals and groups once demanded for themselves in all too many revolutions must become Human Rights that everyone must be accorded. The right to enjoy a clean environment, for example, becomes the equally compelling responsibility to ensure that a clean environment and husbanded resources are preserved for future generations - even if that means less for those of us living today. The concept of Rights is most powerfully enshrined in the UN Declaration of Human Rights — one of the most magnificent examples of this Civil Society already at work in the world.

Opportunity:

We believe that the intellectual, social and economic opportunity we have always demanded for ourselves and our children must become the Opportunity that no one is denied, even if it temporarily means more intense competition for positions from many peoples of the world previously held back.

Some might argue that these ideas are not particularly new. We argue that with the emphasis on universality — the realisation that these five keys to civilisation cannot endure even for the rich and mighty unless the poorest, weakest child in the smallest, most obscure and autocratic community has them too — our pillars are actually radical and revolutionary.

Some might argue that a like-minded, progressive, favourably disposed government is the key to making these pillars a reality. But we believe that the realisation of a Civil Society is a process to which the government is incidental.

Government can't change how people feel about girls' education, or about subtle discrimination against gays or immigrants from different cultures. Only people can do that — with a new state of mind, a new culture of human rights. And only with a Civil Society can that new state of mind gradually mature and expand its grip.

And finally, some might argue that this idea of a Civil Society is the utopian fantasy of dreamers, and that we must be more accepting in practice of the real world as we find it.

But we argue that the progressing world we live in today was created by individual, initially isolated and powerless individuals who wouldn't accept things as they were. South Africa's Mandela and India's Gandhi didn't change the world because they were powerful, they became powerful by first changing the world — by building a Civil Society and changing the culture of the mind.

Albeit likely in a smaller and more modest way, that's what all of us can do.

My dear David, *mon frere,* always supplied his grounded wisdom as a counterpoint to my unfettered idealism. The journey of *Us* carries him as the essence of the genetic code that informs the substance and the practicality of all the paths we explore. And I already know and freely acknowledge that this book is diminished by his absence. Even so, I offer you a glimpse of his singular personality, his world-mending impulses, as an illumination of all we lost upon his early and untimely death.

One of the challenges we discussed, to which there is no easy path to clarity, is the demise of the medium that formed us: the era of print journalism, and the value of curated news. Our training as journalists led us to "referee" the flow of information: to offer accounts that were verifiable with facts, to bring balance and perspective and context: even to opinion writing, which had to be grounded in a bias readily discernible to the most casual reader.

In this I declare a bias which may seem like snobbery. For trained journalists, as my friend and longtime colleague Marc Horton puts it, "citizen journalism" is rather like performing surgical procedures at home: possible, yes, but is it really desirable? For the inescapable reality is this. We have gone from curated news (even within the strictures of corporate media) to the anarchy of social-network driven "information."

This incitement is fed by deeply subversive outlets like the reptilian Rupert Murdoch's money-minting Fox News: spouting glossed up propaganda with ranting presenters who are the antithesis of responsible journalism, while having the audacity to claim it is fair and balanced.

In this world of propaganda masqueraded as objectivity, there are no filters, no curation, no editing: anyone is free to make the wildest accusations entirely ungrounded in reality. This is how "freedom of expression," the great hallmark of democracy, actually becomes a cancer eroding the very health and vigour of democratic discourse. As Gandhi put it in enunciating his seven public sins, here is knowledge without character, politics without principle, commerce without morality.

To illustrate, one need not go beyond the deranged and unhinged 280-character "tweets" from the perpetually aggrieved president of the United States, whose bilious spew of anserine rants from 2017 to 2019 offers an inflammatory parade of clotted ignorance, entirely devoid of facts or evidence. King Lear raging on the heath, with no Fool to contain him.

As social media algorithms herd users towards "information" that confirms their biases, the civic space for reasoned public dialogue diminishes. And given the vicious nonsense spouted by cowards hiding behind the cloak of anonymity on comment sections and message boards, it takes a brave person indeed to even attempt to speak truth to power.

This adds another challenge to the quest for pluralism and respectful dialogue, which are at the heart of the civil society David and I described in our manifesto. You, my dear companions, will find your own ways to navigate through the anarchy of the internet, with the simplest filter of all: where are the bodies of evidence behind this flow of "information"?

The vision David and I evoked did not arise from the ether. Rather, it built on the tenets of the Universal Declaration of Human Rights, adopted into the customary law of nations worldwide after being proclaimed by the United Nations in 1948.

Despite this, by the turn of the millennium, it was abundantly clear that most nations paid only lip service to the declaration. The gap lay in people's knowledge of their human birthright, as set out in the declaration.

In the fall of 2001, scant weeks after Saudi terrorists flew hijacked jets into the twin towers of New York's World Trade Centre, my life was enriched by another singular personality, Shulamith Koenig. Like Gurcharan she is an octogenarian force of nature. And like him, she would become a guru, one who would help me clarify and distill my journey in human rights.

I first hear about Shula in late 2001 in the cafe of a downtown Edmonton hotel, as I take breakfast with Walther Lichem, then the Austrian ambassador to Canada: a breakfast that will bind Walther and I in abiding friendship. Walther is the keynote speaker at a conference which I am chairing. Over his morning muesli in we confirm the grand outline of his proposed remarks. Then he tells me about Shula's vision of Human Rights Cities, communities that would build a supportive and inclusive future for all, using all our shared learnings about being and belonging on a foundation of dignity.

So, at the conference, I sketch out a summary of the vision Walther relayed. I ask the 400 attendees whether they would like Edmonton to become a human rights city. Every hand shoots up.

Two days later, the phone rings. I am greeted by a voice as compelling as the mid-century actor Katharine Hepburn's, the same pitch and timbre but with the accent of Middle European English. "My name is Shulamith Koenig," she says, "my friend Walther Lichem tells me you have done something extraordinary." After five minutes I am sold.

When we meet a few weeks later, she offers a full embrace and introduces me to a remarkable international table. Her world is anchored in a rent-controlled flat near Columbia University, every available surface filled with books and art and artifacts ranging from Chagall to Bacon to reclining Buddhas and intricately inlaid brocanterie: a home shared with her husband, the poet and actor Jerome Koenig. Shula concocts her own batch of *satyagraha* to instill a clear and simple message: people must know their human rights, claim their human rights, and build a better world.

Shula was a teenage soldier when she and her comrades proclaimed the foundation of Israel in 1948: only to leave Israel in dismay as the ideals of the founders devolved to a more trenchant and hard-edged politics (after the 1967 war brough tracts of Arab land into Israeli control). By the 1980s, she had begun what remains her lifelong quest: to ensure people learn of the rights with which all are born.

So by the end of 2001, I join — at Walther Lichem's instigation — the board of Shula Koenig's pioneering effort. In 2004, Shula convenes an extraordinary meeting in New York, a few dozen metres from the United Nations, to frame what needs to be done to ensure people are fully empowered with their human right to lead a life of meaning and purpose. After a vigorous discussion that consumes most of a day, Shula collars my board colleague Stephen Marks (occupant of the unique Chair of Health and Human Rights at Harvard) and me to draft the consensus, which would soon become a widely-endorsed document called the Global Appeal for Human Rights Learning. This is what we write, for publication on Human Rights Day 2004:

> The Universal Declaration of Human Rights remains a beacon to the world, a powerful instrument that expressed the aspiration of human beings to live in dignity and with one another. Yet the Declaration's hope and promise of "freedom from fear and freedom from want" remains an unrealised vision for too many. Human beings are consumed by barbarous acts that continue to outrage the conscience of humankind.
>
> All people must know their human rights in order to live together in justice and dignity; to become agents of transformation and establish human rights as a way of life. Humanity—standing on the brink of devastation, with millions of people mired in poverty, environmental destruction, violence and

oppression—aspires to live in a world of human dignity, freedom, and social and economic justice.

Learning human rights bridges the chasm of despair. It liberates us from the prison of ignorance, and empowers us all to know, claim and make real our universal and inalienable human rights.

...

The United Nations was founded with a vision of a world order built on the recognition of the inherent dignity and of the equal and inalienable human rights of all. To secure this vision, all people must learn and act according to our universal human rights, which define a shared moral and legal framework for living in dignity within our varied communities.

Learning together also means unlearning the inhumanity, violence and injustice that plague the human condition. Learning from the experiences of people is as valuable as traditional teaching to embed the qualities of humility, empathy and mutual respect that underlie human rights. The voices of people deprived of human rights—and thus of their human dignity— are indispensable guides to learning our shared duties to the community, and to constructing a world where every individual and all organs of society secure universal respect for human rights for all. Through dialogue, interaction and learning we move from information to knowledge to realisation of the imperatives of social and economic justice within a human rights framework. Learning human rights harnesses the energies of all people to develop a shared global culture of human rights.

As with the civil society concept David and I evoked, the Global Appeal remains a road-map to build a culture of peace, embedded in civil society and human rights as a way of life.

There is, however, a missing element. To achieve a culture of peace, one must confront the pervasive violence the world over — one abetted and nourished by the international trade in arms.

To this end, I accepted my friend Andy Knight's invitation to contribute a chapter to his deeply influential book *Building Sustainable Peace,* published by the United Nations University Press in 2004. The book would contribute significantly to the creation, in 2005, of an ambitious international effort to build and sustain peace and social justice, particularly in parts of the world emerging from conflict: The United Nations Peacebuilding Commission.

As you consider your aims and the actions you can take to build a sustainable future, I would ask you to consider my central idea here: a tax on military (defence) expenditures, to fund peacekeeping, peacebuilding, and the establishment of human rights as a normative framework of civil life.

Here is the gist of what I proposed to the United Nations, as published in the book, edited by professors Tom Keating and Andy Knight of the University of Alberta.

> A more formal mechanism is vital to ensure long-term, stable funding. The most reliable instrument, if it can be implemented, might be a global tax on militarism. A legal framework would be challenging to develop. One way to proceed might to build on the jurisdictional liberty offered to the International Criminal Court (ICC). If criminal laws are applied interna-

tionally, can the same not be done with certain civil laws, particularly relating to international trade and taxation?

Yet the absence of an international legal framework to permit global taxation of the legal portion of the arms trade need not be an insurmountable barrier. Countries like Canada, and the other vigorous champions of peace, might begin by "taxing" their own defence and military spending — by designating 10 per cent of their military budgets specifically for a global peace-building fund. In Canada's case, this would come to an annual "tax" that would yield roughly four times as much money as Canada now pays in United Nations dues. Budgets taxed at that level would yield about $75 billion Cdn a year. This would be entirely voluntary, but it would set an example. It would fit in well with the evolving "soft power" regime in international relations, because it would stand as a classical instance of using moral suasion to achieve a greater good. If Canada and other military powers began to set aside parts of their own defence spending, and levied a special export tax on their arms manufacturers, it would set a compelling example for others. More practically, it would enable the beginning of what would end up as a permanent fund to enable peace-building and post-conflict reconstruction. There is little chance that it would yield the dividends of a full-fledged international tax on the arms trade, an initial target should be to raise enough to make the very idea of the tax credible — perhaps an amount as large as the annual budget for all other UN operations.

If one carries the fantasy a step further, one can see that a viable international tax on the world's $1.5 trillion war spending could yield the revenues to fund peacebuilding. A relatively modest tax would bring substantial funds — taxing the arms trade and defence expenditure at five per cent, for instance, would also bring $75 billion Cdn a year.

Taxing the arms trade and defence spending would be relatively straightforward, if a consensus were built to do so — the rationale being that the developed countries of the world, including the leading democracies, are the principal suppliers of arms that fuel conflict the world over. They are also the principal suppliers of peacekeepers, and of the meagre funds that are eventually used to build peace in the wake of these conflicts.

There is surely a sense of proportion and natural justice in the thought that those who provide the tools of war should pay to provide the tools of peace. Moreover, not all of this money would be poured into a conflict zone. A sizeable fund would enable the development of the civil capacity needed to build a peace. Funding would enable the creation of surplus civilian police, doctors, nurses, teachers, judges, engineers and so forth. Canada, for instance, might use a good portion of its contribution to global peacebuilding to increase municipal budgets, so that municipalities would be able to develop surplus capacity that could then be channelled to post-conflict situations as the need arose. This capacity development in turn would enable rapid deployment of peace-builders, which could be assembled just as troops are for peace keeping.

Nonetheless, there remains the practical issue not just of tax collection, but of tax administration and disbursement. Who would control the fund?

It is possible to foresee a United Nations-led or —mandated entity modelled on Britain's quangos (quasi autonomous governmental organisations) to gather and distribute a tax on the arms trade and defence spending. This agency or entity would effectively extend taxation influence, if not power, away from national governance to global governance.

The evolution of peace building and the necessity for post conflict reconstruction requires new ideas and new approaches. A stable and permanent global fund built by a tax on defence spending and the arms trade, and a UN high commissioner to make use of that fund, would be logical extensions of Kofi Annan's bold strides towards making human security the very raison d'être of the United Nations. They could indeed provide the building blocks for ensuring that sustainable peace becomes a reality in many parts of the globe where the culture of violence has, in the past, prevailed.

The idea didn't make it very far, given that the UN Security Council is dominated by five permanent members which include four of the biggest arms merchants in the world (Russia, France, Britain and the United States), whose economies are heavily reliant upon selling weapons of death and destruction.

Nonetheless, it might gain new vigour, if a new generation of activists makes it part of a quest for social justice. The proposal is still there for the taking, if any of you wish to pursue it (and I am glad to help as requested and required). No major country has, to date: and is unlikely to, unless it becomes a popular demand that transcends national boundaries.

So let's keep it simple. Let's think of how we might update that idea, and demand its implementation. In 2018, military spending worldwide hit a record: $1.82 trillion. Indeed, military spending has nearly doubled in the last quarter century.

Imagine a tax of 10 per cent levied against that spending. That's $182 billion a year. A $182 billion sustainability fund. To rebuild communities, rebuild lives, fund peace-building, help the ravaged recover from violence. To bring freedom from fear. And freedom from want.

Moreover, as we shall see in our next destination, sometimes it only takes one voice standing up to injustice to bring awareness and inspire change on a global level.

Chapter Ten

Leadership is in the mirror

Edmonton, Canada, January 2009

I am on the BBC website, reading a wrenching first-hand account written by Gul Makai (Cornflower), an 11-year-old schoolgirl, who is losing the gift of education.

The Taliban have occupied her home town in Pakistan's Swat valley. And they have enforced at gunpoint the decree by their religious leaders that girls should not go to school. They have shut down more than 200 girls' schools, blowing many of them up with explosives so they cannot be reused.

Gul Makai is impressively articulate. The diary she keeps first found its way to the BBC Urdu service, before posting on the English site.

Her diary carries the authenticity of a child's voice, yet she writes with a directness and clarity that would elude most adults, as in this posting from 15 January 2009:

The night was filled with the noise of artillery fire and I woke up three times. But since there was no school I got up later at 10 am. Afterwards, my friend came over and we discussed our homework.

Today is 15 January, the last day before the Taliban edict comes into effect, and my friend was discussing homework as if nothing out of the ordinary had happened.

Today, I also read the diary written for the BBC (in Urdu) and published in the newspaper. My mother liked my pen name 'Gul Makai' and said to my father 'why not change her name to Gul Makai?' I also like the name because my real name means 'grief stricken'.

My father said that some days ago someone brought the print-out of this diary saying how wonderful it was. My father said that he smiled but could not even say that it was written by his daughter.

As I read the diary entry, I have one of those moments you reflect on: "There but for fate…"

My own daughters are celebrating their 21st and 16th birthdays this month, in the city of their birth, schooled in a public school system consistently ranked one of the finest in the world. They are on the arc of self-discovery, knowing they will be free to choose their own path in Canada's excellent state-funded universities.

And halfway across the world, Gul Makai, so full of promise, won't even be able to go to school. All because of a perverse and twisted interpretation of scripture.

The clarity of Gul Makai's voice, her courage in sharing her diary with the world, also is a stirring act of leadership.

Proof once again that one voice can make a difference, if indeed it is given voice.

And an affirmation of a basic truth: leadership begins in the mirror.

If not you, who?

If not now, when?

This is the call answered by leadership, and in Gul Makai's accounts, one can already see the emergence of an extraordinarily focused and clear-eyed champion of justice.

She wrote on Sunday January 4, 2009:

> Today is a holiday and I woke up late, around 10 am. I heard my father talking about another three bodies lying at Green Chowk (crossing). I felt bad on hearing this news. Before the launch of the military operation we all used to go to Marghazar, Fiza Ghat and Kanju for picnics on Sundays. But now the situation is such that we have not been out on picnic for over a year and a half.

> We also used to go for a walk after dinner but now we are back home before sunset. Today I did some household chores, my homework and played with my brother. But my heart was beating fast - as I have to go to school tomorrow.

And here is her entry for the next day, January 5, the school day that evoked her apprehension:

I was getting ready for school and about to wear my uniform when I remembered that our principal had told us not to wear uniforms - and come to school wearing normal clothes instead. So I decided to wear my favourite pink dress. Other girls in school were also wearing colourful dresses and the school presented a homely look.

My friend came to me and said, 'for God's sake, answer me honestly, is our school going to be attacked by the Taliban?' During the morning assembly we were told not to wear colourful clothes as the Taliban would object to it.

I came back from school and had tuition sessions after lunch. In the evening I switched on the TV and heard that curfew had been lifted from Shakardra after 15 days. I was happy to hear that because our English teacher lived in the area and she might be coming to school now.

I am captivated by the courage and the clarity of this young woman. I wonder who she is, and how her diary found its way into the media.

Months later in 2009, it emerges that Gul Makai's father is a social activist, and headmaster of an anglophone private school for girls in Swat. The family would flee their home and the school later in 2009, along with hundreds of thousands of other civilians, as the Pakistani army fought to wrest back the Swat valley from Taliban control. Eventually, after months of battle, the towns were safe enough to take back those who fled, and the schools reopened.

By this time, Gul Makai's identity was revealed. She turned out to be a grey-eyed Pashtun girl who still wore a child's smile as she explained her ambition to become a doctor — even though her Dad thought her real calling was to be a politician, because he saw within her the capacity to change society for the better. Her smile, and her bravery, were evident on film as New York Times journalists featured Gul Makai and her family in a half-hour documentary called *Class Dismissed: the Death of Female Education,* which was posted on the newspaper's website — part of their in-depth reporting on the Taliban's spread in Pakistan and its threat to the U.S. military mission in neighbouring Afghanistan.

Edmonton, Canada, October 2012

In absolute horror, I am following events in faraway Swat. The girl the world first came to know more than three years before as Gul Makai is clinging to life in a hospital in Peshawar. Breaking her incognito and outing her face and her voice to the world was a singular act of courage. Now, it may cost her life.

On Tuesday October 9, Taliban gunmen stopped a school bus in Mingora, the capital of Swat.

Ten gunmen surrounded the school bus.

Three climbed aboard with weapons drawn.

They asked for Gul Makai. By her real name.

"Which one of you is Malala? Speak up, otherwise I will shoot you all," said one of the gunmen, later identified by security officials as 23-year-old Ataullah Khan.

Whereupon Malala Yousafzai declared: "I am Malala."

Ataullah and another would-be assassin opened fire, shooting Malala in the head and neck. Their bullets felled two of Malala's schoolmates, Kainat Riaz Ahmed and Shazia Ramzan. Their wounds, though serious, were not life-threatening.

The Taliban took a deep satisfaction in shooting these girls, Malala in particular. "She has become a symbol of Western culture in the area; she was openly propagating it," declared a Taliban spokesman, Ehsanullah Ehsan. Her advocacy of girls' right to learn was an "obscenity", and if she somehow survived the attack — a bullet was lodged close to her brain — she would be targeted again. "Let this be a lesson."

It was indeed a lesson, but perhaps not as the Taliban intended.

Pakistanis were outraged at this brazen attack: whatever the political considerations, none in government or authority could condone fanatics shooting a girl who asserted that girls had every right to education.

(In June 2015, Pakistan announced it had sentenced 10 people involved in attacking Malala to life imprisonment. Ataullah Khan, however, was not among those in court. He was believed to have escaped to Afghanistan. It later emerged that 8 of the 10 convicts were secretly acquitted and fled to Afghanistan — and there was considerable doubt raised as to whether any of the actual shooters were among those who were tried and convicted.

Three years later in June 2018, Mullah Fazlullah, the leader of the Pakistan branch of the Tehreek-e-Taliban, the organisation behind the attackers who shot Malala, was killed in a drone strike by the clandestine forces of the United States. He was targeted after organising a 2014 massacre in Peshawar, in which 132 schoolchildren were murdered.)

Malala was shifted to Birmingham, England for medical treatment. The Pakistani government gave her father a diplomatic posting so the family would have a base while she recovered.

And the bullets did nothing to silence her. After a recovery that appears miraculous — regaining cognitive functions and resuming a nearly normal life within months of the attack — Malala used her voice to speak for the voiceless, to empower girls worldwide.

Two years after she was shot, Malala stood on an eminent stage and prepared to speak about her experience of being an agent of change, of responding to the truth that leadership begins in the mirror. Here is what she said on 10 December 2014, Human Rights Day, the 66th anniversary of the proclamation of the Universal Declaration of Human Rights by the United Nations:

> Education is one of the blessings of life—and one of its necessities. That has been my experience during the 17 years of my life. In my paradise home, Swat, I always loved learning and discovering new things. I remember when my friends and I would decorate our hands with henna on special occasions. And instead of drawing flowers and patterns we would paint our hands with mathematical formulas and equations.
>
> We had a thirst for education, we had a thirst for education because our future was right there in that classroom. We would sit and learn and read together. We loved to wear neat and tidy school uniforms and we would sit there with big dreams in our eyes. We wanted to make our parents proud and prove that we

could also excel in our studies and achieve those goals, which some people think only boys can.

But things did not remain the same. When I was in Swat, which was a place of tourism and beauty, suddenly changed into a place of terrorism. I was just ten that more than 400 schools were destroyed. Women were flogged. People were killed. And our beautiful dreams turned into nightmares.

Education went from being a right to being a crime.

Girls were stopped from going to school.

When my world suddenly changed, my priorities changed too. I had two options. One was to remain silent and wait to be killed. And the second was to speak up and then be killed.

I chose the second one. I decided to speak up.

We could not just stand by and see those injustices of the terrorists denying our rights, ruthlessly killing people and misusing the name of Islam. We decided to raise our voice and tell them: Have you not learnt, have you not learnt that in the Holy Quran Allah says: if you kill one person it is as if you kill the whole humanity? Do you not know that Mohammad, peace be upon him, the prophet of mercy, he says, do not harm yourself or others."

And do you not know that the very first word of the Holy Quran is the word "Iqra," which means "read"?

The terrorists tried to stop us and attacked me and my friends who are here today, on our school bus in 2012, but neither their ideas nor their bullets could win.

This eloquent voice would not have been heard from that particular stage, were it not for her miraculous delivery from the Taliban's failed assassination attempt. For this was the podium reserved for laureates of one of the world's highest honours. Malala spoke as the co-winner of the 2014 Nobel Prize for Peace.

Malala's journey, from a schoolgirl writing a compelling diary about the loss of her education in 2009, to the Nobel podium in Oslo in 2014, is an outstanding example of what ordinary people can achieve, if they dare to lead. It is of course a rare example. Far too often, the voices of tomorrow's prophets are derided in their own time, fall on deaf ears, find no audience. Yet faced with that reality, as Malala put it, you have the choice to keep quiet or speak out.

As she said on the Nobel stage:

> This award is not just for me. It is for those forgotten children who want education. It is for those frightened children who want peace. It is for those voiceless children who want change.
>
> I am here to stand up for their rights, to raise their voice... it is not time to pity them. It is not time to pity them. It is time to take action so it becomes the last time, the last time, so it becomes the last time that we see a child deprived of education.

She is making good on that pledge. Today, the Malala Fund aims to help every girl learn and lead without fear. By trying to silence one voice, the Taliban accidentally unmuted the voices of hundreds of thousands of girls the world over. And as to the Gul Makai who first wrote those diary entries for BBC? Today, Malala has convened a global network of champions. Her Gulmakai Network "supports the work of education champions in countries where girls face the greatest challenges to education. Local educators and activists understand the issues girls face in their communities — and they are best placed to develop solutions."

Malala's story is an inspirational spot to pause and reflect. Perhaps it would lead us to consider how and where we might wish to make a difference in the world. We might wish to start with the wish list developed by the United Nations: key areas on which people can work individually or together to bring positive change to the human condition. They are called the Sustainable Development Goals, a 21st century blueprint for moving beyond the culture of violence towards a culture of love.

You can determine how few or how many of these United Nations Sustainable Development Goals you wish to pursue.

- Goal 1. End poverty in all its forms everywhere

- Goal 2. End hunger, achieve food security and improved nutrition and promote sustainable agriculture

- Goal 3. Ensure healthy lives and promote well-being for all at all ages

- Goal 4. Ensure inclusive and equitable quality education and promote lifelong learning opportunities for all

- Goal 5. Achieve gender equality and empower all women and girls

- Goal 6. Ensure availability and sustainable management of water and sanitation for all

- Goal 7. Ensure access to affordable, reliable, sustainable and modern energy for all

- Goal 8. Promote sustained, inclusive and sustainable economic growth, full and productive employment and decent work for all

- Goal 9. Build resilient infrastructure, promote inclusive and sustainable industrialisation and foster innovation

- Goal 10. Reduce inequality within and among countries

- Goal 11. Make cities and human settlements inclusive, safe, resilient and sustainable

- Goal 12. Ensure sustainable consumption and production patterns

- Goal 13. Take urgent action to combat climate change and its impacts

- Goal 14. Conserve and sustainably use the oceans, seas and marine resources for sustainable development

- Goal 15. Protect, restore and promote sustainable use of terrestrial ecosystems, sustainably manage forests, combat desertification, and halt and reverse land degradation and halt biodiversity loss

- Goal 16. Promote peaceful and inclusive societies for sustainable development, provide access to justice for all and build effective, accountable and inclusive institutions at all levels

- Goal 17. Strengthen the means of implementation and revitalise the global partnership for sustainable development

These are broad agendas, giving you the opportunity to create your own space, carve out your own niche in deciding how you can most effectively become an agent of change.

And because there is a structure and a common purpose behind these goals, yours will not be a lonely voice, destined to fade unheard. As you pursue whichever goals you choose, you will find like-minded people, and strengthen your cause in collaboration with one another.

To be an effective advocate of change, you need to find common ground: in the values that shape you and drive you. Sometimes these are the values that have shaped you, sometimes they are the values you came to embrace.

Finding these values requires coordinated efforts. As we shall see in our next destination — rather a long stop — sometimes one needs to invoke values that will endure across religions, across languages, across cultures. And ideally, values that will endure amid political and societal upheaval.

I found what remains, to me, the most compelling instance of how these values can be applied in a country which was formed out of the faraway lands of my childhood lore. From the Java and Bali whence came stories of exotic lands and peerless princesses. Lands that were part of the ancient globalisation that bound India and Southeast Asia, where people of mixed and divergent heritage came together, in the country they called Indonesia.

Chapter Eleven

Common values, common ground

Jakarta, Indonesia, 29 December 1997

As President Suharto lies ill in his palace on a muggy December Thursday, the mid-summer heat enveloping Jakarta in a smog-laced haze, I am looking for a safe pedestrian crossing amid the afternoon chaos clogging Gajah Mada Street.

I wait on the boulevard between Hayam Wuruk Street and Gajah Mada. Spotting a motionless lull in the crawling traffic jam, I hold up my hand, make direct eye contact with every driver, and zig-zag through the river of cars and trucks belching black smoke. I arrive in front of the *Pengadilan Negeri Jakarta Utara*, North Jakarta city court, where one of the opposition-quelling machinations of Suharto's 32-year-old New Order government is playing out in a courtroom.

A crowd is beginning to congregate, in anticipation of a ruling. I fish out my photo ID, the press card issued by the Ministry of Information, as a first defence if authorities challenge me.

Even though I have a rusty working knowledge of Bahasa Indonesia—it takes me about a month of immersive life to return to basic fluency — I carry within me an instinctive understanding of the societal and cultural norms of Java and Bali.

My ancestors first came to this archipelago in the fifth century of the Christian era, and there was a lively commerce and intercourse between the coastal kingdoms of eastern India, and the cultural heartland of these islands. The historic name for my ancestral land in India was Kalinga, now modern Odisha.

Each coastal city in Indonesia has a *Kampung Keling,* or Kalinga village, which was the settlement and trade centre for those ancient Indians.

As a boy in Odisha, my "christmas" came every spring: the grand festival called Bali jatra (voyage to Bali): celebrating the tradition of Kalinga mariners, artisans and traders. We would float banana husk boats with clay lamps in the rivers leading to the sea, and on the sea beach itself, and gorge on the palm-sugar-laden breads and pastries, made to last several weeks at sea.

I found echoes of Orissan temple architecture in the abundance of Hindu and Buddhist temples and shrines in central Java. Indeed, archaeology marks a clear delineation between the grand epochs of temple building in Java and Odisha.

The great monuments of Prambanan and Borobudur in the vicinity of Yogyakarta (the city of Wisdom) predate the grand epoch of Orissan temples. The Merapi volcano erupted catastrophically in 1006, burying Borobudur in ash and debris, inundating the great temple city of Prambanan. Thereafter, hundreds of

Kalinga and Javanese craftsmen and artisans — sculptors, stone carvers, masons — returned to Kalinga.

Then began what is called the golden age of temple building in Odisha, including gems such as the Rajarani (King and Queen) and Lingaraja (Lord of Creative Power) in Bhubaneswar, the Jagannatha (Lord of the Universe) temple in Puri, and the Sun temple in Konark — a quarter-scale version of it between Yogyakarta and Prambanan was built in the 9th century.

Even more than a shared art history, the cultural reflexes are the same. In central Java more than anywhere else in Indonesia, I have a genetically-wired understanding of how to comport myself given the caste into which I was born, and the obligations of its hereditary status.

I recall walking through the royal palace or kraton of Yogyakarta, to be barred from an area with particularly fine carved pillars, off limits to touch-happy tourists. I clasp my hands in the position of prayer, incline my head to the palace guard, and say "*saya kshatriya dari Kalinga*" (I am a kshatriya, the caste of military leaders and royal administrators, from Kalinga) to be waived in.

Tales of Java and Bali, carried back in oral history, fired my childhood imagination. I grew up on tales of heroic voyages and adventures in Champa (today the area around Hue in central Vietnam), mighty Kambuja (modern Cambodia, home to the monumental Hindu temples of Angkor Wat), and Suvarna Dvipa (golden island, today the largest Indonesian island, Sumatra).

My predisposition to like Indonesia, to match the modern country with childhood myths, made it an easy choice when I was awarded a three month, fully-funded travel and exploration fellowship by the Asia Pacific Foundation of Canada in 1992. I travelled the archipelago, became reasonably conversant with the language, soaked up every aspect or urban and rural communities I encountered.

Now, I approach this time of turbulence with full empathy, even a vague hope for an orderly transition to whatever comes next.

The scene outside the courthouse on Gajah Mada street is infused with the currents of upheaval. The chaos is suddenly silenced by the shriek of police whistles and the sound of boots running across pavement. Quickly, dozens of police with riot shields and batons weave through the sluggish river of vehicles. They force cars aside, open a lane. Then come the lorries spewing black-shirted paramilitary police. First one, then another, then a third. The paramilitary forces tumble out of the back to set up a protective line. They have no firearms. And when I look in their eyes, I see fear.

Within moments a chanting, surging crowd spills out of the courthouse. The court has just upheld a ruling that the government was fully within its rights to oust the Chair of the leading opposition party, the Indonesian Democratic Party, and replace her with a government-backed appointee "elected" at a hastily-convened "special congress."

The crowd cries for justice. They shout that democracy will not be denied; their day is at hand. They come close to the police lines, but not close enough to justify force. There is a discipline in this crowd, as they chant, "Mega, Mega, Mega": a battle cry for their ousted leader, Megawati Sukarnoputri. But the police keep their distance. They sense, like the demonstrators, that they are witnesses to a time of change and the old rules of easy repression cannot so readily apply.

Indeed, with each shout of "Mega", the police line stays rooted to its spot. Not one single baton, not one single shield, is deployed in any threatening or menacing posture.

Beyond the court rulings and the politics at play, there is a deeper connection here to Javanese cultural roots: Megawati is the daughter of Sukarno, Indonesia's post-independence leader, and the dynastic bloodline carries deep import. Javanese believe that the animating energy of leaders, their *teja,* is passed on by blood. And because Megawati has Sukarno's *teja* within her, the police are far more circumspect than they might be with a run of the mill opposition protest.

I have a special interest in Megawati. Members of my extended family on both sides are connected politically and personally with the family of the late Bijayananda (Biju) Patnaik, a former Chief Minister of Odisha (ancient Kalinga). In 1947, Sukarno asked for India's help in rallying the world against the Dutch colonists who were trying to reclaim Indonesia.

Biju, an expert aviator, and his wife Gyan flew to a remote airport in Java to pick up Sultan Sjahrir, later to become Indonesia's prime minister, and take him to an international conference in India where he could press Indonesia's case.

As a gesture of thanks, Sukarno asked the Kalinga aviator to name his newborn daughter. Biju turned to Sanskrit to name Sukarno's daughter "the radiance of the clouds", Megawati Sukarnoputri.

Each family bred a political dynasty. In May 2019, Biju and Gyan's son Naveen was elected to an unprecedented fifth term as Chief Minister of Odisha, fresh off his deft and thoroughly competent management of the disaster wrought by the Cyclone Fani.

Sukarno and the leaders of Indonesia's independence movement came upon Demokrasi Pancasila, or Five-Principle Democracy, as a means of binding a country together.

Nearly 60 per cent of Indonesians were ethnic Javanese. There was a natural fear that Java would dominate, and that the Sumatrans with their distinctive cultural identities would be forced to submit to Javanese rule.

So Sukarno and his Sumatran colleague Mohammad Hatta made a radical choice: while people could speak regional languages and dialects as part of their cultural practices, there must be one unifying national language.

For this they chose the language spoken in the Riau archipelago, lying between Indonesia and Malaysia, that was the crossroads of the world's great trade routes. The population of Riau was less than one per cent of the Indonesian total. Their language had sprinklings of Malay, Javanese, Sumatran, Sanskrit, Persian, Arabic, even a smattering of Chinese: a language built by trade and commerce, easy to learn for any native speaker of Indonesia's more dominant tongues. They decreed that this would be the language of the Indonesian people: Bahasa Indonesia.

Next came the challenge of religion, of reconciling the rigid monotheism of Islam, followed by a majority of Indonesians, with the panoply of gods and goddesses in Hinduism (seen as different manifestations of one overarching cosmic presence beyond human comprehension), and the precepts of Christianity and Buddhism. Hindu and Buddhist culture had continued to shape and define life in Java and Bali even with the advent of Islam, expressed in Sukarno's native Java as "budaya Hindu, agama Mussulman" (Hindu by culture, Muslim by religion).

This is the Five-Principle Democracy Indonesia's independence leaders created.

· A Divinity that is an ultimate Unity (reconciling monotheistic and polytheistic beliefs) *Ketuhanan Yang Maha Esa.*

· A just and civilised humanity *Kemanusiaan Yang Adil dan Beradab.*

· Indonesian Unity *Persatuan Indonesia*

· Democracy, led by the wise representatives of the People Kerakyatan Yang Dipimpin oleh Hikmat *Kebijaksanaan, Dalam Permusyawaratan Perwakilan*

· Social justice for the entirety of Indonesia's People *Keadilan Sosial bagi seluruh Rakyat Indonesia.*

The key question, the night of the Gajah Mada demo where the police backed down, is whether the transition from Suharto to another leader ("76-year-old men eventually die in this country," a Canadian diplomat tartly observes) will be accompanied by chaos, violence, or, at worst, an eruption of civil war among the many factions — repressed Islamists not the least among them — who have come to see the new order government as a de facto dictatorship.

Indonesia's two most recent transitions of power have been remarkably bloody. Suharto came to power on the pretext of quelling a communist coup in 1965-66 — with the clandestine support and vigorous encouragement of the United States, which feared even a socialist Indonesia would mean the fall of Vietnam, where it was fighting a protracted war against Ho Chi Minh's Communists.

To give the coup plotters cover, Suharto claimed that the revered national patriarch, Sukarno, was the unwitting victim of the Communists. Anyone suspected of belonging to the PKI, Partai Komunis Indonesia, was slaughtered by the military — the historians' consensus is around half a million killed. The great majority of them were ethnic Chinese.

Discrimination against Indonesians of Chinese ancestry has a long and terrible history in Indonesia — the enterprise and tenacity that has historically led Indonesian Chinese to flourish in business and commerce makes then a target whenever rulers need scapegoats. In 1740, the Dutch East India Company slaughtered 10,000 ethnic Chinese in Java, to break their grip on Indonesia's economy: a genocide against a mercantile class with few parallels in history.

The Suharto-era pogrom had a particular grounding in the geopolitics of the day. At the time, China itself was going through the upheavals of the Great Proletarian Cultural Revolution, in which education and advanced ability were held suspect, and millions were arrested and sentenced to toil in communes and factories.

The earlier transition was no less fraught. Indonesia declared independence from its Dutch colonial masters in 1945 as the Second World War ended. The Netherlands was ravaged by the Second World War and its long occupation, with barely two sticks to rub together. Astonishingly, it nevertheless tried to return and reclaim rule over Indonesia. It would take three years before the Dutch would give up and leave.

In the three decades since taking power, Suharto has become Indonesia's absolute ruler. "He is like a banyan tree, allowing nothing to grow underneath," as one of Indonesia's leading political scientists told me in a necessarily clandestine conversation.

The machinations against Megawati are a case in point. Suharto's New Order government is led by an all-pervasive political party which in fact denies it is partisan. It is called the Working Circle (*Golongan Karya*), shortened to the acronym Golkar. It is in keeping with the consensus-building governance of independent Indonesia's constitution: a deliberate, audacious attempt to forge a unitary republic from bewildering diversity incorporating many religions and ethnicities. It is in fact the modern world's first great experiment in asserting shared values to build a viable future.

One of the few reasons Suharto has been able to hold on to power is the fear of the chaos that might ensue: workable democracy is far down the list of outcomes, which range from military dictatorship to the rise of Islamic fundamentalists (whose leadership has been arrested and imprisoned under Suharto as threats to secular unity).

As Suharto put it after consolidating power:

> Pancasila democracy endeavors to strike a balance between the interests of the individual and those of society. It seeks to prevent the oppression of the weak by the strong, whether by economic or political means. Therefore, we hold that Pancasila is a socio-religious society. Briefly its major characteristics are its rejection of poverty, backwardness, conflicts, exploitation, capitalism, feudalism, dictatorship, colonialism, and imperialism. This is the policy I have chosen with confidence.

Eventually, this national identity was made compulsory. A parliamentary resolution in 1983 made Pancasila the state ideology that must be followed by all organisations. It is taught to children from primary school onwards, under the banner of the national motto, *Bhinneka Tunggal Ika* (literally "many becoming one", most often translated as Unity from Diversity: an echo of the United States motto of "*e pluribus unum*").

Yet the resistance is everywhere, although most will speak to me only in anonymity in the weeks I have been here.

One morning, I learn to my astonishment that I have been granted a most unexpected interview. This is the moment I understand that there are guardians of Indonesia's values-based governance, Demokrasi Pancasila, who will protect and perpetuate a form of democratic governance as the only means of delivering peace and order after Suharto. The Indonesian Journalists' Union (Persatuan Wartawan Indonesia), under whose cloak I was an officially accredited foreign correspondent ("He's a Hindu from Kalinga, wishes our country well"), has confirmed an interview with a "retired" leader who had been a key figure in Suharto's government: Rudini.

I am not sure what to expect as I see him in a hotel meeting room. Rudini is a distinguished general, the former chief of the Indonesian military; for five years, a senior government minister under Suharto. I wonder whether he is going to hold forth on the party line. I introduce myself, taking in the steely-gaze beneath the cordial smile. He is a small man, yet he projects a larger-than-life presence.

He insists his comments be on the record, and his name used. I am expecting a subtle Javanese apologia for Suharto, the stagnancy and incipient corruption of a party too long in power, more talk of the need for patience. I have seldom been as surprised by an influential political leader's remarks.

"Grassroots people are already aware of their rights and will push their demands for a better life," Rudini tells me. "They cannot be cheated any longer." He offers a laugh — one of those "but what do I know?" flashes of self-deprecation — and says he is merely a retired senior citizen, serving as the head of Indonesia's Strategic Studies Institute after his government service. Still, there is no laughter in his voice as he asserts: "Low-income people have been revolting against the state apparatus because they feel the State only sides with certain groups just to earn additional money."

Indeed, the Indonesian fondness for wordplay has journalists and academics remarking that Suharto is an acronym for "suka harta orang," or "likes rich people." As for the official pronouncements of the New Order delivered by Suharto's information minister Harmoko, even shopkeepers in Pasar Baru market have dubbed Harmoko a contraction of "hari-hari omong kosong", or "daily dose of bullshit."

What is needed, Rudini says, is a total reform of Indonesia's political, economic and judicial norms. "We must return to the principles of Pancasila."

Perhaps more easily said than done, since Pancasila itself has become interlinked with the stifling rule of the Suharto-led New Order. But Rudini has a point.

Indonesia is the world's fourth most populous country (after China, India, and the United States). Geographically, it is vast. Superimposed on the United States, it would stretch beyond the western and eastern costs. Placed over Canada, Indonesia would stretch from the westernmost point of the Yukon to the Grand Banks of Newfoundland. It is also the largest Muslim country in the world. And, despite the controlled and weakened opposition parties, it is recognisably a democracy.

The specifics of a return to Demokrasi Pancasila, and how to curb the potential for chaos in the transition, remain unclear. The courthouse crowd on Gajah Mada Street, however, has its own kind of answer. They want Megawati to be restored to her rightful place as head of the tamed and constrained opposition.

Just before the riot police arrived, the court dismissed a petition by Megawati, protesting the coup against her leadership, which gave the post instead to a government-backed functionary. The coup shook Jakarta with riots in July of 1996, yet it took a year and a half for the petition to be heard. This is the "Javanese way" of calming upheavals and waiting for the healing power of time.

The judicial panel rejected her petition because they could not determine an intent of malice. In another classic of the Javanese way, they suggested that she appeal to a higher court. Or that she launch a civil suit against her replacement, and even one against the government. But it is clear that in this instance, the Javanese way has failed.

As the full details of the ruling become evident, the crowd starts a march down the street, but starts dissipating after a few blocks. They have made their point, cowed the police into restraint, and they know that the change they seek can be neither delivered nor blocked by court decree.

The beginning of the end of the Suharto era is in fact signaled 17 days before the Gajah Mada demo, hours after my arrival on assignment in Indonesia. About 1 p.m. on 12 December 1997, the government announces that Suharto is too ill to travel for a regional meeting of leaders in the Malaysian capital Kuala Lumpur, barely a two-hour flight away. The rupiah immediately plunges in value; the government didn't have the wit to delay the announcement until the markets closed.

Rumours of Suharto's death sweep the city. Witless authorities then decide to close the streets around the presidential palace. I make my way down towards Merdeka (Freedom Square), to find the entries to north Freedom Street (Jalan Merdeka Utara) completely blocked, and a crowd speculating whether the president has died in hospital or in the palace itself.

I walk the full kilometre down one side of Freedom Square, stopping now and then for a chat with animated bystanders eager to share the rumors. As I approach the Arjuna Wijaya sculpture — a monumental piece of Hindu iconography showing Krishna leading Arjuna to triumph in the epic poem known as Bharata Yudha in Indonesia and as the Mahabharata in India — a police check asks me for ID. After I show my press card, young men start gathering around me: "wartawan, wartawan (journalist, journalist)," they repeat as others join. Sadly I have no facts to either bolster or dispel their rumours. They turn away, disappointed.

It is not lost on me that Sukarno took his name from Karna, who in the Indonesian version of the epic emerges as the hero of Bharata Yudha, because he rejected ultimate power for the sake of loyalty and friendship. And Arjuna's victory turned to ashes when he learned that Karna, the foe he had bested in battle, was in fact the older brother whose identity he never knew. Suharto set Sukarno aside to seize power, and now his own days are fading, while the crowds once again call for another Sukarno to lead them.

That evening, I am invited to dinner at home by the noted Indonesian journalist and human rights activist Andreas Harsono, whose identity I kept secret in my reports back then to protect him from retribution. Andreas is intoxicated by the taste of freedom in the air. "I will always remember this day," he says. "When I look back, I can say that this was the day it all began."

We are sitting in his comfortable suburban living room, 50 kilometres away by expressway from central Jakarta and my lodging at the Hotel Indonesia. The indoor garden is open to the sky, filling the room with the aromas of a summer night and a velvet mist of humidity.

Andreas' toddler Norman, ignoring the stuffed bear I have brought him, is playing with the box it came in. A maid clears the table, and a nanny is preparing to take Norman (who in March 2019 would become a full-time journalist with the Jakarta Post) for his evening walk. This slice of middle-class life, with all its material comfort, perfectly illustrates the social contract of the Suharto years. He has made all this prosperity possible, but the price is obeisance.

Free thinking, alternative ideas, challenges to the political order, are all among the things not to be done. This is the flip side of the social harmony and advancement promised in Five-Principle Democracy. Individual demands for freedom and liberty are seen as selfish acts intruding upon the well-being of family and community, the foundational values of Javanese culture.

For Andreas, the events of the day carry the hope that Norman will grow up in a far different Indonesia. Andreas was born in 1965, the year after Sukarno foresaw, in a mix of Indonesian and Italian, as "tahun vivere pericolosamente," shortened to Tavip, the Year of Living Dangerously.

Sukarno had been admitting more and more communist leaders into the government, to play them off against the influence of the military, which was mandated to have both military and civilian roles — called *dwifungsi* or dual function — the civilian role being intervention in weak civil governance to save the people and the nation.

The Year of Living Dangerously ended with the slaughter of Communists — by 1965, the PKI counted three million members in Central Java and Bali — and the bloody civil war which left Sukarno sidelined and half a million dead. As the pogrom continued, Andreas hid with his family in a hole in their garden, to avoid a vigilante rampage. "My earliest memory is being in the dark, on my mother's lap, with no one saying a word."

When Suharto came to power, six in ten Indonesians were too poor to feed themselves. By mid-1997, only one in twenty is mired in absolute poverty — unable to feed, clothe and shelter themselves, with hunger and malnutrition as their chronic companions. In my first extended visit to Indonesia in 1992, funded by a fellowship from the Asia-Pacific Foundation of Canada, I had ample occasion to strike out on my own to see these changes for myself.

In March 1992, my travels took me to a modest village outside Yogyakarta. The landscape was suffused with the dazzling greenery one only finds in rice paddies bathed in the central Javanese light, so vivid it almost hurts the eye. Cloudscapes shifted across the smoking cone of Merapi volcano. Entering this quiet village was like stepping into the feudal world of what I once knew as Home: my mother's village in India. Munarsih, a journalist in Yogyakarta who is showing me what I came for, asks the driver to pull the jeep into a bucolic lane. "Here we are," she says. "This is where the President's family lived."

The moment I saw Suharto's boyhood home, time and distance fell away: it might have been part of my mother's village, right down to the abundance of the mango trees, the foraging chickens, and the hanging roots of the spreading banyan trees. I knew the architecture all too well from my childhood in eastern India: an inner courtyard formed by rammed-earth wings, freshly thatched, the rooms bound by a common verandah two steps up from the courtyard.

This was a typical village home, where several generations of a joint family lived together in the various wings: a community within a community, which was the pattern of human settlement until post-independence Indonesia sprouted its skyscrapers and cities — and the rise of an urban middle class which lured the children off the land.

Indeed, the only encroaching modernity to be seen, adjacent to Suharto's village, is the agricultural university he bequeathed: Bangsa Manggala (Blessings for our Folk).

It was this sort of "generosity" that kept people faithful to the New Order government, and its proclamation of Demokrasi Pancasila. Universities, abundant crops, decent health care, good education, full bellies: all the benevolence expected from a ruler who had begun to assume the aura of a Javanese god-King. And of course, none should be so impolite or ungrateful as to organise dissent.

The Suharto years gave Andreas a decent life, a good education, an immense love of Indonesia — and the confidence to criticise and challenge the ever-spreading absolutism of Suharto's power. As we have dinner, a pasty-looking Suharto appears on television, mustering a weak smile, to say he is ill but recovering. That puts an end to the swirling rumours, but does nothing to dispel the hope stirred by the events of the day.

Full bellies and captive minds might have been enough, once upon a time. Yet when a surging middle class gains the education and the economic power to afford the truth, even a God-King can seem no better than a common thief, once the magic fades.

As it turned out, the transition did indeed happen in a way no one expected.

Jakarta, Indonesia, 21 May 1998

Riots have ravaged Indonesia for more than 10 days, leaving some 1,200 dead across the archipelago, provoked by a fatal shooting of student protesters in Jakarta.

It is the culmination of the deep economic plunge in the country, accompanied by widespread social unrest, which has been building to a breaking point since the beginning of 1998. Indonesia, with its open banking system and free flow of capital, is a victim of the Asian financial crisis of the era: a drive-by-shooting of perfectly healthy and growing "tiger economies" by international investors intent on turning a quick buck.

As the comfort of the middle class eroded, the Suharto era social contract began to unravel. In a foretaste of the transformation awaiting the world, the catalyst that led Suharto to step down was the first widespread use of technology and fledgling social media to show the world the brutality of the Suharto government's crackdown on dissent.

At 10 a.m. on 12th May, some six thousand students gathered in the parking lot of Trisakti University. They lowered the Indonesian flag to half-staff and demanded Suharto's resignation. It was the latest of many campus protests that had been building in Indonesia since the middle of 1997. The demonstration carried on throughout the day. Finally, Indonesian special forces commandos stepped in where the police would not. Under the orders of Lieutenant-General Prabowo Subianto, they opened fire at 5 p.m., as the protest was winding down.

Pictures of the shooting were uploaded to the fledgling internet through dial-up connections (the only widely-used browser was Netscape Navigator), and within hours the images were there, broadcast for the world to see.

That was the point of no return for Suharto. The Trisakti shootings targeted the children of the middle class that had benefited most from Suharto's rule, and upon whom he relied for his support. Riots have broken out across Indonesia, leaving more than a thousand people dead, and they show no signs of abating. It does not help that Prabowo Subianto is Suharto's son-in-law (though the Indonesian political upheaval would cost him his marriage).

There is a very real risk that the riots — which, as a subtext, continue a pogrom against ethnic Chinese Indonesians — will lead to the widespread chaos that brought Suharto to power in 1966. Even now, with an announcement scheduled, there is no clear indication of how the government will respond. Anything is possible, from a military crackdown applied with renewed vigour, to some sort of delaying tactic with promises to listen and consult.

Suharto shuffles up to a bank of microphones, looking more like a placid grandfather than an absolute ruler. With characteristic Javanese understatement and opacity, there is no indication from the opening phrases of Suharto's speech that his rule is coming to an end. He says:

> During these recent times, I have been following carefully the development of our national situation, especially the aspirations of the people for reforms in all sectors in the life of our nation and state.
>
> Based on my deep understanding of these aspirations and prompted by the conviction that these reforms need to be implemented in an orderly, peaceful and constitutional manner for the sake of maintaining the unity and cohesion of the nation, and the continuity of the national development, I declared a plan to form the committee for reform and to change the composition of the Seventh Development cabinet.
>
> But, the reality to date has shown that the said committee for reform cannot be materialised because there was no adequate response to the plan to form that committee.
>
> In the wish of implementing these reforms in the best manner possible, I deem that faced with the impossibility of forming the committee, changes in the composition of the Seventh Development Cabinet are no longer necessary.
>
> Considering the above development, I am of the opinion that it would be very difficult for me to implement in a good manner, duties in governing the state and in development.

Therefore, in line with article 8 of the 1945 Constitution and after earnestly taking into consideration the views of the leadership of People's Representatives Council and the leadership of the factions in it, I have decided to declare that I have ceased to be the president of the Republic of Indonesia as of the time I read this on this day, Thursday, May 21, 1998.

Looking characteristically composed, he finally declares that his entire government is resigning:

For the assistance and support of the people while I led the nation and state of Indonesia, I express my thanks. And I seek forgiveness if there were any mistakes and shortcomings. May the Indonesian nation remain victorious with Pancasila and the 1945 constitution.

As of this day too, the Seventh Development Cabinet is outgoing and to the ministers I express my thanks.

To hear him, you would not know that this is a man whose rule became increasingly ruthless as his years in power stretched to three decades. Suharto looks on as his vice president, Bacharuddin Jusuf Habibie, takes the oath of office to complete Suharto's term as President of the Republic of Indonesia.

The day after, it becomes clear that all of Suharto's family, and his closest cronies and friends, have been stripped of power.

Months after Suharto's resignation, darker truths began to emerge. The riots enveloped a terrible pogrom — systemic, organised rapes of ethnic Chinese by gangs of marauders taking advantage of the upheaval, sometimes escalating to murder: a chilling echo of the 1965 anti-Communist rampage wherein Chinese Indonesians were a particular target.

These were carefully documented in the first months after Suharto's fall, in an effort led by the Jesuit priest Sandyawan Sumardi and a nationwide network of volunteers united as *"Untuk Kemanusian"*For Humanity. Through persistence, and outreach to survivors, they chronicled details of 152 rapes of ethnic Chinese and several murders during the intense days of rioting on May 13, 14, and 15.

Typically, a band of looters would destroy a shop, gang-rape the women within, set the shop ablaze, and occasionally toss their victims into the inferno. And as is so often the case, the investigation is hindered because the victims are too ashamed to come forward; and family memories remain of the widespread slaughter during the coup that brought Suharto to power.

Indonesia's military elite, quickly emerging as a stabilising force in the aftermath of Suharto, are uncomfortable with these dark truths, preferring to look ahead and forget the past. A senior military commander warns fledgling human rights groups not to exaggerate accounts of rape.

By September 1998, Suharto's son-in-law, Major-General Prabowo Subianto, is emboldened enough to take personal responsibility in the kidnapping and disappearance of political opponents in those turbulent months leading up to that momentous May. He says he misinterpreted the orders of his superior officers, thereby absolving Suharto and his immediate circle from any blame. He would later use this shouldering of responsibility to further his own political ambitions.

A series of compromise governments followed Suharto, bringing foes into uneasy alliance. Habibie, an enthusiastic technocrat who preferred to be known as BJ, lasted only a few months (his choice brought more than a few sniggers from journalists, given the similarity of Habibie and *habibi* — Arabic for "darling" — and the rather vulgar meaning associated with BJ in English).

Parliament then chose the popular spiritual leader Abdurrahman Wahid, head of the Brotherhood of Muslims, whose considerable charm and affability was in inverse proportion to his governing competency. These ineffective alliances continued until a day three years later, in July 2001, when Parliament ousted Wahid and named his vice-president of 21 months, Megawati Sukarnoputri, as President of the Republic of Indonesia.

Megawati became the sixth woman to lead a Muslim-majority democracy, but three years later, failed to win election to a second term. Ultimately, she even sought the presidency on a ticket that included Prabowo Subianto as vice-presidential candidate, only to be defeated by a former general, Susilo Bambang Yudhoyono, who over two terms patiently led Indonesia to ever-firmer bolstering of its emerging democracy.

You may find, dear companion, that there are compelling lessons for our own time, in considering Indonesia's experience in evolving from autocracy to a flawed but functioning democracy. As you consider the change you wish to create in your community, it may be worth reflecting on the durability of the shared values that arose from the accommodation of many cultures and influences across the archipelago — and the implications they have for finding common values, and thereby nurturing democratic traditions and institutions, in our own pluralistic societies.

The party Megawati founded, the Indonesian Democratic Party of Struggle, would eventually prevail in 2014 national elections, electing the popular governor of Jakarta, Mulyano (popularly known by his childhood nickname Joko Widodo, contracted to Jokowi), as the seventh president of the Indonesian republic. Jokowi was named as the presidential candidate by Megawati after her own bid for the presidency failed in 2009.

Like Sukarno, Megawati, and Suharto, Joko Widodo is from Central Java — the cradle of the Hindu-Buddhist-Muslim syncretism that gave rise to the values of *Demokrasi Pancasila*. The 2014 result was bitterly contested by Prabowo Subianto, who did not accept that he narrowly lost the election.

Suharto never did face punishment for the abuses of his rule. As it turned out, he would not be prosecuted, nor exiled, nor lose his assets — an estimated fortune of at least $15 billion skimmed from state business in the years of his rule.

Immediately after resigning, Suharto is admitted to hospital. In the months and years that follow, Suharto's lawyers declare he is too ill to face prosecution and trial. A team of 20 doctors is dispatched, in the early 2000s, to give a definitive evaluation of his fitness to stand trial, and conclude he has sustained irreversible brain damage.

Subsequent corruption investigations convicted his son Hutomo Mandala Putra, but Suharto was not personally blamed. When he finally died of sepsis on 27 January 2008 aged 86, a decade after he stepped down, he was facing a civil suit by the Indonesia government to recover some $1.6 billion of state assets.

The president of the day, Susilo Bambang Yudhoyono, went on national television to announce the passing of one of the great sons of Indonesia, and asked for a period of national mourning. Suharto was entombed in Surakarta, the cultural capital of Central Java, with full military and state honours.

At the time of this writing in 2019, Indonesia has had its share of advances and setbacks. Nonetheless, there have been elections that are recognisably free and fair ever since the turn of the millennium. The world's most populous Muslim country remains a democracy, albeit one increasingly influenced by Islamists.

(They succeeded in jailing a Christian mayor of Jakarta, Jokowi's successor Basuki Tjahaja Purnama, for insulting the Koran. And it cannot be denied that political Islam has surged from a zero base under Suharto's rule.)

Still, the true lesson is that the arc from Sukarno's repressive populism to the government Indonesians elected in April 2019 has seen the endurance of building a nation on shared values. The April election became a watershed, because it was the first time that Indonesia chose its President, Vice President, and parliamentarians (to the People's Consultative Assembly) on the same day.

The election campaign was a rematch between the incumbent President Joko Widodo and the indefatigable Prabowo Subianto, fully resurrected and rehabilitated as a political leader, making another bid for the presidency.

Perhaps the real sign of progress is that Prabowo made no attempt to seize power after losing the 2014 election. And neither of the leading candidates has questioned any aspect of Pancasila.

Seven decades after independence, Indonesia continues to demonstrate that a nation built on shared, core values can weather potentially-calamitous political upheavals. And that despite setbacks and struggles, democracy is the enduring value that animates modern Indonesia.

In the April 2019 elections, the results were a mirror image of 2014. Once again, Megawati's PDI-P and its candidate Jokowi prevailed, with Prabowo a clear second: official returns showed the president re-elected with 55 per cent of the vote. Once again, a sulking Prabowo threatened legal challenges. After Prabowo lost the vote by a 10-point margin to Jokowi, he claimed fraud and did nothing to prevent his whipped-up supporters from running amok in central Jakarta for a few days in May. And left it at that. While fomenting rioting and demonstrations, he never evoked the possibility of reversing the will of the people through armed intervention.

"Whatever the results may be, we should just be happy. I'd participated in the presidential election previously; I didn't kick up a fuss when I lost. Never mind, just laugh it off and have a meal together, as that's the choice of the people," Megawati told a Jakarta TV channel as Prabowo glowered and the Islamist Amien Rais threatened political uprising instigated by his losing party, Partai Amanat Nasional (National Mandate Party). "Whatever the results may be, we should be joyous about it."

Indeed, it is worth remembering that between April and May 2019, the 200 million Muslims in India and 250 million Muslims in Indonesia experienced fully democratic elections, and were able to choose their leaders and shape their governance.

Furthermore, 80 million Muslims in Turkey were able to deliver a rebuke to the autocratic tendencies of President Recep Tayyip Erdogan by opting for opposition politicians to govern Ankara and Istanbul in local elections at the end of March. Although the government ordered a rerun of the Istanbul vote, after the breadth of the rebuke became clear, Erdogan's candidate lost the mayoral election by an even wider margin on 23 June 2019.

These facts — that more than half a billion Muslims celebrated democratic values in the spring of 2019 — should not be lost in the relentless focus on the Middle East which has consumed European and American media and policymakers for the entirety of my lifetime

Indonesia's five-principle democracy (Demokrasi Pancasila) remains the core value on which a modern nation is forged from a dazzling diversity. And in an outcome aligned with the glory of Karna, hero of the Javanese epic story of the Bharata Yudha, Sukarno's lineage continues to control the levers of power.

The power of values that transcend cultural differences is amply demonstrated in Indonesia. And those values become ever stronger as mass education spreads, demonstrating once again that knowledge is power.

Yet as we shall explore in our next stop on the journey, some of our most deeply held beliefs are being challenged by a set of values increasingly embraced by the people of the most populous country in the world — to the bewilderment of once-raucous democracies, whose responses range from defiance to helplessness to denial to an outright embrace.

In houses of political power across the often-dysfunctional liberal democracies of the planet, the question is repeated in baffled exasperation: what do we do about China?

Chapter Twelve

The China Challenge

Chengdu, Sichuan, China, November 2018

A bevy of black swans glides by the lake shore, bobbing for a bite, briefly taking flight, their vivid red beaks and sable plumage inscribing an exotic alphabet against a cerulean sky. The lake, the carefully-curated foliage, the flowers, bamboo groves, all evoke a meditative peace. Across the ridge behind me, the happy chatter of hordes of schoolchildren wafts down, interspersed with the commands of tour guides trying to keep their charges to a tight schedule. The pleasure of being a solo visitor to the Chengdu Research Base of Giant Panda Breeding brings no demands on my time, allows me to harvest a soul-calming serenity from my contemplation among the swans.

It is barely six weeks since my nephew left New Hampshire by air ambulance for Toronto, where he is just settling in for an extended stay at a rehab hospital not far from his home. This lakeshore interlude in Chengdu is a welcome moment in my own healing as I struggle with the feelings forcibly repressed in those weeks of my boy's illness when his survival was by no means assured.

I take a sip of my bottled green tea, tasting vaguely of flowers and honey, as a twenty-something couple sharing the bench with me ignore the swans for the allure of their matching Oppo smartphones. They are giggling uncontrollably at a video of "hot moms", modeling new fashions on the popular Chinese TV show Mamma Mia.

Eventually, they gesture to ask whether I could photograph them with the swans, offering me sweet smiles as I agree to comply.

"Where are you from," they ask, practising their English. "Yindu?"

I shake my head, "Yindu laizi Jianada."

Faces alight at my reply, that I am a Canadian of Indian ancestry, they fire out a query in Putonghua. When I shrug in bemusement at their question, they realise I have reached the limit of my hello-goodbye-thank you command of their language. "You like pandas?" At my affirmative answer, they flash me a thumbs up and say "bye-bye" in English, happily heading up the path towards the rose garden.

Having scoped out the walking map, I find a back-path between the well-travelled guided tour routes, headed back toward the habitat where panda cubs are frolicking away the morning. I am quite alone on the path. A foraging peacock emerges from the shrubbery, the only company I keep until I come to the long flight of stairs leading uphill to a habitat where half a dozen pandas are sharing a convivial lunch: sitting in a circle, passing around bamboo stalks to peel and eat.

These are indeed sights to unbend the mind. And it is the last place I expect to find Gandhi. But there he is, setting the standard for judging the panda sanctuary: a lacquered wooden plaque in Putonghua and English, quoting the Mahatma: "The greatness of a nation and moral progress can be judged by the way its animals are treated."

Making my way out, past the panda-monium of the packed restaurants and gift shops overwhelmed by hundreds of school-children, I am accosted by half a dozen vendors selling panda replicas at half the price of the official souvenirs inside. Having already bought a soft-toy panda climbing a bamboo stalk for my grandson, I hold up my souvenir with a smile, even as the vendors shout, "Take one more!"

I stop at the row of food carts for a *jianbing*, a savoury crepe-omelette of mung-bean batter griddled in front of you while you wait, topped with two eggs, cilantro, scallion, and a generous dash of hot bean paste before being folded and served. The crepe and a large cup of chilled sweet watermelon from a fruit cart add up to a delicious $5 lunch.

Strolling down the broad boulevard beside the Panda centre, with no particular destination, I wander into the side streets of this mostly residential neighbourhood, bungalows and apart-ments, a walkable district mingled with parks and greenery all around. I sit on an intricately-tiled bench under a shade tree and take in the vista.

The laid-back pace of Chengdu is so different from the knees-and-elbows hustle of Hong Kong and Guangzhou, or the nev-er-stop-moving pulse of Shanghai. An imperial capital since the third century BC, lying at the base of the Himalayan foothills, today's Chengdu is a city of 15 million people, with a metropolitan population approaching 20 million. Like so much of modern China it is impeccably clean, served by a network of super-efficient subway lines, and a high speed rail hub.

I am staying in the city centre, a few steps from Tianfu (Heaven's Gate) Square, bordered by the stunning New Hall of the Chengdu museum, and the rather overwhelming statue of Chairman Mao, benignly saluting from the front of the Science and Technology Museum, in the city that was the last redoubt of Jiang Jieshi's (Chiang Kai-shek in colonial transliteration) Nationalists before their defeat and retreat to Taiwan. A 20 minute ride on Metro Line One brings one to the world's most spacious shopping, commercial and hotel complex, the 18 million square foot New Century Global Centre: an undulating symmetry of glass rising and spreading 100 metres in every dimension. Thrice as large as North America's largest, my home city's West Edmonton Mall, New Century's indoor beach even has a giant screen to project images of sunrise and sunset over the ocean.

Still on my aimless walk down Xiangmao Avenue from the Panda centre, I stop at a canal-side café called River Bank Flavour, order green tea, and open up that morning's China Daily. Although it is a government-viewpoint journal aimed at expatriates and an anglophone Chinese elite, it is a pleasure to read: the professionalism of the writing and editing is exceptional. And its commentaries about international relations offer a clear window into Chinese government policy.

Today's front page carries a harrowing tale of a 15-year-old girl forcibly married off to a man in his fifties: a marriage chosen by her father, in which the girl had no recourse. The tale of her subsequent rescue, and her entry into technological school thence a well-paying job, is an uplifting account of patriarchy thwarted: one of many young Chinese women rescued from a backwards form of cultural imprisonment — a cultural detention, if you like — which runs completely counter to the egalitarian and secular values that inform the lives of most young Chinese. Now able to earn a living and support herself, this young woman is an exemplar of someone lifted from a form of feudal servitude into modernity.

She is an ethnic Uygur from Xinjiang, and the way her story is framed and presented in China Daily is of a piece with China's vigorous and unapologetic advocacy of a policy most western countries officially abhor: forcing a rural Muslim population still mired in medieval and feudal cultural practice into conformity with the Chinese state; through mass detention and "re-education" in camps across Xinjiang.

Governments with a tradition of liberal democracy call it a gross and unjustified violation of human rights: the detention and brainwashing of hundreds of thousands of people against their will, and the conversion of the Xinjiang capital Urumqi into a virtual prison camp with surveillance everywhere.

Yet from the perspective of the Chinese government, this is a necessary measure for which the world should be giving thanks. As a China Daily editorial published on 16 October 2018 put it:

> When the Xinjiang Uygur autonomous region suffered from explosions, assassinations, arson attacks along with attacks on innocent people and riots from the early 1990s until 2015, the Western media mostly blamed the Chinese government for all this.

When not a single such incident has occurred in the past more than two years since tightened security has been administered and measures have been adopted to undermine the root causes of terrorism, extremism and separatism, they accuse China of infringing on the human rights of the local people.

It should go without saying that the Chinese government must do anything it can to crack down on the three evil forces to ensure people's safety. It would be unimaginable for both the central and local governments to sit idle while residents of different ethnicities in the region were being deprived of their right to enjoy a peaceful life and economic development.

The interview with the Xinjiang government chief published on Tuesday is meant to tell the world what the Chinese government has done and achieved in this regard.

The fight against terrorism, extremism and separatism in the region is complicated. In its undeveloped southern part, the penetration of religious fundamentalism was deep as poor education resulted in the lack of awareness about the rule of law, and abject poverty allowed for the acceptance of religious extremism among local residents.

As a result, training was organised so that those not deeply involved in terrorist and extremist activities could be made aware of their wrongdoing and at the same time be taught some kind of professional skills, as well as Putonghua, to help them land a job.

The rationale behind the training is that only by providing local residents with a means for them to make a decent living will they be able to resist the temptation of participating in terrorist and extremist activities.

The tightened security control and what has been done to squeeze the room for the presence of the three evil forces has paid off.

In 2017, the region's GDP grew by 7.6 percent, and the per capita disposable income for urban residents increased by 8.1 percent, that for rural residents by 8.5 percent. The number of tourist trips to the region was more than 100 million, an increase of 32.4 percent over the previous year. The number of visits it had received from January to September already reached 132 million.

Little wonder that better security and social stability are bringing an economic boom to the region, and economic prosperity will in return help rid the region of extremism, terrorism and separatism.

This is a virtuous cycle.

And therein lies what I am calling the China challenge. For me, a passionate champion of human rights lived as a way of life, China's "re-education camps" are an affront to my belief in full political freedoms, including freedom of religion, freedom of speech, and freedom of assembly.

Nonetheless, my own faith in human rights cannot be a blind faith. It must recognise the existence of a completely different perspective: the Chinese one, where the denial of political rights and freedoms is presented as a guarantor of stability. China is a test of my faith and the beliefs and principles dearest to me. It forces me to ask: what if I am wrong? What if human rights, as that clever disruptor Yuval Noah Harari would have it, is simply another collective abstraction dreamed up by Sapiens in our specious ability to invent lies to abet social cohesion?

In the sixth century before the Common Era, about 2600 years ago, an atheist school of Hindu philosophy challenged the existence of God, and all the precepts of the major Hindu philosophies in the Vedas and other sacred books. The philosopher Carvaka argued that the Hindu holy books existed only to advance the power of priests. The only valid knowledge came from perception: what you could actually observe or perceive. This is much like the perspective of Garcia Marquez's patriarch Jose Arcadio Buendia, who was deemed a madman and tied to a tree for insisting the earth is round, and demanding to see the daguerreotype of God as proof of the existence of a divine being.

For Carvaka, inference — making leaps of logic based on the evidence of one's senses — was equally wrong. As my father J.P. Das put it in his book *Consciousness Quest: where East meets West*, Carvaka exalted the pursuit of sensory pleasures — with no concepts like guilt or sin — as the point of human existence.

> Carvaka is not using consciousness and its associates, such as the power to reflect, review and acquire an insight to the existential tragedies as well as joys of human beings, in order to

promote the continuation of our human race, or our communities, society, and the physical world.

In spite of the unethical exhortation of seeking sensual pleasure, Carvaka's metaphysics could be justified, as it appeals to direct sense experience rather than to represent it through inference and through references to priests and scriptural knowledge. Inferential knowledge, as many of us will agree, has a fatal flaw -the assumption of the truth of major and minor premises. Analogical reasoning, its sister, is prone to fallacies. In fact, reasoning by analogy, like reasoning based on logical propositions or syllogisms, is a valid source of knowledge, but only under certain conditions. So what are we left with except direct sense-perception as a source of knowledge?

China, like Carvaka, challenges my notion of freedom of speech and freedom of thought and action as the necessary foundation of a fulfilled life.

What use are such human rights as freedom of speech and freedom to form different political parties, if one is starving, or cannot fend for oneself? Is one free to be hungry, to fall ill, to die because medical care is unavailable, to watch one's children waste away from malnutrition while enjoying political freedom?

The Chinese social contract since the political uprisings of 1989 has been to provide an ever-improving standard of living to its citizens, so long as they do not question or challenge the governing political order.

Absent politics, both society and economy operate much more efficiently. Rather than the diet of political scandals and shenanigans that confront citizens daily in India and most vigorous democracies, the diversion in Chinese social media is family soap operas, shows extolling the great things accomplished by empowered women, the takedown of corrupt officials, cheating husbands getting their comeuppance, and endlessly-popular singing contests.

Political stability (because there is no means of dissent outside the strictures of state-sanctioned policy debate) brings economic prosperity and social peace. This view is so ingrained in the young Chinese people who practice their English with me, that they stare blankly when I describe the workings of Canada's political system.

"You mean the people prefer instability?" asks a young woman studying English translation at Chengdu's university for training interpreters. She is among a group of two dozen or so interpretation students assigned to assist a visiting delegation from Alberta in its interactions with local firms in Sichuan. "But why?"

Hong Kong Special Administrative Region, China, 31 October 2014

I am trying to make my way uphill on d'Aguilar Street from Queen's Road, jammed in the densest evening crowd I have ever experienced.

It is good-natured cavorting by an impossibly compressed mass of people shuffling a few centimetres at a time, excited and lavishly costumed people: a few princess crowns, lots of devil's horns, at least a third with the classic black mask of the masquerade.

Streetlights and neon are everywhere, and the polite but firm police in their blue uniforms are doing their best to keep everyone moving along. Traffic was waved off these side streets hours ago; I was able to get in only by taking the tram from my modest business hotel in Sai Wan to the heart of Central, literally melding into the crowd, impelled by the steady motion of the never ending river of people. I am in the middle of the Halloween carnival in Lan Kwai Fong, the throng of clubs and cafes that is the lustrous night-time heart of Central.

Perhaps noticing my age in the overwhelmingly younger crowd, a constable asks me where I'm headed. To Wing Wah Lane, the pedestrian street chock a block with cafes and restaurants, where I've agreed to meet an acquaintance from the Eco Expo I've visited the past few days. He gives me a gentle push in the back, pointing me uphill, declaring "make way for Uncle" in English and Cantonese. A space opens up where none had been, and the stream of bodies carries me towards my destination.

Lan Kwai Fong is an entirely new experience for me on these once-familiar streets. During my days as a journalist, a leisurely walk from the Hilton — the preferred bar of expatriate reporters, with a plaqued table reserved in the name of the legendary Australian scribe Richard Hughes (the inspiration for the characters Old Craw in John le Carre's novel **The Honourable Schoolboy** and Dikko Henderson in Ian Fleming's *You Only Live Twice*) — would lead you up Ice House Road to the Foreign Correspondents Club, whence a long flight of steps led downhill to the Central business district.

The Hilton is long gone, torn down in 1995 to be replaced by the 68-storey tower of Cheung Kong Holdings which opened in 1999. And the nondescript streets you once reached by the downhill stairs from the Foreign Correspondents Club are now the throb and bustle of Lan Kwai Fong, which tonight seems to be the destination of every young person on the island.

The controlled stream of flowing bodies on the main street, deftly guided by the patience of unarmed police, sends a tributary flowing into Wing Wah Lane. I let myself be swept forward to this pedestrian precinct where every restaurant and bar has outdoor tables set up.

By 8pm, I find my acquaintance and take a perch on a trestle table stool, as the flow of the costumed young continues scant inches away on either side. Servers try to find space for those who hesitate anywhere near a table, miraculously picking out solo seats and the occasional spot at the inside tables. They are formidably skilled in carrying trays of cold beer, meals, and cocktails with balletic grace: setting them down at one end of the trestle and passing the drinks and snacks with pinpoint accuracy, before punching "order complete" on the mini-tablets tucked into their aprons. It is a marvellous display of symmetry and coordination.

The Sri Lankan server who delivers a frosty pint of San Miguel and a heady plate of succulently sweet flash-fried chili prawns apologises for the wait. "It's good you got here before the dinner rush."

The happy swirl of Lan Kwai Fong on Halloween night is a vivid contrast to my experience earlier in the day, when I came toward the Admiralty by double-decker streetcar from Causeway Bay. The streetcar comes to a final stop barely midway through its route in the densest heart of Hong Kong's affluence, the passengers filing off with a stoic resignation to make their way to the nearest metro station. It has been like this for weeks now, the pulsing heart of a hyper-charged city brought to stillness and silence by a pure and unvarnished example of Mahatma Gandhi's civil disobedience. The cause of this disruption is a tent camp in the middle of Central and Admiralty, normally the most congested of routes traversing the island.

This is what remains of the protests that began some six weeks ago: when hundreds of thousands of people marched through the night, demanding unfettered democracy of a type that had never existed in Hong Kong. Launched by two professors, Benny Tai and Chan Kin-man, and cleric Chu Yiu-Ming, the Occupy Central with Love and Peace movement is a conscious act of Gandhian civil disobedience. Mr. Chu explicitly embraces the core concept of *satyagraha,* the power of truth, impelled by a blazing moral conviction that exists completely independent of the evanescent impulses of the day. A truth perpetrated by people committed to paying the consequences of breaking a law they believe unjust and untenable.

The protests arose because China, which had resumed suzerainty over Hong Kong once a 99-year lease to the British expired in 1997, wanted the right to vet the candidates pursuing the highest elected office in Hong Kong. Under the transition agreement, China was to enable Hong Kong's autonomy for a half century, under a "one nation, two systems" arrangement. The protesters believed that in a true multi-party democracy, the parties should be able to put up candidates without any screening or vetting by the Chinese government. Weeks later, the crackdown many anticipated has not come.

Dozens of tents, with several hundred encamped protesters, occupy the main thoroughfare. I make my way into the encampment. The first people I come across look up with curiosity from the camp chairs placed between tents. The camp itself is a vivid rainbow of tents arranged cheek-by-jowl, with a single lane of open road for the protesters to meet, congregate, chat. There is a bit of a holiday atmosphere, with animated conversation of varying intensity: and a sense of the surreal, at these four to five-deep rows of tents installed amid the skyscrapers that are the most expensive real estate in the world.

The Chinese authorities have decided to wait them out. The remaining protesters are mostly in their twenties. I strike up a conversation with three of them (I have given fictitious names to preserve their incognito, as they were neither arrested nor charged). Lily, Jasmine, and Brian are members of the Hong Kong Federation of Students, which now provides the bulk of the protest. Each is a product of the Hong Kong elite: their extended families include immensely wealthy *tai-kun,* members of the legal profession, two university professors. They are fluidly multi-lingual, their English inflected with the plummy tones of their former colonial masters.

For Jasmine, "democracy is the free will of the people. How can we be free, if we are told which leaders we can choose?"

Brian is clear-eyed about the irony: during British colonial rule, the London government appointed a governor under whose aegis people elected a multi-party legislature and enjoyed a judicial system based on English Common Law. There was no question, Brian acknowledges, of anyone resolutely anti-British ever emerging to compete for the top elected role. "We were promised true democracy. The Mainland government wants to control our choice, just as the British did."

As Lily puts it, "the agreement gave us the full right to choose our own destiny. And the Mainland government has to live up to the accord."

All three are clear that they do not wish to emulate British or American democracy: where leaders of viable political parties must accept the power and influence of big money and perpetuate the agendas of the wealthy if they are to govern with any durability or sustained success.

As Jasmine observes, "We are saying the people should have complete freedom to delegate their power to their chosen representatives. The Mainland wants us to choose between leaders who won't challenge the Mainland government."

They were prepared to be dragged off to jail, seeking victory in martyrdom. What was meant to be a two to three day occupation in 2014 turned into 79 days, gaining the sobriquet "umbrella revolution" as protesters unfurled umbrellas against tear gas and pepper spray, leaving civic authorities two choices: patience, or violence.

The camp between Causeway Bay, Admiralty and Central is the main protest site on Hong Kong island. Across the harbour in Kowloon, the normally traffic-choked streets of Mong Kok are filled with another bank of tents.

Many of their fellow residents have had enough. A day earlier, walking down from mid-levels towards the Star Ferry, I was stopped three times by petitioners, collecting signatures to demand an end to the protest. "They have made their point, but now we need our lives back," says Grace, whose family runs a clothing boutique. I note that I am a foreigner. Whereupon she reaches for another form at the back of the clipboard: ever orderly, there is one petition for signatures of residents, another for visitors.

Indeed, the visible support for the camps is no longer as strong as it was. While some of their fellow compatriots are circulating petitions, others are indifferent about the disruption: it is what it is, and life will just flow around it. In the evening crowd in Lan Kwai Fong, the protesters are out of sight and out of mind. "This is the greatest city in the world," says Stanley, the acquaintance I agreed to meet. "Look around you. There is nothing like it anywhere. No one is going to change that."

As more and more mainland Chinese settle in Hong Kong, the demographic wave is eroding the singularity to which the protesters aspire. English is less of a presence than it once was in the everyday street discourse between foreigners and merchants. Everywhere, there are ads for free or cheap lessons in Putonghua — the dominant Chinese language in Hong Kong also is spoken in neighbouring Guangdong province, differentiated in the Hong Kong dialect of English as "Mandarin Chinese" and "Cantonese."

The protest camps would last another six weeks, and end with a whimper rather than a bang. On 15 December 2014, police would move in to break up the camps in Mong Kok and central Hong Kong. While there were scuffles and some minor street violence on the Kowloon side, the 200 or so remaining Hong Kong protesters surrendered in the spirit of peace and order which animated their disorder. Alex Chow, the leader of the

Hong Kong Federation of Students, even as he acknowledges that there was little tangible outcome from the protests, maintains "the young generation will be the engine of reform."

In the spring of 2019, nine defendants went on trial for their role in instigating the Occupy Central movement. All were convicted of fomenting a public nuisance. In contrast to the anglophone and anglophile judges and barristers, 75-year-old cleric Chu Yiu-Ming chose to address the court in Cantonese. "Today, old and gray, I find myself in the defendants' dock, making a final plea as a convict. It looks so absurd," Chu said. "Yet my heart tells me that I have found the most honourable pulpit of my ministerial career."

On 24 April 2019, Chu was sentenced to two years imprisonment, with the sentence suspended due to his advanced age. Earlier, Hong Kong's Court of Appeal had overturned an eight-month sentence for the student leader Alex Chow. Benny Tai and Chan Kin-Man were jailed for 16 months, for "conspiracy to commit public nuisance."

Judge Johnny Chan noted there was no regret expressed by the defendants for the disruption of a 79-day occupation of Hong Kong's central business district. "By regret, I do not mean the defendants should give up their political beliefs or actions," he said, but the sentence might have been mitigated had they expressed remorse for the "excessive inconvenience and suffering" borne by ordinary people.

Thus Gandhi's point about civil disobedience — oppose unjust laws if you are willing to face the legal consequences — is firmly proven. In March 1922, Gandhi was in court to face a charge of "bringing or attempting to excite disaffection towards His Majesty's Government established by law in British India, and thereby committing offences punishable under Section 124 A of the Indian Penal Code." To which Gandhi pleaded guilty. And turned down any possibility of a suspended sentence or other lenience. If released, he said, he would cheerfully incite opposition to British rule.

Gandhi's words at that time convey the essence of *satyagraha,* and offer a clear-eyed perspective of what non-violent civil disobedience entails: "The only course open to you, the Judge and the assessors, is either to resign your posts and thus dissociate yourselves from evil, if you feel that the law you are called upon to administer is an evil, and that in reality I am innocent, or to inflict on me the severest penalty, if you believe that the system and the law you are assisting to administer are good for the people of this country, and that my activity is, therefore, injurious to the common weal."

Shanghai, China, June 2018

In the wildly fashionable district of Xintiandi, the aromas and tastes are far more evocative of Paris or Barcelona than any classical face of China the imagination may evoke. This was once France, of course, the French concession that was forbidden territory to Chinese inhabitants, part of the terrible reckoning the English and French brought with them in a particularly brutal application of colonialism in the 19th century.

The Anglo French expeditionary force led by Lord Elgin — Sikhs and Madrassis from India among them — looted and vandalised the cultural patrimony of China. On 18 October 1860, the British expeditionary force occupying Beijing set ablaze the Yuanming Yuan, the summer palace of Chinese imperium: after having stripped the compound of untold riches that continue to adorn the museums of Britain and France, and to fund the inheritance of the looters' descendants.

This was a prelude to the colonial drug trade, the so-called Opium Wars in which the governments of Britain and France became wealthy (the rapacious equal of any Central American cartel warlord of the present) by enslaving millions of Chinese in addiction, fuelled by the opium poppies they grew on the Indian subcontinent.

That past is only evident in the utilitarian grace of the old industrial buildings and the occasional merchant's house which bespeak a concerted effort to implant a piece of French prosperity on the other side of the world. On a balmy afternoon, there is a spattering of foreign faces amid the unending sea of Shanghainese taking the Sunday air with children in tow.

All the material bounty of western life is here: from the leg of authentic Iberian ham ($30 for 100 grams, thank you very much!) displayed prominently on a carving table fronting a tapas bar; next to a modern Thai bistro sporting the name and logo of the American bus line Greyhound (don't ask!); to a pizzeria across the road with Roman, Florentine and Neapolitan styles of pizza listed separately on the menu and tankards of draught beer delivered directly in kegs from Germany and the Netherlands.

In between are a score of boutiques with designer offerings aimed at Shanghai's burgeoning upper middle class (the Tesla dealership is down the road, next to a Bose shop offering high-end audio); never mind that much on offer is absurdly beyond the means of a middle-class westerner. Even so, there is an incongruity here. Barely 50 metres away, across the road from a modern Canadian flagship, a lululemon boutique, there are two solid 19th century stone buildings that are completely immune from commerce. One can imagine a Michelin-starred restaurant in the space, or a collection of designer storefronts. But that will never come to pass.

In these buildings is a museum commemorating the birthplace of the wealthiest and most powerful entity on the planet today, an institution that has seamlessly married the wealth-generating capacity of capitalism to the robust social control of the authoritarian state: the Communist Party of China. It is perhaps an evolution completely beyond the imagining of its founders: the Chinese intellectuals (with a Russian and a Dutchman among them) who in these buildings on 23 July 1921 held the founding meeting of the Communist Party of China.

There is a striking portrait of a young Mao Zedong from those days, long before he became the addled ruler in whose name a cabal of sinister revolutionaries launched the Great Proletarian Cultural Revolution of the mid 1960s: a pogrom of educated and capable Chinese which fomented unprecedented chaos. The Mao of the photograph radiates intelligence and determination, the eyes piercing yet thoughtful, determined that the party with its embrace of Marxism and Leninism would free China from the feudal yoke of colonial masters working hand-in-glove with pitiless warlords.

It is difficult to conceive that the Mao of that era would recognise the Shanghai of today, a place of dizzying modernity and technological prowess that rose from the ashes of the Cultural Revolution and powered ahead with breathtaking rapidity in the years after Mao's death. Indeed, as they met furtively in that windowless building in the French Concession, it is difficult to conceive that they could have foreseen the Xintiandi of today, let alone a China that bestrides the world as an economic colossus, investing $700 billion a year — roughly what the United States spends yearly on its global military reach — in the critical public infrastructure of countries whose resources it covets.

With no trace of irony, China's leader, Xi Jinping sees this stunning evolution as the culmination of the socialist principles that underpin Chinese communism, and swears fidelity to the principles of Karl Marx (see what the party of workers can do when they control the means of production!). Indeed, Xi posits China's progress as a rebound from the humiliation of the opium wars and China's enslavement — of which the 99-year lease of Hong Kong was a by-product — even as a state-directed command economy churns out unprecedented wealth and an ever-rising standard of living that has pulled 850 million Chinese people out of poverty.

Indeed, according to the World Bank's 2018 report Poverty and Shared Prosperity 2018, which used economic data from 2015, fewer than one percent of Chinese — actually 0.7 per cent — live in absolute poverty: lacking the ability to feed, clothe or shelter themselves. The same report shows that in the United States, 1.2 per cent of people live in absolute poverty. Since Deng Xiaoping launched China's economic reforms in 1981, freedom from want has become a reality for hundreds of millions of Chinese.

To put economies into a comparable perspective, the World Bank measures economic wealth using "purchasing power parity." Conventional measures of economic output are based on a currency's value relative to the U.S. dollar.

Purchasing power measures, or PPP, compare the purchasing power of the currency as opposed to its value against the U.S dollar. By this measure, China was the world's largest national economy in 2017 and 2018, according to both the World Bank and the International Monetary Fund. China was followed in the top 10 by the United States, India, Japan, Germany, Russia, Brazil, Indonesia, the United Kingdom, and France.

China further profits from its rapidly-developing economic alliance with some of these leading economies in a grouping called BRICS (Brazil, Russia, India, China, South Africa) which coordinates policies and activities to build greater prosperity. This includes the New Development Bank (NDB) launched with $50 billion in working capital, led by the Indian banker K.V. Kamath, who intends to allocate up to 60 per cent of that fund for renewable energy projects.

In fact, China's unstoppable pursuit of an "all of the above" energy policy, guided by state-led investments, makes it one of the world's leading clean-tech innovators, even as it remains one of the world's leading polluters.

For all the technological marvels and the tangible gains of freedom from want, there is a distinct difference from the other Asian behemoth: the equally-polluted and equally challenged India, which has been demonstrably less successful in lifting people from poverty. The missing element in China is political freedom: freedom of speech, freedom of assembly, the right to dissent. In the current iteration of Chinese governance, these are known as the roots of instability, a threat to the safe, peaceful and ever more prosperous life citizens enjoy.

To drive home the point, China's media need to do nothing more than run daily articles from international media on the further impoverishment of the poor and marginalised in the United States, alongside the myriad reports on the inchoate actions of a reality-show huckster who gained the U.S. presidency.

And the fickleness of unfettered democracy is amply illustrated by straightforward reporting on the chaos of Brexit: where a deceitful referendum on breaking Britain from the European union was won by a bare majority, even though it is clear such a rupture will impoverish Britons and imperil their standard of living for decades to come.

The quotidian chaos of the American president, and the supine fecklessness of the British leadership, need no embellishment to reinforce the view that China's political stability is far preferable to the caprices of democracy.

Furthermore, as I saw in Hong Kong in 2014 during the civil disobedience of the umbrella revolution, the band of determined protesters who still occupied central Hong Kong to claim a pure form of democracy (one that never existed under British colonial rule, and is nowhere to be seen in the largest democratic countries) are today considered unpopular Utopians in the face of surging Chinese prosperity.

Even though there is an abundance of motorbikes and scooters amid the luxury cars of Shanghai, one cannot readily conceive that the modern denizens of this city would swap the life they have for one infused with turmoil in the name of free speech and free assembly.

The fear of instability is a direct result of upheavals few of us in liberal democracies can imagine: first, the two decades of civil war, interrupted only by the existential fight against Japanese invaders, which finally ended in 1949. Followed by an even greater calamity: the cataclysm of the Great Proletarian Cultural Revolution which began in the mid-1960s, where being smart and accomplished was a crime, and the so-called revolution of the common people reduced everyone to the lowest common denominator.

The apocalyptic darkness of the Cultural Revolution left deep scars. And led to continued repression of democracy movements that challenged the power of the state. Which is why the grand bargain offered by the Communist Party prevails. It is the social contract established after the military crackdown on the 1989 uprising demanding a freer polity in dozens of Chinese cities (culminating in the killing of protesters in Beijing's Tiananmen Square by elite security forces, after ordinary soldiers refused to shoot at their compatriots). It is simply this: don't involve yourself in questioning the authority of the state, and we will give you an ever higher standard of living.

This social contract has one significant point of dissent: the Hong Kong Special Administrative Region.

In June 2019, mass demonstrations filled the streets of Hong Kong, protesting a proposed extradition law that would allow Hong Kongers to be sent to Greater China to answer serious crimes committed outside the Hong Kong Special Administrative Region. The legislation arose from the case of a young man accused of (and confessing to) strangling his girlfriend while holidaying in Taiwan, and stuffing her body into a pink suitcase. To the minds of the protesters, this would open the door for the Mainland to extradite any Hong Kong resident on any pretext. The Hong Kong government of Carrie Lam withdrew the bill, yet the protests devolved into anarchy.

On 1 July 2019, the 22nd anniversary of the territory's return to Chinese control after 99 years of British rule, masked and helmeted rioters stormed the legislative council, defaced paintings, spray painted slogans, smashed the glass windows. Riot police withdrew in the face of the violence; returning later to clear out the crowds with tear gas.

One should imagine whether the police response would have been similar, if violent rioters stormed the United States Capitol, the British Houses of Parliament, or the Parliament of India. Even so, there were calls in Hong Kong for an investigation of police brutality. And a demand for absolute freedom of a type that exists in none of the world's democracies.

Sadly for the millions of non-violent residents who want to secure continuing, meaningful participation in their own governance — at a minimum, to strengthen and protect their multi-party democracy and legislature — the anarchist outburst lends even further justification for future repression.

The choice facing those Hong Kongers who yearn for both economic well being and full democratic freedoms is fraught indeed. About a fifth of them live in poverty — a far higher proportion than their compatriots across the border in the Pearl River delta — due to astronomical housing costs and a severe shortage of affordable housing.

Many low-wage residents live in illegally subdivided flats, sometimes with two or three people sharing a six-square-metre space with barely enough room to move. The only thing preventing them from moving to neighbouring Guangdong province is to seek better economic prospects, they would have to give up the freedom of speech and freedom of assembly they treasure.

Life in Hong Kong became even bleaker for the protest movement on 21 July 2019, when white-clad members of the criminal underworld, the triad gangs that run most illegal activities, attacked demonstrators with batons. Protesters were beaten to the point of requiring stitches, while the police were slow to intervene: claiming their resources were stretched to the limit merely with the task of policing the mass protests.

Unlike the abrupt and reckless partition of the Indian subcontinent, the 1997 Hong Kong transition was scrupulously planned and executed: a half century of division, then full reintegration into China. The utterances offered by the departing colonisers — of course we shan't give you the right to settle in Britain and certainly not a British passport, but not to worry old chap: China will be a liberal democracy by then, don't you see? — close still another chapter of the corrosive incompetence of the British ruling class.

In a city-state gamed to support the interests of a wealthy elite, there appears to be no upper hand to be had for the exploited, low-wage workers whose only affordable housing option is a shared room scarcely bigger than a cage. It seems they must either put up with their lot, or trade their political rights for a significantly better quality of life in the modern and ever-wealthier Chinese cities all around them.

At the time of writing, protests are ongoing. But the clock is ticking toward 2047; and it will take a tenacious — and pragmatic — societal consensus if Hong Kong's singularity is to be preserved.

When the magnificent film Black Panther filled the screens with its exuberant fantasy in 2018, my social media overflowed with the declarations of connections who want to live in Wakanda. To which there's a short answer. You can. It's called the People's Republic of China.

Wakanda, for all its breathtaking technology, provided no glimmer of democracy. An absolute monarch was expected to rule benevolently, the power system had its own arcane rules of succession, but there was no denying the attraction of life therein. To be an ordinary Wakandan, in Ryan Coogler's film, was surely to lead a blessed life of comfort and privilege.

The feeling resonates in Shanghai. Although the broad levers of the economy are directed by the state, retail commerce is fierce and competitive: from street side stalls to dazzlingly fancy emporiums (the Gucci store on Nanjing Road is six storeys of luxury), the entire bounty of capitalist consumption is there to enjoy.

This government-framed economic structure is familiar to a Canadian. In my home province of Alberta, for instance, a government-owned Crown commercial enterprise and agency controls and licenses the operation of the gambling, liquor, and cannabis industries. None can legally sell liquor or cannabis at a retail outlet without explicit government approval, and the government controls and sets the wholesale price: guaranteeing itself hundreds of millions of dollars in profit, as it skims taxes and distribution fees from the types and volume of cannabis and alcohol preferred by consumers.

The Alberta government culls a far greater portion of gambling revenue than most "free market" casinos, and distributes them among not-for-profit organisations and charities that serve to enrich community life. Within the framework of government regulations and controls, business and competition is both encouraged and unfettered. And to ensure business can flourish, the government-owned bank that operates as a retail arm of the Alberta treasury, ATB Financial, has a mandate to support small business — to the extent that in 2016, the Government of Alberta made a special allocation of $3.2 billion designated to help entrepreneurs. Similarly, Chinese banks may be state-directed, but their lending choices are still governed by the economics of each enterprise's business case.

This framing of competition under the aegis of the state is broadly the Chinese government's approach not just to the economy, but to socio-political organisation. Government-directed companies own hotels and real estate, even setting up rival companies within the same retail sector. Competition makes life affordable, even for those who long for luxury clothing and scents: the metro stop of the Shanghai Science and Technology Museum is overflowing with tailors who will replicate Gucci and other designer fashions for a fraction of the price (and it's best not to probe too deeply into the provenance of cut-price scents).

On the two-kilometre-long pedestrian precinct of Nanjing Road, leading from the Shanghai Bund to People's Square, the glitzy facades give way to side streets crammed with little restaurants, shops selling T-shirts and handbags, neighbourhood barber shops and hardware stores. Malls abound everywhere.

Towards the People's Square end of Nanjing Road is the number one Food Hall, surely the most abundant food court of any mall I have ever seen, spanning four floors in a restored heritage building. From oversize lychees bursting with heady juice, to perfectly ripe guavas sliced and packed, one goes deeper to find every manner of Chinese and international cuisine on display.

Western consumer capitalism is everywhere. The lineup at the vast Apple store on Nanjing road is continuous, no matter what time of the day and night. Coming out of the western end of People's Square, you will come across the largest Starbucks coffee shop in the world: a three-story circular building branded the Starbucks Reserve Roastery.

Yet it would be quite wrong to think that materialism and its absolutist focus on consumption is the only driving ethos for Shanghainese — where educated young professionals earn more in a week than their parents earned in a year in the pre-1990 economy.

Down the road from Starbucks on Nanjing Road West, atop one of the busiest stations on the Shanghai metro, stands Jing'An, a sprawling Buddhist temple complex, an anachronism amidst a forest of sleek glass and stone skyscrapers. All its statues and images — including the lions and elephants adorning the sweeping lines of the rooftops — are newly gilded, lustrous even under a cloudy sky.

I decide to return one afternoon to the Jade Buddha temple, which I had last visited in 2016. The place is almost unrecognisable, in the span of only 20 months. In 2016, the 11th century jade carving of a reclining Lord Buddha had been in the upstairs hall of a vintage building within the temple. Now, it is in a grand pavilion of its own, the temple compound five times larger than it once was, with the addition of a restaurant, a residence for monks, and a tea house, within an easy walk of three major metro stations.

At the freshly gilded Jing'An, there is a commodious residence along one side of the compound for novices and ordained monks, and their abbots. At the shrine to the bodhisattva Guan Yin, the One who hears the cries of a bereft world (known in English as the Goddess of Mercy), there is a queue of three people waiting to speak with an elderly monk, while younger monks tend to the queries and needs of a steady stream of worshippers. When my turn comes to meet with the abbot, whose gentle demeanour carries a compelling resonance of the Dalai Lama, I fold my hands and bow my head. "Yindu?" he asks. I smile and bow again, and receive a blessing to awaken wisdom and compassion.

The spiritual vacuum left by the "godless" communism of the past has given way to not just the revival, but the restoration of traditional Chinese faith traditions of Buddhism and Taoism. Approaching the temple compounds, the smell of incense cuts through the traffic fumes, and the temples themselves are havens of serenity in the midst of urban rush. There is a price for all this: an admission fee that's a little more than the price of a hand-crafted reserve roast coffee, or the cost of a beer and bao in the mall.

One day over lunch near People's Square, I have a chat about culture and religion with an octogenarian survivor of the Cultural Revolution, whom I first met in Canada as part of my work as a strategic adviser to leaders. A trained engineer, he emerged from more than a decade of hard-labour confinement on a rural Chinese farm to become a senior financial official in the Shanghai municipal government. The state-owned enterprise for which he worked was largely responsible for the dazzling development of Pudong, an iconic global skyscape of 100-storey towers in what was once a mosquito swamp, across the river from the Bund. He has a home in Xintiandi, and takes satisfaction in the China that emerged, like a phoenix of myth, from the ashes of the Cultural Revolution.

"My wife and I, we attend services at a Christian church," he observes as we savour a classical Shanghainese dish, *hóngshāo ròu*, lacquered pork belly with quail eggs. Even in the senior ranks of the Communist Party, there is no contradiction between following religious practice and being a party member: so long as your faith does not challenge the primacy of the secular state. I ask about the Uygur Muslims in Xinjiang. "Ah, that is a different story," he says in his lightly accented English, polished through decades of diplomatic and business interactions with foreigners.

What worries the Chinese state is the prospect that among the tradition-bound Uygur, allegiance to Allah supplants loyalty to the state. And after murderous attacks by Uygur separatists in Beijing in 2013 and Kunming in 2014, China took the course of mass detention and "re-education" that many of us bred in liberal democracies regard as a form of conversion therapy, if not outright brainwashing.

The practice of separating children from parents, infusing the young with a belief in the virtue of the state and the "backwardness" of their parents' beliefs and traditions, is very much part and parcel of what is essentially cultural deracination. The physical and mental abuse imposed on those who resist being "re-educated" is, in effect, bludgeoning people into submission: the very practice Canada followed for decades in residential schools designed to take the "savage" out of every indigenous child.

China is fully determined to pitilessly eradicate any spark of Islamic militancy that would harness the power of religion to challenge the authority of the state. The ultimate aim is to "tame" Islam in China into a compliant cultural tradition, bringing the mosques into the same realm of state-sanctioned spiritual practice as the glittering Buddhist temples of China's metro cities.

And this is the trade-off: as long as you are going about your daily life within the bounds of civility, as long as you shun the belief that your version of god evokes a loyalty stronger than your allegiance to the nation-state, as long as you accept that the state knows what is best for the common good and refrain from publicly questioning or criticising its actions, life in big-city China is thoroughly Wakandan.

Shanghai is one of the safest and most alluring places anywhere on the planet for both citizens and visitors: its gleaming, modern subway system spans hundreds of kilometres of track. Its high-speed trains make the 2,100 kilometre trip to Guangzhou in six hours and fifty minutes. This is the convenience and comfort that is the flip side of the surveillance state. Your fingerprints are scanned after you arrive at the airport; a digital match is made between your fingerprints, your Chinese visa, and your visage mapped with facial-recognition software. Days later at the railway station, there's no need to produce your passport for ID, or even a print copy of the train ticket you booked online. You are in the system, and after a quick camera confirmation, here is your boarding pass. Shades of Wakanda, indeed.

Yet one step outside the law takes you down the rabbit hole: with no concept of the legal protections and judicial procedures found in the traditions of the Commonwealth and la Francophonie.

The tangible benefits of Shanghai's state-driven prosperity vigorously challenge the western model of democracy. The Chinese model forces us to take an honest look at the "all things are possible" world of merit we worship — even as we turn away from the reality of gross inequity in everyday life; and the entrenched privilege bestowed by wealth, socio-economic status, and ethnic origin.

I am sharing these glimpses on our journey because the Chinese model already is a preferred means of being and belonging for one sixth of humankind within China, and is envied by others beyond its borders. And even though we know that education affords the population the luxury of pursuing truth, I have to acknowledge that the truth as understood by Chinese citizens, within the Xi Jinping interpretation of socialism with Chinese characteristics, is the engine of a nationalistic pride that rightly affirms the emancipation of an ancient people from the ravages of colonialism.

I will take the warts-and-all democracy of Canada over the Chinese model, because I sincerely believe that the Canadian evolution of pluralism and democracy offers a kinder future for humankind and a better path to establishing the full enjoyment of human rights as a way of life.

In essence, the right to be human includes the agency, empowerment, and autonomy to state what I believe to be true; so long as my version of the truth does not wilfully incite violence nor hate. The right to speak freely and without hindrance, including the unfettered right and responsibility to challenge, with evidence, any "official" version of the truth put forward by governments and their agents.

Even so, I cannot deny the Chinese Communist Party's signal achievement in turning the chaos of the Cultural Revolution into the prosperous and stable life its citizens enjoy today. Canada is a small population in a large geography. China and India are the world's most populous countries: and the dozens of Indians I know who have travelled in China — including Indian software engineers and bankers who make up a Shanghai expat community thousands strong — look upon China's achievements with envy, particularly when it comes to safety and cleanliness.

China's blend of communism and capitalism is seamless, embodied in a shared ideology of "Xi Jinping Thought on Socialism with Chinese Characteristics for a New Era." It even has its own app, called Xuexi Zhongguo (learn, and make the nation great). Launched in January 2019, the app registered 100 million users within the first 100 days. You earn points by answering quizzes, tracking policy, reading Xi's speeches — and redeem them for discounts in restaurants, travel and retail stores.

In this iteration of socialism, if you look hard you can still find Chairman Mao's Little Red Book that was the polemical rallying point for the Cultural Revolution. I found it tucked away in a corner in the bookstore of the Communist Party museum in Shanghai, next to Walt Whitman's *Leaves of Grass*.

Chapter Thirteen

Greening our planet, greening our growth

Gianyar, Bali, Indonesia, February 1992

I am making my way up moss-laden steps to a hilltop shrine to the Mother Goddess, when boulders amid the foliage catch my eye: here are unmistakable patterns of waves, etched into the ancient sandstone tens of millions of years ago, now lodged on a steep hillside in the verdant landscape of central Bali.

A few minutes later I am atop Bukit (hill) Dharma Durga, making my way to the platform adorned with an 11th century sculpture of the Great Goddess slaying the buffalo-headed demon Mahisasura. Mahisasura represents ego and arrogance, in the Hindu telling. The ancient bas-relief depicts the serene goddess performing an act of liberation, to free us from the demon of egotism and pride, so that we may acquire the knowledge and wisdom that all living beings are part of the same animating force. To acknowledge the divinity that is both within us and surrounds us, the *schöner Götterfunken* (beautiful spark of divinity) sung in the European Union's anthem, Friedrich Schiller's *Ode to Joy*.

Looking out from the hilltop to the vast sprawl of greenery all around, I marvel at how humans and nature so readily mingle in Bali. I have been on this island for weeks now, visiting villages, walking through forests, along the dikes of terraced rice paddies where the only sound is the gurgle of water, the buzz of insects, the tangled melodies of birdsong.

These rambles bring me to a sense of peace after a grief that shook the foundations of my being: Mita and I lost a son only fifteen weeks after we conceived him, just days before I was to depart for Indonesia on a media fellowship awarded by the Asia-Pacific Foundation of Canada. The brother our four-year-old daughter Silpi will never know.

I descend a few steps from the platform atop Bukit Dharma Durga and find a place to sit at the foot of the shrine; my meditation occasionally interrupted by the footfalls of pilgrims passing me in silence, with baskets laden with offerings of flowers and fruit and little rice cakes. I sense the stirring of breeze: able by now to distinguish the sound of winds through palm fronds, leafy foliage, and banana groves. I feel the bonds of ego slip away, the sorrow lifts from me, a physical sensation of liberation, as an entirely unsolicited clarity enters my soul: this is how a human life unfolds, with as much grief as joy, to be borne with humility and grace. It is an illumination that finally dispels all illusion that we are masters of our own destiny; that we can shape or bend our world to our will.

My weeks in Indonesia, especially Bali, have brought me to a humbling belief: we are all cohabitants of nature's bounty; and our modern human arrogance blinds us to the richness and value of a life lived in harmony with the natural world. In Indonesia itself, the rural life woven deep into the country's traditions and culture carries coexistence with the natural world as its animating force.

This connection to the earth and its gifts, however, has not stopped human hubris from building a skyscraper-laden city like Jakarta on a sea-level floodplain, where scholars already are warning of rising sea levels as the planet warms in human-abetted climate change.

And I wonder whether we will ever be able to understand the allegory of the goddess slaying the demon ego, and apply this wisdom, to give us humility in accepting our duty of stewardship to the environment bequeathed to us by hundreds of generations of our ancestors.

Edmonton, Canada, 15 March 2019

I am following an extraordinary event unfolding the world over, startling evidence of the difference that one ordinary person can make in the world.

On the Ides of March, the schoolchildren of the world are teaching their adult "guardians" a lesson.

All across the world, in nearly 100 countries, children are leaving their classrooms to join a "strike", demanding meaningful action to address catastrophic climate change.

Following reports and videos as the protest spreads, I am seeing unfold before me a 2019 version of the *satyagraha* Gandhi once led.

Within six months, what began as a solitary act of silent protest by a reserved and plain-spoken Swedish child has become a global movement. It is inspired by Greta Thunberg, aged fifteen, who is speaking today at a rally in Stockholm — one of tens of thousands of students in some two thousand gatherings in communities spanning the globe.

"We have only been born into this world, we are going to have to live with this crisis our whole lives. So will our children and grandchildren and coming generations," Thunberg says. "We are not going to accept this. We are striking because we want a future and we are going to carry on."

Like Autumn Peltier, the Canadian teenager who told the United Nations to give water personhood to preserve Mother Earth's most vital force, the children are leading where adults dare not venture in responding to climate change. All the demonstrations have been organised using social media. In Singapore, with its strictures against public assembly, the rally is a virtual one, held in real time on social media platforms.

And as it has since Greta's movement began, the movement is fuelled by a simple act of defying authority: skipping school on Fridays to demand action on climate change.

Since Greta's act of civil disobedience began 30 weeks ago, an ever-increasing movement of students have been skipping school on Fridays to spur action. The March 15 rallies are the biggest global event yet, timed to coincide with the end of the five-day United Nations Environmental Assembly in Nairobi.

And well-meaning though the summit was, you can see why the young are frustrated. The final communique was a masterful exercise in recognising the obvious, and promising in elegant diplomatic language to, uh, do, er, something, you know?

The dead giveaway is that these are non-binding resolutions.

Greta's generation understands far better than its elders what they face. "Climate change is worse than Voldemort," declared one rally poster in Wellington, New Zealand. The trouble is that many of the adults who run the world have no idea what that means.

The scientists, however, do. The Intergovernmental Panel on Climate Change (IPCC) is the United Nations body for assessing the science related to climate change. In its October 2018 status report, it amplified the conclusions and warnings of previous ones.

To put it in plain language, we have between two to three decades — at which point Greta and her peers will have barely reached middle age — to achieve net zero emissions of carbon dioxide before the planet becomes unsustainable for human life as we know it.

The tragedy is that we've known so for decades.

The intensity of climate change has become ever more prominent since that momentous day in November 1989, when the British Prime Minister of the day, Margaret Thatcher, aroused the United Nations with an urgent call for action to avert climate catastrophe.

"What we are now doing to the world, by degrading the land surfaces, by polluting the waters and by adding greenhouse gases to the air at an unprecedented rate—all this is new in the experience of the earth. It is mankind and his activities which are changing the environment of our planet in damaging and dangerous ways."

Margaret Thatcher's ardent conservatism was founded upon the word "conserve": proper preservation and stewardship of all we have and are, tending our patrimony for the benefit of generations yet to come. And as the only scientist among the world leaders of the day—she read chemistry at Somerville College, Oxford, and worked as a research scientist before turning to law and thence politics — she was keenly aware of the perils of anthropogenic climate change.

Since her warning, carbon emissions have continued to grow well beyond the 1990 emission levels that were set as an international benchmark. Lady Thatcher's remarks were both precise and eloquent in defining the challenge our elected leaders face.

> We must use science to cast a light ahead, so that we can move step by step in the right direction. But as well as the science, we need to get the economics right. That means first we must have continued economic growth in order to generate the wealth required to pay for the protection of the environment. But it must be growth which does not plunder the planet today and leave our children to deal with the consequences tomorrow.

Indeed, the moral imperative to meaningfully address climate change for the sake of the world's most vulnerable gained new prominence on June 18, 2015. On that day the Argentine cleric

Jorge Mario Bergoglio, whom Roman Catholics revere as Pope Francis, publicly released an encyclical entitled *Laudato Si,* calling for a profound transformation in human behaviour to become humble stewards of our environment.

The pope noted the significant challenge facing the Paris talks, writing that: "International negotiations cannot make significant progress due to positions taken by countries which place their national interests above the global common good."

Proof of the pope's point is the absolute dominance of the military-industrial complex, which even leaders of great rationality like Barack Obama and Emmanuel Macron cannot tame in their quest to abet the common good. That, and the reluctance to see both the environment and economy as two facets of the same coin: that sustainable economic growth, by definition, must mitigate the ecological damage that is the inevitable result of any profitable enterprise.

Pope Francis, whom 1.2 billion Catholics believe to be the Vicar of Christ on Earth, unwaveringly declared that ecological stewardship and social justice are one and the same:

> The urgent challenge to protect our common home includes a concern to bring the whole human family together to seek a sustainable and integral development, for we know that things can change. The Creator does not abandon us; he never forsakes his loving plan or repents of having created us. Humanity still has the ability to work together in building our common home. Here I want to recognise, encourage and thank all those striving in countless ways to guarantee the protection of the home which we share. Particular appreciation is owed to those

who tirelessly seek to resolve the tragic effects of environmental degradation on the lives of the world's poorest. Young people demand change. They wonder how anyone can claim to be building a better future without thinking of the environmental crisis and the sufferings of the excluded.

The pope's perspective was amply confirmed by international scientific consensus. As United Nations Secretary General Ban Ki-Moon noted in response:

> The secretary-general welcomes the papal encyclical released today by His Holiness Pope Francis which highlights that climate change is one of the principal challenges facing humanity, and that it is a moral issue requiring respectful dialogue with all parts of society. The secretary-general notes the encyclical's findings that there is "a very solid scientific consensus" showing significant warming of the climate system and that most global warming in recent decades is "mainly a result of human activity."

Indeed, what was clear to the British prime minister of 1989 has repeatedly been confirmed by international scientific consensus.

The best we can hope is to moderate the effects of climate change.

The predecessor to the October 2018 report, the November 2014 synthesis report of the IPCC also cast the necessity of global action as a moral imperative, evoking issues of social justice and the disproportionate effect of climate change on the poorest and most marginalised populations of the world.

As then-IPCC Chair Rajendra Pachauri noted in the public announcement of his panel's report, "Many of those most vulnerable to climate change have contributed and contribute little to greenhouse gas emissions. Addressing climate change will not be possible if individual agents advance their own interests independently; it can only be achieved through cooperative responses, including international cooperation."

Today's consumer society— with scant regard for the consequences of consumption on our natural heritage — has come to define "conservative" as one who stands for the reckless worship of pecuniary profit, rejecting any restraints or inhibitions on the pursuit of material gain.

The attitude of "anything goes" in the name of commercial success is the impelling force behind the degradation of the environment, and its profound effect on the climate of the biosphere we share.

In the three decades since Lady Thatcher's clarion warning, we have spent far too much time arguing over whether human activity is driving climate change, all the while producing and consuming fossil fuels at a rate that continues to imperil the biosphere.

Deniers of science, including the current president of the United States, continue to ignore the evidence staring them in the face, actively unravel the meagre protection and mitigation already established, and insist that the answer to tomorrow lies in perfecting yesterday.

We have seen well-meaning initiatives like the toothless Kyoto Accord, which had no penalties for countries that didn't meet their emission goals. We tried to create carbon offsets so heavily polluting countries could buy credits from non-polluting ones.

It really hasn't made a dent in the emissions that fuel our consumer lifestyle. Until and unless we have sustained, long-term, investments of billions of dollars per annum in alternative and renewable energy sources, we will not be able to move the needle on the consumption of fossil fuels. Even if we do make that investment, the best we can hope is to moderate the effects of climate change.

As Greta and the hundreds of thousands of students protesting with her on 15 March 2019 demanded, the adults in power must seriously answer: How will we meet the challenge of coping with catastrophic climate change?

Yet to be answered with any comprehensive or mandatory strategy, this is the existential question of our age. We have known since the first decade of this millennium that climate change can't be stopped or prevented. The mind must shift to adaptation and mitigation.

For Greta Thunberg's generation, the adult leadership of the world has been in a dither her entire life, with high-sounding resolutions that lack teeth. To the children who are just now learning what the adults have done to further the destruction of their future, the political insistence on maintaining the status quo is not only unthinkable, but immoral. As Thunberg, now 16, told the European Parliament in April 2019:

> If our house was falling apart leaders wouldn't go on like you do today. You would change almost every part of your behaviour. As you do in an emergency…

If our house was falling apart the media wouldn't be writing about anything else. The ongoing climate and ecological crises would make up all the headlines.

If our house was falling apart you wouldn't say you have the situation under control and place the future living conditions for all living species in the hands of inventions that are yet to be invented.

And you would not spend all your time as politicians arguing over taxes and Brexit.

If the walls of our house truly came tumbling down, surely you would set your differences aside and start cooperating.

Central to the youth climate strike movement is the demand that those with power wield that power responsibly — and ironically, it is the children who feel they must reprimand the adults, impelling them to grow up and do what is necessary.

In Greta Thunberg's black-and-white thinking (a gift, as she identifies it, of her existence on the autism spectrum), it is inconceivable that the scientific solutions exist, but the political will to implement them does not. As she reminded EU politicians in her address, the month before elections for the European parliament:

When I tell politicians to act now the most common answer is that they can't do anything drastic, as that would be too unpopular among voters.

And they are right of course. Since most people are not even aware of why those changes are required. Which is why I keep telling you to unite behind the science — make the best available science the heart of politics and democracy.

The EU elections are coming up soon. And many of us who will be affected the most by the crisis , people like me, are not able to vote. Nor are we in a position to shape the decisions of business, politics, engineering, media, education or science. Because the time it takes to educate ourselves to do that simply no longer exists.

And that is why millions of children are taking it to the streets, school striking for the climate to create attention for the climate crisis.

You need to listen to us. We who cannot vote. You need to vote for us, for your children and grandchildren.

What you are doing now can soon no longer be undone.

In this election you vote for the future living conditions of humankind.

And though the politics needed do not exist today, some alternatives are certainly less worse than others. And I have read in newspapers that some parties do not even want me standing here today because they so desperately want to avoid talking about climate breakdown.

Our house is falling apart.

The future — as well as all we have achieved in the past — is literally in your hands now.

But it is not too late to act.

It will take a far-reaching vision. It will take courage. It will take a fierce determination to act now to lay the foundations when we do not know all of the details about how to shape the ceiling. In short, it will require "cathedral thinking".

I ask you to please wake up and make the required changes possible.

To do your best is no longer good enough.
We must do the seemingly impossible.

In 2002, the year before Greta was born, I was in a car on the freezing streets of Edmonton, traveling to the airport on my way to a human rights meeting in Vienna. My mobile phone rang. It was the Alberta justice minister, David Hancock.

"What did you say to the Premier last night?"

"Why?"

"He said you told him how to get around the Kyoto Accord?"

I suppose I had. Ralph Klein, a populist chief minister with stupendous political skills and a short attention span, had been venting as the two of us dined at a trendy Asian fusion restaurant, Wild Tangerine.

He was beside himself about the Kyoto Protocol on climate change and how the federal government had signed on to it without the province of Alberta's consent. His ministers and aides had told him this spelled catastrophe for Alberta, because it demanded fundamental changes to society and economy in a very short time.

Ralph and I were battle-scarred adversaries who had become friends with the passage of time. "Every time I opened the paper, you were taking a strip off my arse," he groused about my editorials (to which I felt compelled to respond that such a large derriere made an easier target, an observation that summoned his booming laughter). But now, he turned to me to get "the straight goods" on big issues.

So I told Hancock what I had told Klein: the penalty for violating the Kyoto Protocol was to be given more time to meet its targets... and thus it has been, with every international protocol, accord, and declaration ever since.

Klein introduced the first carbon tax in Canada, a \$15 per tonne levy on heavy emitters — years before carbon taxation became recognised (as affirmed by the 2018 Nobel Memorial Prize in Economic Sciences) as the most sustainable way to change the behaviour that drives planet-imperilling carbon dioxide emissions.

It has been far too much to expect, during Greta's entire life, that mandatory carbon pricing would become a universal measure to fund adaptation and mitigation.

And none can say we didn't know about the urgency and the immensity of the crisis we have unleashed.

Unless we make serious, large-scale and sustained investments to develop enough quantities of alternative energies to replace fossil fuels, we are destined to remain in the hydrocarbon age.

And even the most serious effort for alternatives will take decades before it can meet global energy demand.

In the face of the last three IPCC reports, especially the 2018 assessment, it is clear that the effort to stop climate change, meager and ineffectual though it was, is comprehensively lost. We are done.

Now all we can do is prevent the worst. The question we face, the central question of Us, is how?

It begins with political will.

In the days before Mr. Ban convened world leaders on Sept. 23, 2014 to take meaningful action on climate change, the world witnessed an extraordinary spectacle: Mr. Ban himself joined the cadre of protesters outside the UN headquarters in New York. Seldom does one see the top elected official in the world Parliament joining, in person, a protest against the world's inaction against the existential peril of our time.

The New York meeting in September 2014 was meant to focus attention on the impending release of the Intergovernmental Panel on Climate Change (IPCC), heralded as the most comprehensive scientific consensus on anthropogenic climate change and its consequences for the biosphere.

Released on 2 November 2014, the fifth IPCC assessment starkly affirmed that it is far too late to "stop" climate change — even if "stopping" such change were within the capacity of humans. Indeed, even if all fossil fuel use were to stop now, the greenhouse gases already extant in the atmosphere from human activity over the last 150 years will continue to bring rapid transformation in the health of the biosphere.

The IPCC's synthesis reports for policymakers from the 2014 and 2018 assessments make it abundantly clear that the best chance of taking meaningful preventive action to stop climate change is long behind us.

That's why Mr. Ban's participation in the protest was more than a mere show of solidarity and sympathy with the citizens demanding the world leaders do something. It was also an acknowledgment that the inaction of global leadership is far out of step with citizen expectations. By the time Mr. Ban took to the streets, a full quarter century had passed since a major world leader raised the alarm about climate change from the podium of the UN General Assembly.

As the UN prepared to convene what was billed as a definitive summit on addressing climate change, in Paris towards the end of 2015, there were some signs of urgency afoot in the world. The U.S. and China, by far the leading carbon emitters, announced an accord in November 2014 to coordinate significant action on climate change.

Closer analysis revealed that the ambitious agenda in fact only reaffirmed earlier commitments by each nation to take meaningful action. Moreover, the actions were foreseen to take effect a decade hence, by which time, going by the scientific consensus, the planet will be in even greater peril.

Thus there is an urgent need for both adaptation to a changing climate, and robust efforts at mitigation. The IPCC tells us in effect that we cannot prevent catastrophic climate change because we cannot turn back the tide of industrial history.

The discussion was well framed following the fourth assessment report of the IPCC in a scientific gathering convened in Copenhagen in 2009. More than 2,500 scientists involved in the IPCC deliberations issued a report that called for both mitigation and adaptation.

The 11 universities that convened the Copenhagen Climate Congress hoped to provide a comprehensive picture of the status of world climate science. The peer-reviewed synthesis report from the conference laid out the peril in plain language:

> Past societies have reacted when they understood that their own activities were causing deleterious environmental change by controlling or modifying the offending activities. The scientific evidence has now become overwhelming that human activities, especially the combustion of fossil fuels, are influencing the climate in ways that threaten the well-being and continued development of human society. If humanity is to learn from history and to limit these threats, the time has come for stronger control of the human activities that are changing the fundamental conditions for life on Earth.

It offered an excellent contribution in defining the distinction between adaptation and mitigation:

> Any societal response to human caused climate change should be a combination of **mitigation**, whereby active measures are taken to reduce or change the human activities that are driving climate change, and **adaptation**, whereby society in-

creases its capacity to cope with the impacts of climate change, so far as possible.

Mitigation and adaptation are closely related as response strategies. Adaptation is essential, as even a massive mitigation effort initiated today would be unable to eliminate the impacts of the climate change that are already occurring and those to which society is committed in the future owing to the inertia in the climate. At the other extreme, if no mitigation is initiated and human caused climate change is allowed to continue unabated, the risk of the most dangerous or catastrophic impacts associated with a global warming of several degrees is large. Even the wealthiest of societies, with the best and most well-resourced adaptation activities, would probably not be able to completely adapt to such levels of climate change. This simple reality underscores the fact that effective climate policies should combine both adaptation measures and mitigation activities.

Well-intentioned though the Paris talks were, it turned out that comprehensive international agreements were too ambitious: they require so many compromises, which rob them of effectiveness. The Paris Accord offered nothing but moral suasion to reduce greenhouse gases. The penalty for failing to achieve one's targets, once again, was to be given more time to do so.

It calls to mind the dark prophecy Yeats proclaimed in *The Second Coming*:

> *Turning and turning in the widening gyre*
> *The falcon cannot hear the falconer;*
> *Things fall apart; the centre cannot hold;*
> *Mere anarchy is loosed upon the world,*

The blood-dimmed tide is loosed, and everywhere
The ceremony of innocence is drowned;
The best lack all conviction, while the worst
Are full of passionate intensity.

Which is why the movement Greta Thunberg inspired has hundreds of thousands of students across the world, out of their classes and in the streets on this March day.

Edmonton, Canada, May 2019

Fixated on the screen of my BlackBerry KeyOne, I scroll through WhatsApp every few seconds, looking for any updates or news of my sprawling extended family in Odisha. The dozens of cousins from my mother's side of the family (she had more than 40 first cousins, and their descendants are gathered in a WhatsApp group named after the ancestral village, Moroda) are in the path of Fani, a devastating cyclonic storm that has just made landfall. Two decades earlier, one of these "super cyclones" completely ravaged Odisha, leaving thousands dead, and widespread destruction in its wake. In the age of climate change, cyclonic storms are the "new normal" along the coast of the Bay of Bengal.

News trickles out bit by bit. One cousin's rooftop deck was blown away. Others lost trees and gardens galore. Some lost electricity; many lost mobile phone contact. Water was out for days. The devastation from 200 km/h winds that howled for hours was absolute. Still, very few people lost their lives.

The difference, this time, is adaptation. The Odisha government organised a mass evacuation of more than one million people as Fani began to take shape, shooting out messages by every available medium — nearly every Indian now has a cellphone — getting people to shelters where plenty of hot food, water, and safety awaited. Since the cyclone previous, every village, every neighbourhood, had designated cyclone shelters. In village dwellings traditionally constructed of rammed-earth and thatch, many homes had been rebuilt with at least one solid concrete room that could withstand cyclone winds. And within weeks, that same WhatsApp feed filled with images of clean-up, rebuilding, and restoration.

This is a compelling example of how past experience led a forewarned and competent government to make the changes necessary to adapt to the inevitable; and the immense cooperation and collaboration required between citizens and the several levels of government that served them in order to manage a natural catastrophe, which had been far more devastating when it struck a generation before.

St. Augustine, Trinidad, October 2013

I am sharing a dinner table with Sir Shridath Ramphal, who served the Commonwealth for 15 years as Secretary General. We are talking about practical measures to address climate change: and more specifically, a role for the Commonwealth, the group of 53 one-time British colonies that spans from large energy producers to island nations most threatened by rising sea levels. Over lemon chicken and spicy noodles at a Chinese restaurant in Trinidad, at a gathering convened by my friend Andy Knight, Sir Shridath displays the amazing agility of mind that remains undiminished at age 85.

We recall the Commonwealth's shining hour: leading the emancipation of South Africa, in which then-Prime Minister Brian Mulroney and Foreign Minister Joe Clark led a principled and determined Canadian advocacy within the Commonwealth and beyond.

The dinner conversation bolsters my conviction that the Commonwealth can indeed be a catalyst for finding an effective international approach to dealing with climate change.

The key question is how do we move to a mindset of adaptation and mitigation? I outlined a proposal for a Commonwealth Climate Fund — as an alternative to the diluted and toothless international compromises like the Kyoto Accord and the Paris Accord, which tried to unite the whole world to common purpose. If it can be made to work within the Commonwealth, it could prove to be a scalable model of success.

The rationale driving this proposal is that the greening of fossil fuel production and the development of renewable and alternative energy should occur simultaneously, and even in cooperation and harmony. Already, it is becoming clear that fossil fuel energy companies have the capital and the resources necessary to pursue alternatives: whether this is "green washing" or a serious commitment remains to be seen, but there is little doubt about the capacity.

A significant question for democratic nations, especially energy producers, is this: what is the moral justification for the production and consumption of fossil fuels? In Alberta and Canada's case, the least bad answer is to take the income generated by fossil fuel extraction, and use it to pay for green initiatives to further the goals of adaptation and mitigation.

As owners and stewards of the largest fossil fuel deposit anywhere, Canadians cannot choose the option of leaving our prime resource in the ground. Idealism aside, this is the energy source to which the world is addicted, and its proper control and development is all we can aspire to.

And in the potential we foresee in transition and evolution towards non-carbon energy—wind, solar, hydro, tidal, biofuel, biomass, even nuclear—the either/or mentality isn't particularly helpful. Fossil fuels and "alternative" energy should be complementary, not at odds.

The value of a Commonwealth Climate Fund is that one Commonwealth country, Canada, would be the principal contributor to this production-based fund. The Canadian province of Alberta contains the single largest hydrocarbon deposit in the world: the Alberta Oil Sands.

Thus a Canadian-led fund can establish both the regulatory framework and the public resources necessary to ensuring that greener oil sands production and non-fossil-fuel energy sources can evolve as expeditiously as possible.

Doing so will require sustained, long-term, investments of billions of dollars per annum in alternative and renewable energy sources, to offer a workable alternative to the consumption of fossil fuels.

This is all good reason to leverage the wealth of the Alberta oil sands — once again, the single largest hydrocarbon deposit on the planet, containing some 1.8 trillion barrels of discovered oil in place. Moreover, Alberta is home to more than half the oil reserves available for open free-market investment, in contrast to government-controlled oil resources elsewhere.

In effect, the moral justification of developing the oil sands, while doing so as sustainably as possible, is that we use the wealth generated by them to fund the transition to a more sustainable future for the planet.

What could such a fund look like, and how might it work? The Commonwealth Climate Fund (CCF) would be accessible to all Commonwealth member countries. It would take the lead in funding clean tech, green tech, and climate change adaptation and mitigation. It could be set up as an arm's length entity within the aegis of the Commonwealth Secretariat: the permanent civil service which serves the collective and consensual governance of Commonwealth affairs — much as the UN Secretariat serves the United Nations.

We will need robust, large-scale revenue in order to make a real difference.

Here are the basics as to how we might begin:

Investments and projects should be funded by taxing revenue from fossil fuel extraction, defined as BoE (barrel of oil equivalent). BoE would apply to the production of oil, natural gas, and coal production in all Commonwealth countries.

The funding mechanism would be a Commonwealth Climate Tax of $2 per BoE, a "severance tax" levied on all greenhouse gas-emitting resource extraction within Commonwealth countries, at the moment the resource is severed from the state of nature.

These revenues would flow to the CCF within the Commonwealth Secretariat. Location within the Commonwealth Secretariat would assure transparency, accountability, honesty and integrity.

The idea of a severance tax was proposed in some detail by Alberta's Royalty Review panel created by Premier Ed Stelmach. Chair William J. (Bill) Hunter, economist Andre Plourde (now a professor at Carleton University) and the gifted entrepreneur Evan Chrapko brought considerable passion and insight in advancing the idea. And even though it died in the political climate of the time, it is certainly worth reviving now.

The severance tax would in effect be implemented as the Commonwealth Climate Tax (CCT) applied to the gross value of any natural resource, measured by the market price of the resource at the first "point of sale" upon severance.

There would be fiscal levers: the rate would need to be in the single digits, so that it does not deter investment and innovation.

Moreover, it could vary by the type of resource severed, so that it is sensitive to the particular costs and challenges of a given form of natural resource production.

It could provide a predictable and strong stream of revenue to pay for a clean-energy economy, accelerate the development of low-carbon industries, and greatly increase investment in renewables and alternatives.

A severance tax would address the day when emissions captured from smokestacks, would provide a commercial source of CO_2 to be digested by algae, which would then be harvested for processing biofuels, nutritional supplements (algae are a rich source of Omega-3 fatty acids), and myriad commercial applications.

Thus, the combination of greener fossil fuel production and alternative energies would be a complementary and simultaneous development. Because it is collected upon severance, the extractor can absorb it, diffuse it over the value chain, or charge directly to the end user.

Moreover, unlike the "license to pollute" hazard of cap-and-trade, it would ensure the money provides a tangible, direct link between resource revenues and a green economy.

The weakness is that the CCT idea does not really address consumer demand for fossil fuels. While the severance tax costs presumably are passed on to the consumer, there is no direct motivation to consume less. Thus it is only one part of the solution.

We will need leadership of the type that Sir Shridath and his contemporaries embodied in his day and age: leaders across the Commonwealth who will be animated and engaged by the planetary challenge.

There are several good reasons why the Commonwealth is a good platform, where one could find success:

- The Commonwealth has about 232 billion barrels or about 17 per cent of the world's proven oil reserves, the bulk of them in the Canadian oil sands. Indeed, Canada has the world's third largest reserves, behind Venezuela and Saudi Arabia.

- Oil and gas are key economic factors in 17 Commonwealth countries.

- Most Commonwealth countries produce carbon fuels, including hydrocarbons, coal and wood.

- The Commonwealth can offer a moral justification for the production and consumption of fossil fuels, as presented previously: using the wealth and income they generate to fund the transition to a greener and more sustainable future.

- At today's prices, the Commonwealth has $23 trillion worth of oil wealth alone. Gas and coal, measured in barrels of oil equivalent, amount to trillions more.

- The Commonwealth can be a Clean Energy Model for the World.

- Canada, which produces the most oil in the Commonwealth, can and should be a leader in this moral imperative.

- Canada can set the example within itself, and invite cooperation and collaboration to extend the clean energy model to the entire Commonwealth.

The CCT would be a condition of resource extraction levied by every Commonwealth government on production. This means the largest payers into the fund would be the largest producers.

In essence, with the predictable and strong stream of revenue produced by the tax, the CCF will be able to:

- Pay for a clean-energy economy

- Accelerate the development of low-carbon industries

- Greatly increase investment in renewable and alternative energies

- Build a **carbohydrate economy** to complement the **hydrocarbon economy** (using starches and sugars in crops and forests)

- Create a **zero-waste economy** in which every product and byproduct is processed to optimal value

- Use **biomass** to produce electricity; synthesise gas; provide liquid and solid fuels.

- Use **agriculture** and **wood fibre** to make insulation, textiles, building products, industrial papers, composite materials (even for auto parts), polymers, binders, fragrances, food wraps.

The Commonwealth Climate Fund can be a robust tool for societal development, by accelerating the development of abundant, low-carbon sources of energy with government-funded resources.

These resources can be used to enhance civil society building blocks such as wellness, literacy, connectivity, community, diversity, inclusion and sustainability.

These are a few beginning ideas to spark the conversation, as you find your path along the journey of *Us*.

Yet we are at a place in the Spring of 2019 where — as Greta and her generation assert — we are consumed with what Martin Luther King called "the fierce urgency of now."

Now, as in King's time, the question is one of civil rights and human rights: doing what we can to make the world sustainable for Greta's generation and their descendants. Giving our future generations the full latitude to live a meaningful life of dignity and purpose: the right to be human.

As former U.S. President Barack Obama — himself the beneficiary of the United States movement for civil rights — observed, there are too many leaders who pay lip service to Nelson Mandela's principles, but don't walk the walk.

If anything, the life and example of Gandhi, King and Mandela should inspire us to build the alliances we need to address the climate catastrophe. Whether it is massive geo-engineering to save low lying populations like the Maldives, or Bangladesh's river deltas; or investment in technologies to harvest large quantities of carbon dioxide from the atmosphere, our ability to adapt is only limited by our imagination and our willpower.

The same united effort that led to the Commonwealth persisting in the quest for South African liberation can and should guide us in convening the Commonwealth to address climate change and a greener energy future.

If it succeeds, we will have gone a good distance towards the inclusive and sustainable human society Mandela envisioned.

And perhaps we will find credible answers and durable measures of adaptation and mitigation, that Greta and her generation so stirringly demanded on 15 March 2019.

Remember: even a $2 severance tax on the hydrocarbon resources — at least 100 million barrels of oil equivalent a day — means at least $200 million a day to commit to coping with climate change. That's at least $73 billion a year from oil alone. It's not enough, but it's a good start. A catalyst, to accelerate our transition to a carbon-neutral economy. To abet all the other investment made by companies and countries, to fund the shift towards a sustainable future for our planet.

This is the minimum "do something" climate protesters can champion. A "save the planet" tax of two dollars a barrel.

Echoing Gandhi, Greta has launched the *satyagraha* of our time. Now, we adults must take full measure of the damage we have wrought, and ensure there will in fact be a future for the children.

Chapter Fourteen

Common good, common wealth

Edmonton, Canada, May 2011

"It's a good day for the Infuriator," says my friend David Evans, calling from the Edmonton Journal newsroom that was my home for nearly a quarter century. "I just can't believe they're going to get away with it."

The Infuriator is our homage to M, the head of Britain's clandestine intelligence service in Ian Fleming's James Bond novels: a cheap red wine — Algerian, in M's preference — the spy chief would quaff while fuming about a particularly egregious breach of the human condition.

Within minutes, cheap red duly poured at our habitual bistro where the staff know to leave us in discreet privacy, David is venting about the scoundrels who brought the world to the brink of economic ruin — and U.S. President Barack Obama's reluctance to send any of the perpetrators to criminal prosecution that would lead to imprisonment.

It is four months since the U.S. government's review commission came to its devastating conclusion:

> We conclude this financial crisis was avoidable. The crisis was the result of human action and inaction, not of Mother Nature or computer models gone haywire. The captains of finance and the public stewards of our financial system ignored warnings and failed to question, understand, and manage evolving risks within a system essential to the well-being of the American public. Theirs was a big miss, not a stumble. While the business cycle cannot be repealed, a crisis of this magnitude need not have occurred. To paraphrase Shakespeare, the fault lies not in the stars, but in us. Despite the expressed view of many on Wall Street and in Washington that the crisis could not have been foreseen or avoided, there were warning signs. The tragedy was that they were ignored or discounted. There was an explosion in risky subprime lending and securitization, an unsustainable rise in housing prices, widespread reports of egregious and predatory lending practices, dramatic increases in household mortgage debt, and exponential growth in financial firms' trading activities, unregulated derivatives, and short-term "repo" lending markets, among many other red flags. Yet there was pervasive permissiveness; little meaningful action was taken to quell the threats in a timely manner.

And now, it was abundantly clear that none of these perpetrators would face prosecution.

"I'm telling you, socialism is going to come storming back," David said after a couple of quaffs had served their purpose. "People aren't going to stand for this."

David is my successor on the newspaper's editorial board; a friend of striking integrity, infused with a moral clarity that is inspirational.

David and I were born baby boomers, children of the era that lived in dread of nuclear war, taught in school drills to take shelter under our desks in the event of a nuclear explosion! We were taught to loathe and fear communism as the implacable foe: for it was the brutality of Stalin and the chaos of China during the Great Proletarian Cultural Revolution that dominated the thinking of the day in our ingrained hostility towards the communist world.

Indeed, any morsel of "seeing it from their perspective" I might have entertained about Stalin and Stalinism, once I gained an adult's perspective and came to apply critical thinking and reasoning to the "truths" imbibed in childhood, was completely dispelled by the terrifying and crystalline emotion of Anna Akhmatova's *Requiem*. In Stanley Kunitz and Max Hayward's translation:

> *That was a time when only the dead*
> *could smile, delivered from their wars,*
> *and the sign, the soul, of Leningrad*
> *dangled outside its prison-house;*
> *and the regiments of the condemned,*
> *herded in the railroad-yards,*
> *shrank from the engine's whistle-song*
> *whose burden went, "Away, pariahs!"*
> *The stars of death stood over us.*
> *And Russia, guiltless, beloved, writhed*
> *under the crunch of bloodstained boots,*
> *under the wheels of Black Marias.*

...

I have learned how faces fall to bone,
how under the eyelids terror lurks
how suffering inscribes on cheeks
the hard lines of its cuneiform texts,
how glossy black or ash-fair locks
turn overnight to tarnished silver,
how smiles fade on submissive lips,
and fear quavers in a dry titter.
And I pray not for myself alone...
for all who stood outside the jail,
in bitter cold or summer's blaze,
with me under that blind red wall.

David, a scholar of Russia and its history, was similarly clear-eyed in his revulsion.

We were bred to believe that democracy, for all its flaws, was the only system of governance worth pursuing. That the combination of democratic governance and a capitalist market economy were the ideal goals of humankind.

Yet the rapacious greed of the money barons who nearly brought the world to its knees — who, it is becoming ever clearer, will face no meaningful consequences — sickens us.

Our old myths can no longer be sustained. China proves, month by month, that capitalism in fact works best in the confines of an authoritarian state. Decisions are taken for what the rulers deem to be the common good; the awesome wealth generating force of capitalism is harnessed and deployed to the collective benefit of society while also leaving a substantial amount in individual hands — as witnessed by the personal fortunes of the mega billionaires Ma Yun (Jack Ma) and Ma Huateng (Pony Ma), who remain dedicated members of the Communist Party of China even while amassing private wealth in creating the wildly popular digital platforms Alibaba and WeChat. We have observed with keen interest as Russia's embrace of robber-baron capitalism utterly traduces the ideals with which Lenin, Trotsky and Zinoviev guided post-revolutionary Russia from 1917 to 1925.

The 2008 global financial crisis, driven by a level of venality that seems beyond the understanding of any moral and ethical person, is almost an incitement to embrace communism, in David's view.

"I truly believe this is the end of capitalist society," says David. "It may be a dead man walking for a couple of decades, but believe me, there's no comeback. Just wait and see, people are going to start rising up and take to the streets if there's no consequence for these scoundrels."

Four months later, David's prediction will begin to come true. On 17 September 2011, a group of protesters move into Zuccotti Park in New York's financial district: launching what they called a campaign to Occupy Wall Street. Within weeks, the Occupy movement will become global, purporting to represent 99 per cent of humankind arrayed against the one per-cent who own half the world's wealth. In cities the world over — Edmonton protesters brave chilly winds to set up a tent encampment on a vacant patch of grass in the heart of the city — people will occupy business districts to demand action against inequality.

David lived to see his perspective catch fire. He raptly followed Bernie Sanders' insurgent campaign as a "democratic socialist" for the Democratic Party nomination for the United States presidency in 2016.

He shared my dismay when the party establishment rallied behind Hillary Clinton and pushed Sanders aside, only to lose the presidency to a flailing and self-obsessed New York blowhard who tapped into the seething populism rallied by Sanders, but sold a farrago of rubbish.

The winner of the 2016 U.S. presidential campaign offered bluster and bravado instead of rational governance; a creature so inoculated against normal human emotions that he sported a self-satisfied grin on hearing his genitalia graphically described on television, by a woman who asserted a dalliance with him a mere three days after his wife gave birth to their son.

It became clear in David's lifetime that the president, tainted in ways beyond measure, may indeed be the last gasp of capitalism. Moreover, David felt vindicated by the Sanders campaign and the populist support it aroused. It only reinforced the foresight he offered in 2011—that people would rise up against a prevailing economic order that left nearly all of the people behind while it enriched a few beyond comprehension.

Trier, Germany, February 2013

I recall David's prescient words as I take a cappuccino in this ancient Roman city's commodious central plaza, adorned with a beautifully preserved Roman gate and a sense of culture and history that seems to radiate from the cobblestones. The city centre is a pedestrian zone, lending a sense of timelessness to this ancient gathering place.

I am within a short walk of two startling churches: the ornate Dom cathedral with its stunning stained glass windows and architectural flourishes that inspire awe; and the rather more austere Liebfrauenkirche, the oldest Gothic place of worship in Europe.

From his nearby house on the Bruckenstrasse, at the edge of today's pedestrian zone, one of Trier's most famous citizens was ideally placed to reflect on the streams of worshippers making their way to these churches, built on a scale of such grandeur as to summon humility in the most arrogant soul. In 1843, it led Karl Marx to observe:

> Religion is the sigh of the oppressed creature, the heart of a heartless world, and the soul of soulless conditions. It is the opium of the people. The abolition of religion as the illusory happiness of the people is the demand for their real happiness. To call on them to give up their illusions about their condition is to call on them to give up a condition that requires illusions.

Rambling in the cathedral square, walking where Marx walked, David's foresight weighs heavily on me. Are we, I wonder, approaching the point Marx predicted, where capitalism left unchecked will collapse under the weight of its greed and predations?

In 1867, Marx produced a masterful work which remains one of the most thoughtful and compelling volumes of political science and economics, *Das Kapital. Kritik der politische Oekonomie.* In *Capital: A Critique of Political Economy,* Marx called for limiting work hours, enabling people to retire from work with dignity and security, and an end to colonialism as a system of economic exploitation and the looting of faraway lands. And he neatly defined the power imbalance which would set the stage for socialist revolution in the decades to come:

> The great beauty of capitalist production consists in this — that it not only constantly reproduces the wage-worker as wage-worker, but produces always, in proportion to the accumulation of capital, a relative surplus-population of wage-workers. Thus the law of supply and demand of labour is kept in the right rut, the oscillation of wages is penned within limits satisfactory to capitalist exploitation, and lastly, the social dependence of the labourer on the capitalist, that indispensable requisite, is secured; an unmistakable relation of dependence.

The ideal Marx envisioned was rather different: instead of a power relationship wherein the employer has near absolute exploitative power over a dependent worker, the worker should in fact be amply compensated for the fruit of their labour.

Marx's point is well illustrated in our times, in the ferocious pushback against attempts to raise the minimum wage, let alone to establish a living wage that would enable the working poor to afford a life of dignity.

Enabling and empowering workers to have the economic independence to afford a meaningful life of dignity and purpose cannot work in capitalism, even as it is practised today. As Marx observed, the whole notion of capital is to harvest the surplus value of someone else's labour and use it to enrich oneself.

Marx's *Capital* described, in terms of political economy, the political philosophy he and his collaborator Friedrich Engels had set out more than two decades earlier. Just as workers' uprisings began to sweep across Europe in 1847 and 1848, Marx and Engels produced a political pamphlet regarding the rights of workers against the higher orders in the societal and economic hierarchy of the day that exploited the working people.

They called it *Manifest der Kommunistischen Partei,* or Manifesto of the Communist Party, published in February 1848. Published in London, in German, by the *Kommunistischer Arbeiterbildungsverein* (Workers' Educational Association), the manifesto was distributed in small quantities across Europe, in the hopes of forming a workers' party that would unite across countries to stand up to an exploitative socio-economic order.

It fell into obscurity until the publication of *Capital:* whereafter Marx brought it into renewed prominence through the offices of the International Workingmen's Association. The Association was formed in 1864 in London, to continue the fight for social justice at the root of the 1848 uprising — brutally quelled by authorities across Europe, followed by the suppression of organised demands for social and economic justice.

The Peoples' Spring of 1848 represented a revolt against the feudal system embodied in monarchies that still prevailed: it continued an arc that began with regicide during the French Revolution of 1789-1799.

Its core demand for a new social order foresaw nation-states replacing hereditary monarchies, where aristocratic rule was perpetuated by intermarriage between different royal houses across Europe. (The modern cliché of "reading the riot act" originated in this period, as Britain quelled rebellion by forbidding what it considered unlawful assembly, any gathering of 12 or more people).

The International Workingmen's Association, which became a vehicle to realise the vision of *The Communist Manifesto*, eventually formed The First International, which lent is name to a stirring anthem set to the music of the French revolutionary anthem, La Marseillaise.

While there are many English translations of the 19th century verses, Billy Bragg's contemporary English rendition of The Internationale conveys its spirit and makes it particularly applicable to our times:

> *Stand up all victims of oppression*
> *For the tyrants fear your might*
> *Don't cling so hard to your possessions*
> *For you have nothing if you have no rights*
> *Let racist ignorance be ended*
> *For respect makes the empires fall*
> *Freedom is merely privilege extended*
> *Unless enjoyed by one and all*
>
> *So come brothers and sisters*
> *For the struggle carries on*
> *The Internationale*
> *Unites the world in song*
> *So comrades come rally*
> *For this is the time and place*
> *The international ideal*
> *Unites the human race*

Let no one build walls to divide us
Walls of hatred nor walls of stone
Come greet the dawn and stand beside us
We'll live together or we'll die alone
In our world poisoned by exploitation
Those who have taken now they must give
And end the vanity of nations
We've but one earth on which to live

So come brothers and sisters
For the struggle carries on
The Internationale
Unites the world in song
So comrades come rally
For this is the time and place
The international ideal
Unites the human race

The international anthem became the rallying cry for revolutions that would sweep away the established order in the 20th century, most notably in Russia and in China, which would sing its own lyrical evocation.

With the theoretical weight of *Capital* behind it, the *Manifesto of the Communist Party* ignited a wave of worldwide revolts, aiming to establish a new social order in which exploited workers of the world would at last find justice and human dignity.

Marx, who created the final draft of the work conceived with Engels, wrote in conclusion:

In short, the Communists everywhere support every revolutionary movement against the existing social and political order of things.

In all these movements, they bring to the front, as the leading question in each, the property question, no matter what its degree of development at the time.

Finally, they labour everywhere for the union and agreement of the democratic parties of all countries. The Communists disdain to conceal their views and aims. They openly declare that their ends can be attained only by the forcible overthrow of all existing social conditions.

Let the ruling classes tremble at a Communistic revolution. The proletarians have nothing to lose but their chains. They have a world to win.

Working Men of All Countries, Unite!

Marx's philosophy did not arise in and of itself. It is built on the revolutionary thinking distilled into political philosophy by his predecessor Jean-Jacques Rousseau. In 1754, Rousseau produced his *Discours sur l'origine et les fondements de l'inégalité parmi les hommes,* or a Discourse on the Origins of Inequality among Humankind.

Rousseau spoke of humans emerging from the state of nature to form organised societies, and to evolve into the concept of private property. This change was the beginning of inequality: individual wealth versus the common wealth, and individual good as separate from the common good.

Eight years later, in 1762, Rousseau refined and distilled his thinking into advocating a "social contract" to enable humans to live in liberty, fraternity, and equality. His book *Du Contrat social ou Principe du droit politique (Of the Social Contract or Principle of Political Rights)* opened with a declaration that was revolutionary because it articulated a self-evident truth: "Man is born free, and everywhere he is in chains."

These were the chains the Communist Manifesto aimed to break. And the words that influenced the revolution-fed constitution of the United States, declaring the highest human aspiration to be "life, liberty and the pursuit of happiness."

Rousseau laid the foundations for the American Revolution, the French Revolution, and all the 19th century movements that replaced monarchy with some form of representative governance — with agency and empowerment to come together in collective endeavours.

Whereas the state of nature endows a human with absolute freedom, there is a value to tempering that freedom to act collectively, in the common interest, predicated on the rule of law. Rousseau's Social Contract is the foundation of what we would later come to describe as the common good and the common wealth. As Rousseau put it:

> The passage from the state of nature to the civil state produces a very remarkable change in man, by substituting justice for instinct in his conduct, and giving his actions the morality

they had formerly lacked. Then only, when the voice of duty takes the place of physical impulses and right of appetite, does man, who so far had considered only himself, find that he is forced to act on different principles, and to consult his reason before listening to his inclinations. Although, in this state, he deprives himself of some advantages which he got from nature, he gains in return others so great, his faculties are so stimulated and developed, his ideas so extended, his feelings so ennobled, his whole soul so uplifted, that, did not the abuses of this new condition often degrade him below that which he left, he would be bound to bless continually the happy moment which took him from it forever, and, instead of a stupid and unimaginative animal, made him an intelligent being and a man.

Let us draw up the whole account in terms easily commensurable. What man loses by the social contract is his natural liberty and an unlimited right to everything he tries to get and succeeds in getting; what he gains is civil liberty and the proprietorship of all he possesses. If we are to avoid mistakes in weighing one against the other, we must clearly distinguish natural liberty, which is bounded only by the strength of the individual, from civil liberty, which is limited by the general will; and possession, which is merely the effect of force or the right of the first occupier, from property, which can be founded only on a positive title. We might, over and above all this, add, to what man acquires in the civil state, moral liberty, which alone makes him truly master of himself; for the mere impulse of appetite is slavery, while obedience to a law which we prescribe to ourselves is liberty.

This was a radical thought indeed for its time, that civil society and the rule of law would supplant the entrenched hierarchy of nobles and serfs; where absolute monarchs claimed to rule by divine right.

In its time, Communism became an extension of Rousseau's principles: elevating the collective benefit of society far above individual pursuit of self-fulfilment, which would by nature be seen as selfish. Indeed, Rousseau considered "le bien commun", or the common good, as the highest aspiration of any organised society. In this he was echoing classical Greek philosophers, particularly Aristotle, who spoke of the common interest.

And in an echo of thinking that spanned cultures, Rousseau's notion of the common good flowed from the Chinese notions of societal harmony, as advocated by Taoist philosophy. Twenty five centuries before our time, Lao Tzu laid the foundations of Taoism, which has been revived today as a revered philosophical example by the current leadership of the Communist Party of China.

Lao Tzu was the head librarian of the royal library at Luoyan, and with his disciple Kong Qiu (who became known as Master Kong or Kong Fuzu, romanised to Confucius) advocated looking within oneself and knowing oneself as the beginning of meaningful participation in community life.

In the 81 cryptic verses of his Tao te Ching, Lao Tzu wrote about the cardinal virtues of harmonious life: be kind, be gentle, be supportive, and revere all life. These virtues are the foundation of the Taoist catechism which has been embraced as a way of living by people in different societies and cultures across the world:

If there is to be peace in the world,
There must be peace in the nations.
If there is to be peace in the nations,
There must be peace in the cities.
If there is to be peace in the cities,
There must be peace between neighbors.
If there is to be peace between neighbors,
There must be peace in the home.
If there is to be peace in the home,
There must be peace in the heart.

Just as the common good is the surrender of absolute individual freedom for the common benefit of society, so is the common wealth an evocation of what all of us collectively own. From the stewardship of the natural world to the modern infrastructure of schools, hospitals, roads, railways and ports; the common wealth is in essence the collection of assets that supports and abets the common good.

The symbiosis between the common good and the common wealth was first expounded by Kautilya — which may well have been a *nom de plume* for Chanakya, prime minister to the emperor Chandragupta Maurya of the Mauryan empire which flourished 2,300 years before our time, spanning a territory that includes much of today's Iran, Afghanistan, Pakistan, parts of Central Asia, and all but the southern tip of the Indian subcontinent, extending east to modern Myanmar and south-western China.

Kautilya's book *Arthashastra*, or the Art of Statecraft, envisioned 2,300 years ago what we would regard as the modern welfare state. The duty of kingship, he noted, is to recognise that the monarchy exists to serve the state and the people living within it: to encourage productive economies, collect taxes, and spread the benefits of taxation into a better life for citizens.

It is striking to note the resemblance between Kautilya's prescription and the modern Chinese state: there is immense risk in challenging political power, which is concentrated and absolute, yet the benevolent monarch of the Arthasastra is duty-bound to ensure the well-being of subjects.

In setting out the sources of taxation which would create and sustain the common wealth, Kautilya recommended:

> The Collector-General shall attend to (the collection of revenue from) forts (durga), country-parts (ráshtra), mines (khani), buildings and gardens (setu), forests (vana), herds of cattle (vraja), and roads of traffic (vanikpatha).

> Tolls, fines, weights and measures, the town-clerk (nágaraka), the superintendent of coinage (lakshanádhyakshah), the superintendent of seals and passports, liquor, slaughter of animals, threads, oils, ghee, sugar (kshára), the state-goldsmith (sauvarnika), the warehouse of merchandise, the prostitute, gambling, building sites (vástuka), the corporation of artisans and handicrafts-men (kárusilpiganah), the superintendent of gods, and taxes collected at the gates and from Báhirikas (outsiders) come under the head of forts.

> Produce from crown-lands (sita), portion of produce payable to the government (bhága), religious taxes (bali), taxes paid in money (kara), merchants, the superintendent of rivers, ferries, boats, and ships, towns, pasture grounds, road-cess (vartani), ropes (rajjú) and ropes to bind thieves (chórarajjú) come under the head of country parts.

> Gold, silver, diamonds, gems, pearls, corals, conch-shells, metals (loha), salt, and other minerals extracted from plains and mountain slopes come under the head of mines.

> Flower-gardens, fruit-gardens, vegetable-gardens, wet fields, and fields where crops are grown by sowing roots for seeds (múlavápáh, i.e., sugar-cane crops, etc.) come under sétu.

> Cows, buffaloes, goats, sheep, asses, camels, horses, and mules come under the head of herds.

> Land and waterways are the roads of traffic.

> All these form the body of income (áyasaríram).

All of this existed in the context of what we would today regard as an authoritarian and patriarchal social order. Law-abiding citizens had nothing to fear, spies and surveillance ensured compliance with laws, and public servants were expected to act for the common good.

Indeed, Kautilya wrote at length on more than 40 different forms of corruption and embezzlement of public funds, with harsh consequences for transgressors. But in his description of a duty of the monarch and the rights and responsibilities of citizens, Kautilya asserted that the common good and the common wealth must be maintained within the Hindu societal hierarchy that later came to be known as the caste system, and justified it:

> The observance of one's own duty leads one to Svarga (heaven) and infinite bliss (Anantya). When it is violated, the world will come to an end owing to confusion of castes and duties.
>
> Hence the king shall never allow people to swerve from their duties; for whoever upholds his own duty, ever adhering to the customs of the Aryas, and following the rules of caste and divisions of religious life, will surely be happy both here and hereafter.

Even the most benign of monarchies — which today might be construed as authoritarian states, bringing economic benefit to the people while quelling dissent and denying political freedoms — cannot ensure the nurturing of a just society, because there is no easy means for the citizen to bring enduring change to the societal order imposed by those with power.

No matter the stability or even societal good that unchallenged power may deliver, too many of us have experienced Rousseau's Social Contract, and the liberal democracy it inspired, to ever willingly submit to the strictures of absolute power.

It might be more easily imposed in societies that have never tasted the liberty Rousseau wrought — Saudi Arabia, most Middle Eastern sheikdoms and even Russia and China come to mind — yet for those of us shaped by free association, free speech, and the exercise of free will; there is no compelling enough reason why one must choose between economic fulfilment and political freedom.

Yet it would be foolish indeed to ignore the apathy that pervades so many democracies, the variations on "I didn't vote because politicians are all the same, and it makes no difference anyway."

Part of democratic apathy arises from the lack of two fundamental human rights: freedom from fear and freedom from want. The ever growing ranks of the working poor in what we call the western world, and the inequality in wealth so keenly evoked by the Occupy movement — the millions across Europe denied the dignity of work after the global financial crisis, the generations of welfare-dependent Britons who leave school to go straight on the dole with no hope of meaningful work, the many miners and factory workers who lost their livelihoods when their industries automated or shut down altogether, the legions who survive from paycheque to paycheque — this is the litany of failure in democracies where political freedoms are prized as the highest goal of society.

It is small wonder indeed that many of the dispossessed gravitate to authoritarian rule, even to the siren call of fascism, when demagogues promise to better the material conditions of their lives.

At a certain point, it is futile to debate whether a democratic system or a market-oriented authoritarian system provides the greatest benefit for the greatest number. We should rather be looking at social structures where there is no trade off or false choice between the liberty to be poor and starve, and the strictures of a don't-challenge-the-rulers state that provides citizens with economic security.

And let us remember the great paradox of liberal democracies. Even as they proclaim freedom and liberty at home, their economies churn out armaments and weapons that enable murderous repression by non-democratic regimes. Despite their claims of moral superiority, the actions of these nation-states inflict enslavement, terror, and a culture of fear within their borders and elsewhere: as in Saudi Arabia's use of sophisticated American weapons to terrorise millions in its war of choice in Yemen.

Perhaps our measure of success ought to be set against a different standard:

· Do citizens have meaningful opportunity to engage in the evolution of their society?

· Are the building blocks of a clement life — universal access to education, universal access to health care, economic opportunity that provides a living wage — readily available to most if not all?

· Is there a safe means of offering constructive criticism, of advancing ideas and discussions on how best to shape the collective future?

· And above all, is there a critical mass of citizen engagement to ensure that inclement changes are not imposed on the many by the few?

The common good and the common wealth need active citizen engagement if they are to be nurtured and shaped to serve social and economic justice. When we have fewer than six in ten voters actually casting a ballot in most democratic elections (save those few nations with mandatory voting), when the Halloween revellers in Hong Kong outnumber by far the small brigade of their fellow citizens aspiring to a utopian democracy, we realise that the world belongs to those who actually show up and engage in shaping our collective future. Rather than a debate about the relative merits of one particular social system or other, we need to muster the actual consent of those we purport to represent, if we are to achieve meaningful societal transformation.

Moreover, when you look beyond your own community, and your own national boundaries, the greater challenge is to abet the common good and the common wealth among those of our sisters and brothers who live in societies emerging from war and conflict.

This is where the first imperative is the realm of peace-building — rather different from conflict prevention or peacekeeping — and the daunting task to promote a more civil society in places where there is none. This too is a human obligation, if we are to achieve freedom from fear and freedom from want for an ever larger proportion of humankind.

This was a notion that gelled when the United Nations was led by the late Kofi Annan, the United Nations Secretary General from 1997 to 2006. He established a formal mechanism of peacebuilding in the context of establishing human security — including the quite radical notion of Responsibility to Protect, a Canadian-led concept which implied that national boundaries could be breached to protect citizens from the tyranny of their own government.

It is an implicit facet of human security — at least as advocated by Canada and several other middle powers — that the primacy of individual security must prevail in situations where civilians are caught up in internal conflicts. The human security agenda is part of the remaking of world order made possible by the end of the Cold War between the western alliance and the former Soviet Empire. In theory at least, it promises a future wherein human rights are paramount. It flows from an evolving idea of human security — the notion that human rights transcend political boundaries.

In the days of the Cold War, it would have been unthinkable for the UN or indeed any collection of democracies to embark on such a robust intervention for the stated purpose of upholding human rights.

After the collapse of the Soviet Union, with wider latitude to act, two activist Canadian foreign ministers in governments of differing partisanship — Joe Clark and Lloyd Axworthy — pursued a transformative agenda of establishing human security, and building peace rather than merely keeping it. Transcending partisan politics, they held that ultimately, peacebuilding aims at building human security, a concept which includes democratic governance, human rights, the rule of law, sustainable development, and equitable access to resources.

Just as Canada was a pioneer in introducing and fine-tuning the notion of peacekeeping, the ministers reasoned, so it must continue to be a leader in developing and implementing the concept of peacebuilding, in partnership with other like-minded and generally smaller nations.

The notion of building a peace is not a theoretical conceit. It was forged in the cauldron of the decade-long civil wars that consumed the Balkans in the 1990s, as traditional UN roles of peacekeeping were tried and found wanting.

The North Atlantic Treaty Organisation (NATO) bombing of the former Yugoslavia from March to June 1999, as it intervened in the civil war in the rebellious Serbian province of Kosovo, was a turning point. It marked the first large-scale decision by western democracies to violate a country's borders and its national sovereignty in the name of rescuing people from the persecution directed against them by their own government.

This 'illegal' and unilateral measure — the bombing was conducted without the authorisation of the Security Council — did not sit well with many countries, because one of the founding tenets of the United Nations is that national borders are inviolate.

The Canadian role in advancing the human security agenda was to find the right balance of "hard power", the military role of keeping and maintaining public order, and "soft power", the necessity of building civil institutions within safe and protected areas. The challenge of blending hard power and soft power — enforcing the rule of law so that civil society can be rebuilt — is a fundamental challenge in global governance.

The elements of a civil society must be established before anyone can confidently establish, let alone nurture, the common good and the common wealth.

The rule of law, representative government, the assurance of fundamental human rights, broad access to education and health care: these are the foundations of any lasting peace.

Representative government should ideally include an element of democracy. Nonetheless, in many war-ravaged regions, the guarantee of human rights may be a more important factor in building peace. Given these conditions, a working democracy can evolve from the other elements of a civil society.

Building an inclusive society, based on pluralism and diversity, are elusive goals in communities and nations emerging from conflict, throwing off the yoke of colonialism, overcoming the bitter divisions of racialism.

They are made all the more elusive by the propagation of the arms trade by Britain, France, the United States and Russia; which continue to flood weapons into regions where people are desperate for a secure life.

Is it any wonder millions flee the conflicts generated by the arms trade in utter desperation, taking enormous risks in paying people smugglers fortunes for a fraught passage, to clamour for safe haven and entry at the borders of the United States and Europe?

The quest to establish and foster non-violence, when "free societies" are themselves among the greatest enablers of violence, is the challenge that faced Gandhi, King and Mandela in their time.

As change agents, it also becomes our challenge.

We have learned to enhance the common good and the common wealth in advocating a sustainable biosphere, asserting gender equity, practicing and embracing a pluralistic and inclusive society which values diversity as a strength, and speaking out against injustice — whether it prevails in our own communities or in the wider world.

Nonetheless, we have thus far been unable to change the attitude of those with power.

Yet as we shall explore in our next stop, there are powerful instruments at our disposal — not to mention the experience of those who have gone before us — which we can harness to provoke change, and make the difference we wish to see in the world.

Chapter Fifteen

Changing the attitude of those with power

Los Angeles, California, USA, 8 March 1965

It's a picture perfect afternoon as Chris and I walk to his family home from our elementary school in Brentwood, filled with the delight of nine year old boys with an afternoon of play ahead. Chris's sprawling house at the bend of Wellesley Avenue and Darlington Avenue backs on to a ravine, and our usual agenda is to climb down to the water to poke around. Then we come back up for a snack before going out again to play in the front yard.

These are joyous days, of a piece with our life in the affluent Westwood neighbourhood since we arrived after a year in Nashville. Parents sent children to play outdoors unaccompanied, allowed them to walk to school or to a friend's house, with no qualms around safety. In that era, television was a luxury, not a necessity.

Our parents had met in London a decade previously, as graduate students in Britain. And we, the children who came after their friendship was forged, are readily incorporated into their amity. Chris and his little sister, four year old Karen, become my siblings long before my own sister would be born.

My parents and I live in a commodious apartment on Gorham Avenue, near the Veterans' Administration hospital. Our daily routine is to go play with Chris after school, before my parents come and pick me up on their way home from the University of California at Los Angeles — where my father is a visiting professor, and my mother is pursuing PhD level graduate work.

Yet this particular Monday is imprinted on my memory. It is one of the triggering events that launched me into a career in journalism, thence as a writer: it is the first newspaper headline I remember.

It is the front page of the Los Angeles Times in Chris's house, and I have re-read the story at least three times: unable to process such cruelty, such jarring violence, so alien to the idylls of my carefree southern California life. "Negro Marchers Clubbed," it says, over a huge picture of several light-skinned state troopers. They are bludgeoning a kneeling dark-skinned man, who assembled with hundreds of others to demand the right to vote.

Earlier, the story describes, police rode roughshod over the protesters in Selma, Alabama — who gathered at the behest of Martin Luther King, Jr., in an act of civil disobedience against laws forbidding unsanctioned assembly, to demand the full citizenship right to vote freely in elections.

Millions of Americans living in the southern United States had been robbed of their right to vote, denying them any meaningful participation in changing the power structures that kept them in economic and societal servitude: in effect, a more sophisticated form of enslavement.

Though it may seem difficult if not impossible to believe in the context of today's politics in the United States, those dark-skinned Americans who actually overcame the barriers to vote in the South, voted for the Republican Party. The Republicans ended slavery. The Republicans championed liberty of all.

In the South, because of the obstacles to voting, millions of dark-skinned Americans — and hundreds of thousands of light-skinned Americans mired in poverty and denied an education — were barred from voting, as the registered voting rolls actually shrank. The Republicans were denied their traditional voting base.

The Democrats enjoyed a monopoly on power, essentially one-party rule which sustained and maintained apartheid despite the efforts of the Republican president who ended slavery, only to see emancipation delayed.

Indeed, the unshakable power base of Democrat presidents was the solid voting block of segregationist Americans in the South. One of the reasons Kennedy was slow to respond to King was the real fear that if his party alienated the guardians of apartheid, it would lose its ability to win presidential elections.

The institutions of racial segregation and racial discrimination in hiring were enshrined into law by the southern Democrat Woodrow Wilson, who was elected president in 1912 and again in 1916, succeeding the Republican populist Theodore Roosevelt.

For the many today who believe that xenophobia stems from ignorance, that education and learning are the best ways to overcome racism and discrimination, Wilson stands as the negation to that comfortable premise.

Wilson was the first president with an advanced graduate degree — a PhD in political science from Johns Hopkins University. Although southern born and bred, he was part of the northeastern U.S. elite — serving as president of Princeton University and as Governor of New Jersey before ascending to national politics. And in other aspects of his life, he would prove to be a prescient leader.

In the aftermath of the First World War, he proposed the League of Nations that later would evolve into the United Nations. In one of the great ironies of history, the office of the United Nations High Commissioner For Human Rights in Geneva is headquartered in the Palais Wilson.

In fact, there was an utter absence of human rights in the segregationist legislation Wilson entrenched during his presidency. Segregation, in Wilson's view, eliminated friction between the races.

Thus the military had battalions of dark-skinned soldiers, but they had to be led by light-skinned officers. Workplaces had separate areas based on skin pigmentation — even the everyday necessity of the post-office, in an era where written letters were the universal means of communication.

Wilson's leadership in segregation entrenched the divide, a natural precondition to the sustained efforts of southern Democrats in the intervening decades to deny dark-skinned Americans their right to vote.

They comprehensively undermined the two remarkably progressive pieces of Republican legislation passed in the 19th century. In February 1870, the U.S. Congress ratified the fifteenth Amendment to the U.S. Constitution. It forbade the federal government and each state from denying a citizen the right to vote based on that citizen's "race, colour, or previous condition of servitude."

It was the third of three Constitutional amendments (the reconstruction amendments) meant to give force and permanence to the promise of racial equality and social justice inherent in the Republican President Lincoln's abolition of slavery.

(It is worth noting that none of this encompassed gender equity. Women — regardless of racial origin — were not permitted to participate in their democracy. That would have to wait until the 19th amendment to the American Constitution, ratified in 1920, which finally entrenched the right of women to vote.)

In practice, suffrage was far from universal by the time of King's civil rights movement. The Selma march supported legislation — the Voting Rights Act — to ensure full and fair access to the rights set out in the Constitution of the United States.

To register to vote, for instance, dark-skinned Americans had to answer "skill testing questions" such as how many bubbles there were in a bar of soap. There were "literacy tests" where light-skinned voters were asked to read a simple sentence and dark-skinned ones given convoluted masses of legalese which they were expected to distil into a simple declarative sentence.

On the morning of March 7, about 600 people, a smattering of light-skinned amongst the dark-skinned, gathered to march 90 kilometres from Selma to Montgomery, a show of defiance and solidarity. They left Selma by the Edmund Pettus bridge, only to find their progress blocked.

The Selma marchers knew full well that the police would be waiting — they had been warned. They knew their march would be met with violence. Yet they marched on, crossing the bridge and enduring the gauntlet of police brutality.

They were living the code of conduct King, echoing Gandhi's *satyagraha,* prescribed in his "I Have a Dream" speech in Washington in August 1963:

> Let us not seek to satisfy our thirst for freedom by drinking from the cup of bitterness and hatred. We must forever conduct our struggle on the high plane of dignity and discipline. We must not allow our creative protest to degenerate into physical violence. Again and again, we must rise to the majestic heights of meeting physical force with soul force.

The resolve of the marchers to accept the blows of their oppressors in those printed images and reports — there was no television coverage of the march — conveyed a powerful moral clarity, elevating King and his companions as martyrs in the cause of justice. They gave truth to King's observation, proclaimed in Washington, that "You have been the veterans of creative suffering. Continue to work with the faith that unearned suffering is redemptive."

That day, which came to be known as Bloody Sunday, was the culminating event that changed the attitudes of those with power. Dramatised two generations later in Ava DuVernay's stirring film *Selma*, the events of March 7, 1965, led to the most sweeping change in civil rights since Lincoln's emancipation proclamation ended slavery a century before.

Having signed the Civil Rights Act in 1964, Democrat President Lyndon Baines Johnson signed the Voting Rights Act on August 6, 1965 — five months after Selma's bloody Sunday. In doing so, he knew the Democrats would lose the South.

Sadly, those hardened segregationists subsequently took over the Republican party in the South; where they continue a relentless campaign to restrict and undermine minority voting rights. They are abetted by the proud bigot chosen by the Electoral College to be President of the United States in 2016, after he was resoundingly defeated in the popular vote.

Nonetheless, the lessons of Selma did indeed bring a sea-change in the attitude of those with power.

On the 50th anniversary of that fateful day, one of the survivors — who was bludgeoned into concussion and the brink of death — came to a commemorative ceremony on Edmund Pettus bridge, to bear witness.

John Lewis, who had not only survived but thrived, elected time after time as a member of the United States House of Representatives since 1987, offered an eloquent summation of the significance of Selma:

> On March 7, 1965, a few innocent children of God, some carrying only a bedroll, a few clutching a simple bag, a plain purse or a backpack, were inspired to walk 50 dangerous

miles from Selma to Montgomery to demonstrate the need for voting rights in the state of Alabama. On that day, on that day, 600 people marched into history, walking two by two down this sidewalk, not interfering with the free flow of trade and commerce, not interfering with traffic, with a kind of military discipline.

We were so peaceful, so quiet, no one saying a word. We were beaten, tear-gassed. Some of us were left bloody right here on this bridge. Seventeen of us were hospitalised that day. But we never became bitter or hostile.

We kept believing that the truth we stood for would have the final say. This city, on the banks of the Alabama River, gave birth to a movement that changed this nation forever. Our country will never, ever be the same because of what happened on this bridge.

He spoke in the presence of American leaders who were committed to a more civil and inclusive society: including George W. Bush, the Republican President from January 2001 to 2009, who was the first Republican since Theodore Roosevelt to fully embrace and champion Lincoln's legacy, appointing cabinet secretaries and senior officials of darker pigmentation to his inner circle.

Yet as Lewis remarked, he was there to greet another president whose very existence would have defied belief in March 1965. Lewis said:

It is a great honor for me to return to my home state of Alabama, to present to you—not to introduce to you, but to present to you—the president of the United States.

If someone had told me, when we were crossing this bridge, that one day I would be back here introducing the first Af-rican-American president, I would have said, "You're crazy. You're out of your mind. You don't know what you're talking about." President Barack Obama!

It is surely a great irony of history, given the profoundly rac-ist and segregationist policies of the U.S. Democratic Party for nearly two thirds of the 20th century, that two Democratic pres-idents arose from the ranks of those whom Democrat legislators in the southern U.S. thought unworthy of equality and voting rights promised in the U.S. Constitution. William Jefferson (Bill) Clinton, who grew up in a trailer raised by a single mom, part of the disparaged "white trash" who were excluded from voting as ruthlessly as dark-skinned Americans; and Barack Hussein Obama, who had a legitimate claim to be called African Amer-ican because of his parentage.

Even though the racist backlash against Obama implanted a president who for years as a private citizen peddled vile lies about Obama's birth, the election of two presidents from "un-worthy" origins suggests that the arc of the moral universe, as Dr. King believed, is indeed bending towards justice.

The final irony is that the blustering narcissist occupying the White House since 2017 has completely absorbed the once-noble party of Lincoln into his own quivering mass of moral decay.

On 14 July 2019, this scoundrel — whose own grandfather was expelled from Bavaria by royal decree in 1905 and took refuge in the United States, apparently making his fortune in a brothel in gold-rush-era Alaska — indulged himself in a mendacious Twitter rant against political foes of darker pigmentation.

Much as he had questioned the legitimacy of President Obama's birth, this seditious mountebank, in one of the early morning tirades that are a hallmark of his "leadership", assailed the legitimacy of legislators — elected for the very purpose of making laws that determine how their government is to be run:

> So interesting to see "Progressive" Democrat Congresswomen, who originally came from countries whose governments are a complete and total catastrophe, the worst, most corrupt and inept anywhere in the world (if they even have a functioning government at all), now loudly and viciously telling the people of the United States, the greatest and most powerful Nation on earth, how our government is to be run. Why don't they go back and help fix the totally broken and crime infested places from which they came.

John Lewis, the survivor of Selma, led his colleagues in the United States House of Representatives in condemning the president's racism: the first such formal censure delivered by Congress in more than a century. Only four Republicans stood in solidarity with the Democrats.

Given that the caucus the president assailed included women descended from slaves Lincoln freed, the steadfast and silent assent of nearly all the Republican lawmakers in the House of Representatives and the Senate of the United States of America comprehensively demonstrates the demise of every Lincolnian ideal embodied by what was once the party of emancipation.

As Shakespeare's Feste observed in the epilogue of Twelfth Night, "And thus the whirligig of Time brings in his revenges."

Coyoacan, Mexico City (CDMX), Mexico, February 2016

A long and patient queue snakes outside the artist Frida Kahlo's blue house in this exceedingly pleasant neighbourhood of Mexico's sprawling capital. There is a lovely aesthetic here in Coyoacan: leafy streets and handsome villas, gardens and pocket parks, a lively and relaxed public market where the street food includes metre-long quesadillas deftly stuffed and folded by the ladies behind the grill.

On a bearably hot afternoon, Mita and I are learning to love the addition of chilli peppers to the most unlikely foods: the soft meat of a green coconut, scooped out with a dash of ancho sauce after you've imbibed the water; sliced mangoes tossed with chipotle paste.

As the chile-laced mango bursts with a cascade of flavour across my palate, I send a silent thank you to David Evans: this is his favourite city in the world, and Coyoacan his favoured destination.

Nice as it would be to visit Kahlo's villa, I am here in search of another historic spot: the place where one of Kahlo's dalliances ultimately found refuge. This married paramour — Kahlo gifted him a 1937 self-portrait — was expelled from the Blue House arising from an interlude of reconciliation between Kahlo and her spouse, the legendary muralist Diego Rivera, who himself displayed only a tenuous affinity for the marital bed.

The evicted lover was a Ukrainian, born Lev Davidovich Bronstein to a secular Jewish farming family, whose life journey quite literally changed the world.

Bronstein had come to the Blue House after he was offered refuge in 1935 by Lazaro Cardenas del Rio, a leftist hero of Mexico's revolutionary war who in 1934 became President of the republic.

Bronstein, and his wife Natalia Sedova, found a home two blocks away from the Blue House. It lay within a pleasant walled compound with a semi-arid garden, which today hints its connection to a turbulent history only by the presence, beside Bronstein's grave in the inner courtyard of the red-and-gold hammer and sickle flag of the Union of Soviet Socialist Republics.

An early agitator in the Russian Social Democratic Labour Party while still a teenager, Bronstein was captured by the Czar's secret police, tried, and sentenced to Siberian exile for his troubles at the age of 21. Only two years later, in 1902, Bronstein escaped from his Siberian imprisonment using the stolen passport of a gaoler. He adopted that passport identity as his own, and was known thereafter to the world as Leon Trotsky.

Trotsky was the purest exponent of direct action to overthrow the existing power structure. Rather than trying to change the attitude of those with power through the use of non-violence and moral persuasion, he preached continuous revolution: and a never-ending vigilance — even after the Imperial elite had been toppled — to ensure that the newly-installed revolutionary government faithfully adhered to the democratic will of the working class.

The Trotsky house in Coyoacan offers a fascinating glimpse into a compelling and complex life — including the perfectly-preserved room where one of Stalin's assassins fatally injured Trotsky with an ice-pick in 1940.

The room itself is strikingly spartan: a simple bed, a sturdy desk and chair, windows positioned to catch a cross-breeze. It is jarring to realise that this spare but comfortable accommodation was the last home of the Russian revolutionary whom Lenin anointed to succeed him as the leader of the Soviet Union. The Leon Trotsky who founded the Red Army, growing it from 300,000 soldiers to a million soldiers in the span of six months in 1918, finally defeating the White Army in Russia's 1918-20 Civil War. There he is, in a photograph adorning the walls of his house now turned into a museum: hurtling through the countryside in his armoured train, at each stop exhorting the troops to liberate themselves and their future generations from serfdom. And I wonder anew how the history of the 20th century might have unfolded, had the dying Lenin's wishes borne fruit, and Trotsky's claim to power prevailed.

Trotsky believed that Russia's feudal system couldn't sustain a Communist revolution, because while feudalism and serfdom were clearly oppressive, there was no urban working class producing industrial goods for capitalists. Thus the great flaw in Marxist prescriptions, to Trotsky's thinking, is that in Russia, there was no capitalist class to speak of. What Marx evoked reflected the exploitation of labour in the industrialised economies of Germany and Britain.

So a permanent global revolution would overthrow the ruling order in every country of the world and end exploitation. Simply limiting communism to Russia would inevitably lead to the tyranny of bureaucrats and what we would today call technocrats.

These views were not popular with Stalin and the clique who pursued power for power's sake. Ousted from office by Stalin and expelled from the Communist Party, Trotsky fled Russia.

Marked for assassination by Stalin even in exile, Trotsky continued to denounce the oppression of a totalitarian state administered by an all-powerful; bureaucracy, which stifled the intent and purpose of the Russian Revolution — which Trotsky foresaw as the beginning of a necessary global revolution wherein the working classes worldwide would seize power and institute mass democracy representing the will of the greatest number.

During a six-month stay in Norway in 1935, an interlude in exile which would months later take him to this house in Coyoacan, Trotsky wrote *The Revolution Betrayed,* wherein he asserted the Soviet Union is doomed unless it enables democratic dissent and the lively exchange of ideas and ideals that are the lifeblood of democracy. He observed:

> The bureaucracy is not only a machine of compulsion but also a constant source of provocation. The very existence of a greedy, lying and cynical caste of rulers inevitably creates a hidden indignation. The improvement of the material situation of the workers does not reconcile them with the authorities; on the contrary, by increasing their self-respect and freeing their thought for general problems of politics, it prepares the way for an open conflict with the bureaucracy.
>
> ...

The cessation of visible political struggle is portrayed by friends and agents of the Kremlin as a "stabilization" of the regime. In reality it signalizes only a temporary stabilization of the bureaucracy. With popular discontent driven deep, the younger generation feels with special pain the yoke of this "enlightened absolutism" in which there is so much more absolutism than enlightenment. The increasingly ominous vigilance of the bureaucracy against any ray of living thought, and the unbearable intensity of the hymns of praise addressed to a blessed providence in the person of the "leader", testify alike to a growing separation between the state and society. They testify to a steady intensifying of inner contradictions, a pressure against the walls of the state which seeks a way out and must inevitably find one.

. . .

All indications agree that the further course of development must inevitably lead to a clash between the culturally developed forces of the people and the bureaucratic oligarchy. There is no peaceful outcome for this crisis. No devil ever yet voluntarily cut off his own claws. The Soviet bureaucracy will not give up its positions without a fight. The development leads obviously to the road of revolution.

Indeed, Trotsky foresaw that Stalinist repression would inevitably lead to the restoration of capitalism — not in the bosom of a democratic state, but with the authoritarian architecture of the Stalinist state. Which, as fair minded observers may discern, precisely defines the Russia that exists in 2019.

Fear of the revolution so ardently advocated by Trotsky would shape international thinking for decades after his assassination, in what became known as the Cold War.

From the 1950s onwards, the United States in particular led a virulent capitalist response, backed with clandestine means and military might, to subvert the will of the people in countries the world over — wherever there was even a whiff of communism or socialism.

The U.S. established a doctrine called the "domino theory", wherein American leaders believed that if one country turned socialist, all others would fall in turn. When Communism emerged as the victor from the Chinese Civil War that raged from 1927 to 1949, the U.S. launched a concerted effort to prevent what it saw as signs of the permanent export of revolution Trotsky preached.

Most often, it intervened when populist revolts or guerrilla armies threw off the cruelty and oppression of the harshest authoritarian rule. Too often, this led countries to reach for the embrace of the Soviet Union, which was all too willing to fill the void.

When the vile dictator Fulgencio Batista was toppled by the guerrilla army of Fidel Castro y Ruiz in Cuba as the 1950s ended, Castro's outreach to the U.S. was soundly rebuffed.

By 1962, Soviet missiles were in Cuba aimed at the United States, and the world came to the brink of nuclear war.

When the secular leader Mohammad Mossadegh was appointed Iran's prime minister in 1951, under the Constitutional Monarchy that was evolving Iran's transition from mullah-influenced feudalism to full democracy, he wanted to ensure that the wealth of the nation benefited the people of Iran.

His government began to look into the books of the Anglo-Iranian Oil Corporation, which essentially carried out colonial exploitation with the blessing of Reza Shah of the Pahlavi dynasty. Mossadegh, himself of royal blood (part of the Qajar line that opposed the Pahlavis), set out to nationalise the oil company. In 1951, in a near unanimous vote, the Iranian Parliament approved public ownership of the oil company, to set a foundation for a robust economy and to ensure this ancient culture's advance into the benefits of the modern world.

This was a step too far for Britain and America. In 1953, the secret intelligence services of both countries, the Central Intelligence Agency and MI-6, engineered a coup that ended democracy in Iran. Mossadegh was dismissed by the Shah, and parliament dissolved, in momentous events that would see full monarchy restored at gunpoint.

The CIA envoy, Major General Norman Schwarzkopf, brought the Shah back from hiding. And helped to establish the state security apparatus, *Sāzemān-e Ettelā'āt va Amniyat-e Keshvar* (SAVAK), which conducted a clandestine reign of terror to keep the Shah in power.

The decadence of the Shah's rule — serving up roasted peacock and Chateau Lafite Rothschild to guests, including American vice president Spiro Agnew, at an immense and lavish spectacle to celebrate the 2,500th anniversary of the Persian empire in October 1971; while SAVAK tortured, brutalised and killed democrats by the score — created fertile ground for the Shia clergy and theocrats among them to rally an oppressed and deeply conservative rural population.

For General Schwarzkopf and the United States, this was mission accomplished: Iran was "saved" from socialism, and its national patrimony flowed into foreign coffers. (In 1991, his son General Norman Schwarzkopf Jr., would lead an international military alliance to oust the Iraqi dictator Saddam Hussein al-Tikriti from the oilfields of Kuwait; which Saddam invaded with the consent of American ambassador April Glaspie, after the Kuwaiti monarchy stole Iraqi oil with horizontal drilling technology).

The Iranian coup was essentially carried out to ensure that a foreign-owned oil company could continue to exploit the resources that belonged to the Iranian people. That oil firm eventually became British Petroleum. Yet the Shah's rule lasted a scant quarter century, before the Iranian people, the secular and religious alike, rose in revolt. In 1979 they toppled a monarchy founded on terror and suppression. And SAVAK's impeccable efficiency in excising Iran's secular democracy root and branch led to an inevitable outcome: a theocracy governed by ayatollahs, which prevails to this day.

Nowhere was the domino theory more influential than in Vietnam, where the U.S. backed a series of puppet governments in the southern part of the country to prevent the victory of Communist forces led by Ho Chi Minh.

After nearly two decades of intervention, the Vietnam war ended in a crushing defeat for the U.S. and its allies. One of the most iconic images of my young adulthood was the image of the chaotic U.S. retreat of 1975 as the forces of general Vo Nguyen Giap entered what was then the southern city of Saigon — with U.S. personnel taking the last helicopter from the rooftop of the American embassy, abandoning hundreds of desperate Vietnamese who had been U.S. allies, and who were striving to reach evacuation and safety.

Fear of Trotsky's permanent revolution prodded liberal democracies into markedly anti-democratic actions. And in another irony of history, Vietnam and China in 2019 are the two most striking examples of what might be called capitalism with a communist flavour: the market forces of capitalism flourishing under one-party rule in systems that brook little if any dissent.

Just as I presented the China challenge as a counterpoint to my ardent advocacy of the full panoply of human rights as a way of life, so I present Trotsky and his call for exporting revolution as a counterpoint to the non-violent means of *satyagraha* and creative suffering, whereby Gandhi and King sought to change the attitude of those with power.

It is all the more important, because the place I part company with Trotsky is his embrace of violence — and his insistence that there must be a reversal of roles between the oppressing class and the oppressed class in any revolution: the established order must not only be overthrown, but its perpetrators crushed. In a society that truly embraces the common good and the common wealth, there can be no clear winners and losers. If the oppressed take revenge on the oppressors, they become the oppressors in their own right. A civil society can only exist if it is born out of non-violence and compassion.

Yet in his analysis of injustice, particularly his criticism of Stalin and the Stalinist state, one finds a strong resonance with the societal critiques advanced by Gandhi, King and Mandela.

Even though I do not waver in my belief that civil disobedience and nonviolent resistance are the most appealing means to achieve freedom from fear, I cannot deny that Trotskyism offers a counter-force whose primary goal is to achieve freedom from want: even if it has to be installed by force and by fear.

Ideally, there need be no trade-off between freedom from fear and freedom from want. Indeed, *Xi Jinping Thought on Socialism with Chinese Characteristics for a New Era* purports to have achieved that balance — a view evidently not shared by many Hong Kong Chinese, nor by governments with a tradition of liberal democracy.

Yet sometimes, the attitude of those with power can yield to the might of popular will. And even revolutionary governments established by force can collapse under their own weight.

This is precisely what brought the end of the Soviet empire. The armed agents of the state simply refused to carry out the orders of the rulers, because there were some lines they were no longer willing to cross.

It happens seldom: but when it does, a regime that seems entrenched in permanence can come apart in the blink of an eye. So it was when the Berlin Wall came down in 1989, bringing the collapse of communist rule across Eastern Europe, and the eventual dissolution of the Union of Soviet Socialist Republics.

We know that the quest for civil society remains a work in progress, dear companions, because changing the attitude of those who hold power is seldom done with ease.

The gift of human rights, among those of us who live in societies committed to supporting our autonomy and agency to participate meaningfully in the life of our polity, also comes with a human responsibility: to navigate towards a future where all can seek the education, the economic security, and the empowerment to exercise our right to be human.

And in the communities of mutual interest that manifest themselves in everything from global climate strikes to marches against injustice, you yourself can pursue an ample role in establishing a just society, anchored in the dominion of love.

Chapter Sixteen

The right to be human

Vienna, Austria, August 2008

It is a particularly clement summer evening in an outdoor café in central Vienna, the world around bathed in burnished gold. The late sun sparkles through a frosted glass of rosé wine. Its filtered light limns the contours of Mita's face, as the heat begins to recede, and the waning afternoon softens the grand vista all around us.

We are on the terrace of the Café Landtmann, a few paces from the commodious plaza of Vienna's City Hall. We are enjoying the view Sigmund Freud might have seen on the short walk here from the University of Vienna's school of medicine, or from his home in the nearby Berggasse. Being in Freud's preferred café seems an everyday occurrence in this astonishing city, awash in the history of humankind.

We are a brisk walk away from the majestic Natural History Museum that houses the thirty thousand year old Venus of Willendorf, a Mother Goddess sculpture that may be the oldest surviving religious relic of our species. A walk down the street will bring us to the Beethoven Museum, and a leisurely stroll to Mozart's apartment.

Walking from our bed and breakfast through the back roads leading to City Hall, we pass the memorial plaque marking the onetime home of the actor Oskar Werner, a few paces from a traditional shoemaker who begins with wooden models of one's feet for a perfect fit. Past rambles around Vienna have taken me to many of these markers of prominent Viennese of times past: poet Wystan Auden, novelist Honoré de Balzac; composers, actors and performers, scientists and political leaders — including Theodor Herzl, the University of Vienna law student who became the founder of modern Zionism.

This evening evokes a stirring of hope. Even though the architecture of a bygone age is meant to evoke grandeur and the might of power, there is something electric about being in a great city that has lost the empire for which it was built. Its imposing streetscapes are full of a welcome belied by humility, an open-armed embrace of a bewildering array of humanity which streams to Vienna for everything from the second headquarters of the United Nations to the Organisation of Petroleum Exporting Countries, for the discreet banks whose appetite for receiving wealth is entirely blind to pigmentation and origin. It is made all the more human by the lively cosmopolitan mix of its people, and the welcoming and inclusive ambience that emerged from the turbulent decades of its 20th century history.

Mita and I have just finished a simple yet exceptional meal in this timeless Viennese gem: grilled *lachsforelle*, the wild salmon trout of nearby mountain lakes; turmeric-hued chanterelle mushrooms gathered from the nearby Vienna woods, sautéed with shallots and parsley, their intense saffron-and-pepper flavour wrapped in a barely-set omelette.

We are in amiable company, after a fulfilling day at the Vienna conference on human rights education: Bill Schabas, the eminent Canadian scholar who a few years hence will be appointed to head the international inquiry into Israel's conduct in the 2014 Gaza war; and my friend Steve Marks, with whom I shared the privilege of drafting the Global Appeal for Human Rights Learning.

Steve and I are here at the behest of Shulamith Koenig, the catalyst of the People's Decade for Human Rights Education (PDHRE), who convened the gathering that produced the Global Appeal.

It seems more than faintly ridiculous to be discussing human rights in the gilded halls of the former imperial precinct now turned into a conference centre, not to mention the reception itself in the stunning Marmorsalle, which is the most aesthetically pleasing room in which I've ever hoisted a bun.

All irony aside, the conference itself is exhilarating, mingling activists and academics, a global gathering that is deeply meaningful in creating and bolstering common cause between people already making a difference in the world. We affirm that people must know their human rights to claim their human rights. And we have gathered in Vienna to share best practices on how we go about it.

I feel at ease because my presentation is done; my colleagues not displeased with what I had to say.

I spoke of my experience as a Canadian born in India, and why I believe in inclusion, pluralism and diversity in any holistic vision of human rights.

I explained that my act of becoming Canadian also enabled me to contribute substantially to the national discourse of what it should mean to be one. In the late 1970s and early 1980s, I was among a vanguard of Canadians from diverse origins worried that official multicultural policy served to put people in ghettos, to encourage a benign apartheid wherein cultures were separate and equal.

The fundamentally hollow concept of "tolerance" only invited acceptance of something: it did not lead to sharing, discovery, and ultimately celebration. We worried about the future of a cultural mosaic where every piece in the mosaic was separate and apart from the others.

I described the singularity of my Canadian life. About our belief there could be a means of preserving seminal identities while sharing our lives and experiences with one another. This sat more comfortably in a country that did not believe in forcing assimilation into some overarching national *mythos,* as was the experience south of the border in the United States.

We Canadians were working to reshape a 1970s and early 1980s milieu where "multiculturalism" was defined as giving grants to ethnic and cultural associations to propagate and perpetuate their own traditions.

We believed that this would ultimately lead to an abundance of solitude, if there was no attempt to share across cultures, across ethnicity, across religion. And in this context, we worked to shape Canada as a grand inclusion, in which one could maintain the bonds of heritage and ancestry while bringing them to reshape a dynamic and evolving Canadian identity.

In the early 1980s I wrote an article in *The Edmonton Journal,* titled "Multiculturalism: A Kindly Apartheid?" and was roundly condemned by readers. The subject was so emotional that I could not successfully communicate my intent — to ensure the participation of all those cultural solitudes in the crafting of our collective future.

Nonetheless, those thoughts of inclusion prevailed and ultimately succeeded in the following years. The future evoked by so many of us fighting for a different country, now exists in my modern Canada. A generation later, my country is one of pluralism, multiple identities, cultural sharing, and a surging confidence among the generations coming of age in the digital world.

And then I described the path that all of you, dear companions, can follow. A global community of human rights cities — communities where our daily lives are shaped and guided by the better angels of our nature. The experience is universal: something you can build in your own environs, as you inspire others to be the best *for* the world rather than the best *in* the world.

These are communities that have chosen to incorporate human rights into their everyday lives; to train and empower citizens to know their human rights in order to claim their human rights.

This is an evolutionary process, not a revolutionary one, and aims at collaboration and consensus to change the underlying values and attitudes that contribute to violence and misery.

It thus differs from "code violation" monitoring like Amnesty International or Human Rights Watch in looking for long-term changes in behaviour, rather than the mere chronicling of breaches or violations of human rights. Rather than an imposition, the human rights city evolves from within the community, accommodating its unique cultural norms and behaviours, and its own approaches to consensus and coalition building.

The indispensable foundation is inclusive, participatory and responsive governance. This is found principally within, but not necessarily limited to, democracies; even authoritarian political structures can offer meaningful and responsive governance, especially at the local or municipal level.

More than participation and representation, it is fundamentally about *inclusion,* the right to be fully included in the civic life of one's community, one's state or one's country.

How fully an individual citizen exercises the right to be included and to participate is at the citizen's own discretion, yet the right cannot be denied.

Along with inclusion, the notion of pluralism is at the heart of democratic governance. This is the very act of overcoming "otherness," of affirming that many streams of human experience and of the human condition can live together in dignity, under the rule of law, with diversity seen as a source of strength and resiliency.

As we have learned in this journey of *Us,* there is an apparent link between undemocratic structures and human rights violations. Moreover, even functioning democracies can be weak if they condone the denial of human rights, whether at home or abroad.

Canada, a perpetual leader in the United Nations Human Development Index, has for decades paid lip service to the fact that inclusion has not been achieved for its indigenous people. But it is only in the second decade of the 21st century that the imperatives of reconciliation are at last impelling Canada to address its own serious shortcomings in relations with First Nations.

A complete understanding of the obligations of pluralism and inclusion is essential to the healthy evolution of a democracy. Which is why, to this date, democracy remains the system most conducive to guaranteeing human rights protection and human security.

Entrenching human rights learning is really an endeavour to build human capacity, both individually and in communities, and to enable the blossoming of human potential.

And in an answer to regimes that resist the imposition of "foreign values" and argue dictatorship is best suited for their societies, we should note that human rights are not a "foreign value" unless human dignity is a "foreign value."

Finally, I raised the thought that we may need to move away from a "contested" term like human rights, and transmute it to "the right to be human." This implies a birthright that exists beyond the ambit of legal codes, governments and governance, and speaks to the human birthright to live together in dignity and in community.

By embedding this context and framework for dialogue within, among and between individuals, collectives, institutions, and indeed societies, we can together catalyse the creation of self-learning and self-realisation, whence will come one's own tools for social and economic change.

The goal, I asserted, is to engender societal, civic, economic, and political changes to reclaim and secure the right to be human. This in turn creates happy, secure and productive citizens, living in stable and attractive communities.

In the words of Nelson Mandela: Developing a new political culture based on human rights.

There is a certain serenity that settles in after a serious public engagement. The quiet comfort of watching the play of fading light on Mita's face is a welcome and necessary pleasure after an intense day of stimulating and exhausting talk.

Yet the day is not done. Now, at the Landtmann, we await a moment of transformation in United States politics.

Steve is fiddling with his laptop, connecting remotely with his son in Denver, who has promised to send Steve a live feed of an historic occasion: the national convention of the Democratic Party of the United States, which is about to nominate a biracial candidate forged in multiple ethnic identities as their nominee for their country's presidency.

The relaxed ambience of the terrace and its ample pavement suddenly fills with a sustained roar, as the laptop screen crackles with the energy of a full football stadium. The connection is made. The roar of the crowd surges out of the screen. A lithe figure comes to the podium. We watch and listen, as the crowd awaits in barely-restrained passion. And a wave of emotion explodes in the faraway stadium as Barack Hussein Obama leans into the microphone and declares, "With profound gratitude and great humility, I accept your nomination for presidency of the United States."

The soaring spirits unleashed by his nomination, the election, the heady first months of power — whence Obama was awarded an anticipatory Nobel Peace Prize that foresaw the fulfilment of his promises — could not be sustained.

The entrenched power structure of the United States, the military-industrial complex so starkly foreseen by President Dwight David Eisenhower, came to swallow the Obama presidency. Within months, he authorised a prolongation of the futile Afghan war, consigning America to continued failure in the "graveyard of empires" that had humbled all imperial ambitions over the millennia of recorded human history: from the Greeks to the Persians to the English to the Russians.

Obama, the cool and measured jurist, the Harvard law school star who actually understood the reach and limits of American power, ended up authorising the death of innocents. Brutality pulled him, centripetal, into random and arbitrary murder from the skies. The drone campaign run by Obama's Central Intelligence Agency made little distinction between civilians and combatants as it rained "targeted" bombs and missiles from remotely-controlled aircraft in the wild mountains of Afghanistan and Pakistan.

Under Obama, the United States did not even make a pretence at the due process which is at the heart of the rule of law. The president who took satisfaction, but no triumph, at the commando raid that killed Osama bin Laden, hewed to the precedents set by his predecessors: using the awesome power of the world's mightiest military in the name of advancing peace, democracy and human rights.

It was a stark departure indeed from the hopes pinned on Obama at the start of his presidency. I articulated mine on inauguration day, 20 January 2009, in a column distributed through the newspapers in the Chicago Sun-Times group. Indeed, I expressed my ardent presumption that he and his presidency would at last open the door to a culture of love:

> I will raise a glass and spare a tear today as Barack Hussein Obama pledges fealty to the Constitution of the United States of America to become your 44th President; the first I have shed for any of your presidents since that bleak November day when Jack Kennedy's remains were carried to Arlington National Cemetery.
>
> In this I am joined by much of the world. Seldom has hope been so ardent, the burden of expectations so immense.
>
> As a boy experiencing American apartheid in 1963 — my father held a Kennedy Foundation visiting professorship at Vanderbilt University in Nashville — I recall too vividly the turmoil and turbulence of a foreign childhood, made more complex by "colored" and "white" signs dictating where one might take a sip of water and empty one's bladder. Like millions of your citizens, I never thought I would live to see this day.

Yet here we are. And like so many of your well-wishers in the world — and believe me, those warmed by the American ideal number in the hundreds of millions, particularly in my native India — I am astonished by your nation's capacity to remake itself, to embark on a new arc of history when the old is found wanting.

Like any passer-by experiencing Anish Kapoor's marvelous and mystical "Cloudscape" in Chicago's Millennium Park, those with a fondness for America look at Obama and find a reflection of our most intimate and heartfelt selves. Two thirds of the world shares a variation of his pigmentation, and all know - even the dark-souled terrorists who shot up Mumbai and took planes into the Twin Towers - that the mere possibility of President Barack Obama speaks to the regenerative impulses of your society.

Indeed, as Obama spoke two weeks ago at Baltimore's City Hall, who could remain unmoved by his eloquent evocation of the possibility of America: "What is required is a new declaration of independence, not just in our nation, but in our own lives - from ideology and small thinking, prejudice and bigotry - an appeal not to our easy instincts but to our better angels."

In this aspiration he is joined by millions of Canadians, for we are a country that contradicts your new president's oft-repeated assertion that only in America is his story possible.

We do indeed need a new declaration of independence, one that is both immanent and omnipresent, in our personal lives and in the wider world. More than small thinking and bigotry, we declare independence from the worship of violence, and look to Obama's presidency to lead us toward a culture of love.

Not the naively utopian aspects of love my generation imbibed in drug-hazed 1960s and 1970s, but the abiding and unconditional love taught in every scripture and every faith. The love that evokes the absence of fear and the absence of want in our own lives and the lives of our intimates; the love that enables girls, boys, men and women to live together in dignity, in harmony, in community.

At the end of the day, this is our most powerful response to terrorism, and the myriad threats Obama inherits today. Indonesia, a country that shaped us both, proclaims this ideal in its national motto: Bhinneka Tunggal Ika; Our Diversity Makes Us One.

Obama's presidency, and his precepts, invite us to live and embrace a culture of human rights - not a parsing of the narrow legal codes that dictate "rights and responsibilities," but our birthright to pursue a life of dignity, free of fear and free of want.

Obama's renewed declaration of independence evokes the advancement of human rights, human development and human security - three overlapping and interlinked concepts that are the core of an alternative vision of the world.

Rather than an international order predicated on relationships between nations, this model goes beyond political boundaries to advocate the wellbeing of the individual citizen, no matter where he or she lives. Human rights implies freedom from fear and threats to one's fundamental existence. Human development asserts a claim to the resources and freedoms one needs to develop to one's full potential. And human security evokes freedom from hunger, war, ecological disaster, corrupt governance and other impediments to a life lived in justice, with equality of opportunity for all.

We know the answer to terrorism lies not just in police action against perpetrators, but in creating a more civil and more secure world, where the benefits and the opportunities of human civilisation are available far more broadly than they have been. The most excluded often live in places where there is no human security and little human development, and therefore no human rights.

This vision departs from the conventional idea of nation-states guaranteeing security by building significant military capacity, and using economic prowess to secure their own prosperity with scant regard for the progress of others. Unfortunately, this convention shaped how many in the world perceived America for the better part of the last half-century.

Today, you begin a new American journey, one unlike anything the world has seen. On your shoulders, we your many friends lay our dreams. Godspeed, President Obama, as you build your ladder to the stars and invite us to climb on every rung.

The lesson here is bitter and profound: if a resolute and ethical leader like Obama falls prey to the larger currents that nurture a culture of violence, becomes hostage to the diktats of the military-industrial complex, can we truly expect any change from top-down leadership?

And that, my dear companions, is the very reason the journey of *Us* illuminates the actions of citizens, as much as the actions of leaders. Through collaboration, through commitment to dismantling the structures that trap us in violence and injustice, change will arise and endure. And so we bring you to define and navigate the change you want to be, and to recruit the like-minded to abet the progress of love.

Chapter Seventeen

Becoming the best
for the world

Edmonton, Canada, November 2018

Leslee takes a swig of lemony hot water, clears her jet-lagged throat and plants both forearms on the table. We are at Café Tiramisu, the closest thing Edmonton has to a community gathering place where the lively exchange of ideas is part of the ambience and the charm. She is dressed in her customary black, eyes sparkling with mischief and resolve, eager to embark upon a conversation that will inevitably lead to vehement agreement.

It is lovely listening to her voice, with its delicious modulation of an actor trained in Shakespeare. As an actor, Leslee Udwin played Jessica to Gemma Jones' Portia in The Merchant of Venice on film; and on stage with the late Alan Rickman and Alec Guinness. As a film producer, she offered two bittersweet entertainments of cultural clashes, East is East and West is West. As a champion of advocacy filmmaking, she created a 1990 film that freed the unjustly jailed Birmingham Six.

She is steeped in the precept of *tikkun olam,* the teaching in Jewish culture that impels one to heal the world. And she has pulled me into her mission: an irresistible force of nature, committed to the common good.

Ours is one of those from-the-moment-you-meet friendships. It is a rare gift indeed in middle age: when your patterns of living have been set for decades, and the rhythms of your daily life allow scant opportunity for the abiding bonds most often forged in youth.

We have been at a formal meeting, walked several blocks on slippery streets against a chilling wind, and here we are. We share the comfort and ease of friends of long standing, although we have known each other for only a few years: openness and trust, briskly-exchanged thoughts that eventually align, a delight in deflating pomposity, and an absolute resolve to navigate the seemingly insurmountable skein of violence and injustice that infuses the daily life of humankind.

Our relationship did not start well. Leslee made a remarkable film, India's Daughter, after the unspeakably brutal assault of a 23-year-old Indian medical student Jyoti Singh: trapped in a rogue bus by a gang of rapists as she left a New Delhi mall after a screening of *Life of Pi* on December 16, 2012. Jyoti was injured in the most horrific ways imaginable. And thrown out on the roadside to die.

Leslee's film was set for international release on International Women's Day in March 2015 — and the first news I had of it was that it afforded a platform to Jyoti's unrepentant rapists. I was absolutely appalled. I could not imagine what would possess someone to actually give these unspeakable criminals a voice — and I wondered how she had managed to gain hours of interviews with these monsters in the confines of their death-row gaol.

I went so far as to write to my colleagues on the board of Canadians for a Civil Society, warning that we should not endorse any vehicle that brings publicity to Jyoti's condemned rapists. Then I actually saw the film. And learned to my horror that the condemned rapists emerged from a mindset too grotesque — a culture of rape, in which women must act saintly to avoid being branded as sexual objects that deserve to be defiled — to be resolved by a mere death sentence.

When Canadians for a Civil Society organised an Edmonton screening of India's Daughter on October 6, 2015, Leslee appeared by Skype to interact with our spectators. At the very moment she excused herself with camera in hand to head outdoors for a quick cigarette, I sensed a kindred spirit. A feeling amply confirmed when we met in person months later.

In the years that followed, Leslee was nearly overwhelmed by the worldwide demands for her time to screen and speak about India's Daughter. And in that time, she used the prominence and the exposure to launch an ambitious effort to lay a radically different foundation for societal development: to infuse a deep sense of humanity in the minds of children as they begin to develop a sense of self and a sense of being and belonging.

Which is what brings us together tonight, to enhance an answer to the question I posed in lamenting Obama's failure: What will it take to bring a transformation to a culture of love? Her answer, still a work in progress, is Think Equal.

Leslee's Think Equal project offers you ample room for engagement, especially if you are a teacher. Think Equal, as embodied in its curricula seeks:

> … a system change in education to end the discriminatory mind set and cycle of violence across our world. We believe there is a missing subject in school curricula.
>
> We ask governments to adopt our curriculum and its tangible tools mediating all aspects of experiential social and emotional learning. We ask them to mandate this as a new subject onto the compulsory curriculum of world schools from the earliest years when, according to neuroscientists, the child is optimally modifiable in attitude and behaviour.

Leslee and I are at Tiramisu to tackle a slight hiccup in the Canadian rollout of Think Equal, centred on a particularly enthusiastic group of pre-school teachers in the Peace River country of northwestern Alberta. I sip on a delicious glass of Sangiovese from the Tenuta Montecchiesi in southern Tuscany, while Leslee hydrates her tired vocal chords with hot water.

It is a moment of amiable companionship, as we discuss how to advance Leslee's vision: "We can only break the cycles of violence, negative stereotypes, and prejudicial judgements, if we invest in encouraging values, empathy, and respect for the dignity and equality of others."

It is a sentiment ably articulated by the actor Meryl Streep, one of the luminaries she has attracted to her cause.

Yet Think Equal, like Human Rights Cities, is only a means to an end. The thoughts they provoke, the ideas they plant, can only be effective if they can enlist your active engagement.

People like you, able to navigate a networked world — communities of mutual interest that transcend national boundaries — are ideally suited to achieve the common good.

The common good is nothing more nor less than who we are and what we want to be.

In the journey of *Us*, we have learned of the many paths available to you, as you pursue a future empowered by the dominion of love.

Let me refresh our journey with wisdom arising from two striking poems, written at the beginning and end of the Second World War. Wystan Auden evoked an abiding truth in the face of the horror about to engulf his world, in *1 September 1939:*

> *For the error bred in the bone*
> *Of each woman and each man*
> *Craves what it cannot have,*
> *Not universal love*
> *But to be loved alone.*
>
> *...*
>
> *All I have is a voice*
> *To undo the folded lie,*
> *The romantic lie in the brain*
> *Of the sensual man-in-the street*
> *And the lie of Authority*
> *Whose buildings grope the sky:*
> *There is no such thing as the State*

And no one exists alone;
Hunger allows no choice
To the citizen or the police;
We must love one another or die.

In his song cycle *Kykli (Thrush),* written at the end of the Second World War, George Seferis hauntingly evoked the return of love in reminding us of the possibilities of who we once were, and who we can be once more:

de sou mílo gia perasména, mílo gia tin agápi
stólise ta mayá sou me t'angathya tou íliou
shkoteiní kopélla
I kardiá tou Shkorpioú bhasilepese,
o týrannos mésa ap"ton ánthropo échei fýgei,
ki óles oi kóres tou póntou, Nerydes, Graíes
Trékhoun sta lambyrísmata tis anadyómenis
Ópoios poté tou den agápise th' agapísei
Sto fos...

Which, in my rough translation, leaning heavily on Edmund Keeley and Philip Sherrard, becomes:

I'm not speaking to you of the past, I am speaking of love;
Adorn your hair with the thorns of the sun,
Dark girl:
The heart of the Scorpion has set
The Tyrant within man has fled
And all of the daughters of the sea, Nereids and Graiae
Rush to the brilliance of the rising goddess:
Whoever has never loved shall love,
In the light ...

Dear companions, we have shared many excursions, explorations, provocations and experiences to this point in our journey.

Along the way I hope we have found more illumination than frustration, found resonant experiences that may help to guide your own path.

You have given me the gift of your companionship, and you have my thanks. I offer you my solidarity and my full-hearted blessings as you continue your life's course, towards a different future for us.

May you find fulfilment and purpose as you continue to remain an agent of change in the cultures and civilisations we share.

Along your future pathways, may you use the "experiments with truth" that illuminated our travels.

We have Gandhi's triune of *sarvodaya, satyagraha,* and *ahimsa.*

You can be a champion of *sarvodaya* in your own home, your own neighbourhood, your own community, in nurturing a caring and inclusive place where all are supported. Compatriots living together with dignity, in community, free from fear, free from want, in harmony with one another and our wider world.

You can establish *satyagraha* by looking within yourself, by empowering yourself with Truth, and imbuing all you do with the radiance of moral clarity.

The courage it takes to practice *satyagraha* is amply captured in the life and example of Malala Yousafzai.

It is precisely what Greta Thunberg shows us in inspiring children to civil disobedience to demand action on climate change.

We have learned from Autumn Peltier that *ahimsa* extends to our stewardship of the natural world, that we must do no violence to Mother Earth, and be especially mindful of caring for her life-giving water.

You can advocate *ahimsa* by asking if your words or your actions will help or hurt. The absence of violence arises from the absence of fear.

From the bullied child in the schoolyard to the child abused by persons with power over them; from the women and men who fear coming home to those whose lives would fall apart if they missed a paycheque; a commitment to *ahimsa* means doing all you can to banish fear.

We have Mandela's challenge to build a new political culture of human rights, founded on the dignity of each of us and all of us.

We have King's firm belief, echoing the 19th century abolitionist Theodore Parker, that "the arc of the moral universe is long, but it bends toward justice."

We have explored Shula Koenig's transformative dream of human rights cities, where all will know their human rights in order to claim their human rights; best exemplified in the Austrian city of Graz.

We have encountered the visionary yet practical transformation of Think Equal, the brainchild of the actor, film producer and documentarian Leslee Udwin.

We have seen through Vijayamma's life in the SOS Children's Village in Aluva, the very embodiment of *sarvodaya* in instilling human dignity into the lives of children forsaken and abandoned by others.

We have delved into China's singular model of nurturing the common good and the common wealth: an abundance of societal development; without freedom of speech, freedom of association, and the competitive churn of partisan politics.

We have explored Indonesia's tenacity in embracing democracy based on shared values, to outgrow the dictatorial impulses of its early rulers in uniting a country of immense diversity.

We have noted the evolution of China's venture in harnessing the wealth-generating power of market capitalism and using its fruits to build an ever-improving standard of living — not just at home, but in the broader world.

In coming to understand that capitalism and democracy do not necessarily go hand in hand, we have had to abandon the fantasy that communism and a capitalist economy cannot coexist. And we have seen how the stunned and flailing leaders of liberal democracies are largely impotent in addressing the Chinese model of achieving economic primacy by limiting political rights.

We have faced the hypocrisy of countries founded on democratic ideals of freedom and liberty, which fail to establish a living wage for people that would enable them to enjoy lives of dignity.

We have grappled with the cynicism of the modern global arms trade, whereby democratic nations preach freedom at home while fueling violence and instability abroad; profiting from misery and suffering, then denying entry to the refugees displaced by the lethal chaos these nations and their arms-mongers enabled.

We have encountered the 3-D vision essential for the future of humankind: disarmament, development, and democracy. Demand disarmament, fund and ensure development, so you have a foundation to embed democracy.

We have ideas you may wish to champion in support of this vision, tangible actions which go beyond protest to actually bring change.

A two dollar carbon tax on every barrel of oil or equivalent we consume generates at least $200 million a day. A ready-made pool of not less than $73 billion a year, to fund the shift we need to a sustainable future for our planet. A "save the planet" tax that can become a rallying cry as climate strikes continue to spread across the world.

A 10 per cent "save humanity tax" on the $1.82 trillion dollars the world spent on arms and armaments in 2018 generates $182 billion a year to rebuild communities, rebuild lives, fund peace-building, help the ravaged recover from violence. To bring freedom from fear. And freedom from want.

Save the planet for $2 a barrel.

Save humanity with a tenth of the money we spend on sowing violence.

Pursue disarmament, development, and democracy.

And thereby establish our human birthright to a culture of love.

This is your time. This is the turning point in the history of our species. And it is yours to shape.

So we too come to a turning point of our navigations and explorations. As you continue the trajectory of *Us*, it is time for me to take my leave.

We have come this far together, dear companion.

Now, the mutual discovery and learning you take from *Us* is in your hands.

"Here ends the works of the sea, the works of love," Seferis declared in closing his epic poem Our Mythic History (*Mythistorema*).

All that remains is for you to set sail. To imagine your own journeys, to write your own chapters, in the story of *Us*.

And I know that as you move forward, you will not be alone.

You will find your own companions, mingle your journeys, chart your own destinations, as you revive the reign of love.

Our destiny is yours to shape.

I await with joy the world you will build.

Thanks

Us is shaped by editors who have engaged this project as a labour of love: Linda Goyette, Marc Horton, Beno John, and Silpi Das-Collins. Linda and Beno have known my writing for four decades; Marc was one of my formative editors in journalism. And it is a rare privilege that my daughter, who edits her grandfather's work, now is leading the substantive editing of *Us*.

Sophie Maisonneuve and Minni Sharma designed cover and contents of both the digital and print versions. James Murgatroyd ensured a seamless transition from the online shop to your screen.

Senator Douglas Roche encouraged me to structure *Us* as a memoir, and hosted many lively salons where ideas took shape.

Gurcharan Singh Bhatia kept pressing me to champion the ideas herein.

I learned much from Shulamith Koenig, and her conviction that people must know their human rights and make them a way of life.

Eric Schloss, and Marc Arnal, offered unfailing encouragement. Walther Lichem and Wolfgang Benedek showed me the importance of rule of law in societal development.

Horst Schmid's unfailing support gave me considerable clarity of purpose. Malik Youyou showed me the flair and determination needed to take a big idea to fruition. Christian Demoyen schooled me in serenity.

My late uncle Radhanath offered a compelling lesson in living life to the fullest.

The late David Evans and I debated many of the ideas that found their way into Us.

Kathleen Modrowski and Stephen Marks were an abiding influence in distilling my views, as were Bibhu Prasad Mahapatra, Andy Knight, and John Barrington Leigh.

Leslee Udwin's enthusiasm gave me the energy I needed to cross the finish line.

Elwood Johnson QC provided moral support and generous lunches.

My family stood with me through the decade it took for this book to emerge.

Canadians for a Civil Society was instrumental in the creation of this work. My former colleagues on the CCS board of directors offered estimable guidance and insight.

There were many others along the way, a community of friends whose company provided a rich subtext for the ideas and experiences we will share on the journey. You know who you are. I thank you one and all.

Satya Brata Das
Edmonton, Canada, July 2019

About Satya

Image: Braj Bhushan

Satya Brata Das is a writer, a community volunteer, and strategic adviser to leaders. His career as an editorialist, columnist, and foreign correspondent spanned the last quarter of the 20th century; during the glory days of print journalism.

You may reach him via **satya@cambridgestrategies.com**

A note on the type: Designer Sophie Maisonneuve set *Us* in Mrs. Eaves XL and Mrs. Eaves, modern variants of the classic 1750s serif font Baskerville. Sarah Eaves was the housekeeper and later the wife of typographer John Baskerville. These fonts were cast by Zuzana Licko of the Emigre digital type foundry.

Made in the
USA
Monee, IL